The Career of a Tsarist Officer

DENIKIN, Anton I. **The career of a Tsarist officer; memoirs, 1872–1916,** tr. by M. Patoski. Minnesota, 1975. 333p il map bibl 75-14625. 17.95. ISBN 0-8166-0698-6

tudents who cannot read Russian should welcome this English transla- on of General Denikin's out-of-print memoir, *Put' russkogo ofitsera* 953). Denikin, one of the more responsible White generals whose role s been exaggerated by Dimitry V. Lehovich in *White against Red; the e of General Anton Denikin* (CHOICE, Jan. 1975), gives a straightfor- ard account of his youth and his training as a Russian officer. The ope of the book is from his birth in 1872 to his participation in World ar I in 1916. It thus forms a prelude to Denikin's memoirs on the ussian Civil War, *Ocherki russkoi smuty* (1921–26), translated as *The ssian turmoil* (1922), summarized in one volume as *The White army* 930, repr. 1973) and is highly recommended for undergraduates in- ested in Russia's military system, the Russo-Japanese War, and orld War I. Extensive notes and biographical sketches of major mili- ry figures.

CHOICE   JAN. '76

History, Geography & Travel

Europe

The contribution of the McKnight Foundation to the general program of the University of Minnesota Press, of which the publication of this book is a part, is gratefully acknowledged

The Career of a Tsarist Officer
Memoirs, 1872–1916

by ANTON I. DENIKIN

An annotated translation from the Russian

by Margaret Patoski

UNIVERSITY OF MINNESOTA PRESS, Minneapolis

Printed in the United States of America
at North Central Publishing Company, St. Paul.
Published in Canada by Burns & MacEachern Limited,
Don Mills, Ontario

Library of Congress Catalog Card Number: 75-14625

ISBN 0-8166-0698-6

PREFACE

A translator should, like a puppeteer, remain behind the curtain, his invisibility being one mark of a successful performance. A translation should, moreover, reflect the style of the original without sacrificing freshness in the new language. Denikin's battle episodes translated easily since military descriptions possess the common features of brevity and urgency in any language. More difficult were his descriptions of childhood experiences. There Denikin, surrendering to a natural tendency, occasionally reverted to the archaic language of a world which might as well, for its strangeness to the present, have existed in a distant and forgotten age. I have enjoyed the cooperation of Denikin's daughter, Marina Grey-Chiappe, who graciously provided illustrations for this English edition as well as correcting my misunderstandings of the Russian text, and I especially appreciate her aid in bringing these passages to life. Finding myself onstage, I seize the opportunity as well to acknowledge the encouragement and assistance offered by my husband and colleague, Victor A. Patoski. Research and writing, though personally satisfying, would be lonely work without the company of good friends.

M. P.

INTRODUCTION

The controversial role in history of General Anton Ivanovich Denikin is an unfortunate byproduct of his position as principal leader of the White movement at the time of its collapse. Although no single individual should be held accountable for the fate of the White armies of south Russia, historians have often laid the blame on Denikin's previous inexperience in commanding large forces as well as on his failure to initiate land reforms or to enunciate definite political goals. Less charitable critics have invariably cited his personality and uncompromising character as factors contributing to the Whites' failure.

More than any of Denikin's numerous writings, these early memoirs reveal the environment, training, and experience which shaped his character and mentality, making him a professional soldier first and last — a man with an exalted concept of duty and a devotion to the military calling that amounted to a sense of mission. Denikin's book accurately reflects the milieu and influences which molded the principles he adhered to with unswerving loyalty throughout his life. Modest, inwardly serene, politically naïve, completely devoted to his religious faith and country, Denikin was, like so many men of similar training, ill equipped to survive in the tumultuous Russia of his day.

The man who was briefly to hold the title Supreme Ruler of Russia was born in 1872 near Wloclawek in the Warsaw province of Russian Poland. His father, Ivan Efimovich Denikin (1807–1885), born a serf in Saratov province, had by initiative and native ability reached the rank of major before his retirement from the frontier guards in 1869. Two years later Ivan Efimovich married Elizaveta Fedorovna Vzhesinskaia (1843–1916), a Polish Catholic who was supporting herself and her elderly father as a seamstress. The family of five (the three Denikins, Elizaveta's father, and Anton's nanny) existed, though barely, on Major Denikin's pension of thirty-six rubles a month. When this meager sum was reduced drastically at the elder Denikin's death, Anton Ivanovich was forced at age thirteen to help support his family by tutoring younger pupils while his mother took in student-boarders.

Profoundly influenced throughout his life by his father's devotion to Russia and the Orthodox religion, Denikin never wavered from his childhood determination to become an army officer. Although his academic record was not brilliant, his grades in realschule qualified him to enter the Kiev Junker School in 1890, after preliminary enlistment in the 1st Rifle Regiment stationed at Plotsk. Upon graduation and promotion to ensign in 1892, Denikin chose a vacancy in the 2nd Field Artillery Brigade stationed at Bela in Sedlets province. There he met Vasilii Ivanovich Chizh, whose daughter Xenia was to become Denikin's wife.

After passing competitive examinations for the prestigious three-year General Staff Academy in St. Petersburg, Denikin enrolled there in 1895. He failed the first-year course by a fractional mark. Since repetition of the course was prohibited, Denikin returned to his brigade and doggedly retook the qualifying examinations. This time he was admitted as fourteenth highest of the 150 students accepted yearly, maintained respectable marks, and would have been among the top fifty graduates appointed to the General Staff had not a new academy director arbitrarily changed the requirements for graduation. Denikin's appeal of this irregularity, directed to the tsar himself, had no immediate effect and in 1901 he once more returned to his brigade, having paradoxically been promoted to captain for distinguished academic success but rejected for appointment to the General Staff.

Denikin's duties in Bela allowed him sufficient free time to resume the literary career which he had launched at the academy and which he was to continue for the rest of his life. His articles and tales about the environment he knew best, military life and small provincial towns, were well received, except by the people they caricatured.

In late 1901 Denikin, more to unburden his soul than from any hope of redress, wrote to War Minister Aleksei N. Kuropatkin. Kuropatkin reopened the investigation, manfully admitted his own error, and corrected the injustice done the young officer. Denikin was transferred to the General Staff in 1902, first as a staff officer in the 2nd Infantry Division in Brest Litovsk, then as a company commander. By the autumn of 1902 he commanded a squadron of the

183rd Infantry Pultusskii Regiment in Warsaw. While some neighboring units were assigned to quell the numerous disorders which erupted during 1902 and 1903, Denikin's regiment guarded the Warsaw fortress in which the future head of the Polish state, Joseph Pilsudski, was then incarcerated.

Denikin's account of the background and causes of the Russo-Japanese War, like his interpretation of the origins of World War I, naturally proceeds from the Russian perspective. His views nevertheless conform generally to those currently accepted. When the Japanese war broke out in February 1904, Captain Denikin was a staff officer in the 2nd Cavalry Corps in Warsaw. Although still confined to bed from injuries suffered in the previous winter maneuvers, he applied for combat duty. His eagerness for front-line service was, however, frustrated by an appointment to the staff of the Trans-Amur Region Frontier Guards, whose mission was protecting the eastern and southern branches of the Manchurian railway. He received promotion to lieutenant colonel with a substantial salary increase but his brigade could anticipate no combat action other than occasional skirmishes with Chinese bandits. Continued efforts to seek more active duty were rewarded late that autumn when he became chief of staff of the Ural–Trans-Baikal Cossack Division, part of the 1st Manchurian Army commanded by General N. P. Linevich. Denikin first encountered enemy fire in November when he characteristically volunteered to lead an advance in the Tsinkhechen battle.

The surrender of Port Arthur in January 1905 freed Japanese armies to concentrate on Mukden in March, producing a Russian disaster. In the subsequent reorganization of the top command, General Linevich replaced General Kuropatkin as chief commander and Denikin became chief of staff of General Mishchenko's Mounted Detachment of the 2nd Army as well as continuing his divisional duties. Mishchenko's detachment, which participated in the abortive "May offensive," was continuously in battle until July 1, 1905, and the last engagement of the Russo-Japanese War near Sanvaiza. Denikin's distinguished service earned him promotion to colonel.

Having no desire to remain in Manchuria or Siberia after peace was concluded, Denikin requested by telegraph a division staff position in European Russia, then hastened home. At Harbin, his departure point, he witnessed the administrative havoc wrought by incomprehension of the October Manifesto. Demobilized reserves and soldiers released from Japanese prisons, understandably eager to get home, added to the civil disorder. Denikin virtually fought his way back to St. Petersburg along the Trans-Siberian Railway through the small, revolutionary, self-proclaimed republics which sprang up in the anarchic conditions of 1905. He and other officers organized the troops on their train to prevent a surprise attack, posting guards over their locomotive. From this experience Denikin learned how a handful of determined people, using force or the threat of force, could prevail in revolutionary circumstances. But after facing discomfort and danger to return to St. Petersburg, Denikin found that bureaucrats had again thwarted his plans. No position had been reserved for him; he had to accept a staff vacancy in the 2nd Cavalry Corps in Warsaw. There, at least, he again found time to write.

In 1907 Denikin joined the staff of the 57th Reserve Brigade quartered at Saratov, in the Kazan military district, where he remained for four years. General Sandetskii, the newly appointed commander of the Kazan district, was a martinet without combat experience who paralyzed his staff with paperwork and red tape. Denikin's portrayal in these memoirs of Sandetskii's relations with his subordinates and their reactions to him illustrate the best and worst aspects of the Old Russian army.

Simultaneously a renaissance of sorts was attempted elsewhere in the army. The mistakes of the Russo-Japanese War showed Russian military science to be sadly outdated and veteran officers, Denikin among them, were eager to share their newfound knowledge of modern techniques and weapons. In 1910 Colonel Denikin received command of the 17th Infantry Arkhangelogorodsk Regiment at Zhitomir, in the Kiev military district. He combined old with new, resurrecting the history and collecting the memorabilia of the venerable regiment created by Peter the Great, while welding its personnel into a modern combat force. He was participating with his regiment in imperial maneuvers near Kiev in 1911 when Premier Peter A. Stolypin was assassinated, an event which Denikin perceived to be critical for Russia's future. During the Balkan crises of 1912 and 1913 he tried to prepare his regiment, both physically and mentally, for the war he considered inevitable, ignoring official orders which prohibited officers from discussing contemporary political topics. His results if not his methods were apparently appreciated, for in March 1914 he was assigned to supervise similar training of Kiev district troops. On June 21, 1914, just before the "Sarajevo shot," Denikin was promoted to major general for distinguished service. It was soon to become clear, unfortunately, that the results of the Russian "military renaissance" were inadequate to meet the exigencies of world war.

As acting chief of staff in the Kiev district, Denikin felt the frustrating impact of the emperor's vacillation between partial and full mobilization during late July 1914. Since his chief was on leave, Denikin undertook the organization of staffs and corollary institutions for the 3rd and 5th Armies. But the final mobilization timetable had not yet been announced, and when new regulations finally appeared in early August, Denikin had to repeat all his work.

According to the 1894 Franco-Russian Alliance, if Germany declared war on France, the Russian northwest front was obliged to attack within fourteen days and the southwest front in nineteen. Germany declared war on Russia on August 1 and on France two days later. Russia was unprepared — a fact which Denikin offers in his memoirs as proof that his country did not seek war; nevertheless, Russia honored its alliance and pushed the northwest front to attack by August 17. The front commander, General Ya. G. Zhilinskii, sent two armies under Generals P. K. Rennenkampf and A. V. Samsonov into the Masurian Lakes debacle, a catastrophe for which General Rennenkampf was blamed. Later, while chief of staff at Mogilev (Supreme Headquarters) in 1917, Denikin was to read the results of the subsequent inquest, never released for security reasons, which revealed that while Rennenkampf had committed strategic errors, he had not betrayed his country. But this old soldier, one of Denikin's earliest heroes, was already disgraced and broken in spirit when revolutionaries killed him in Taganrog in 1918.

Denikin became quartermaster general of A. A. Brusilov's 8th Army assigned to General N. I. Ivanov's southwest front. Since Denikin much preferred combat duty to desk work, in September 1914 he requested and received command of the 4th Rifle "Iron" Brigade (expanded in April 1915 to a division), which he headed for two years. Through the winter of 1914–1915 Denikin's riflemen fought in the icy passes of the Beskid range of the Carpathians to prevent the Austrians from relieving Peremyshl. In a number of bloody battles his Iron Rifles were the only units to maintain discipline.

In May 1915, reinforced by German troops from the Anglo-French front, the Austrians forced the Russians back to the San and the Dniester. By June German General Mackensen had recaptured Peremyshl and controlled the central San region. On June 22 the Russians lost Lvov and in July began what Denikin refers to as the "great three-month retreat" on the western and southwestern fronts. His most brilliant accomplishment that year occurred in September, when during a counterattack he captured the Ukrainian town of Lutsk and thereby earned promotion to lieutenant general. However, he was immediately and inexplicably ordered to abandon the prize which had cost the Iron Division forty percent of its personnel. Such are the fortunes of war that he had to repeat the costly capture of Lutsk in 1916.

In the autumn of 1915 Denikin's division was incorporated into the newly formed 40th Corps of the 8th Army. Victory in the battle of Chartoriiskii established the 8th Army on the Styr, where it remained until spring 1916.

Meanwhile Emperor Nicholas II had assumed personal command of the Russian armies, and the tsarist tragedy rushed to its denouement. The inept Nicholas retained General M. V. Alekseev as chief of staff to plan and conduct all operations in the name of the supreme commander, but Nicholas's name had long since ceased to inspire awe and unquestioning obedience. As Denikin notes, prominent generals shrugged off operations orders with impunity.

Because of the failures of Ivanov on the southwest front, General Brusilov replaced him early in 1916 and launched the ill-fated "Brusilov offensive." Denikin's Iron Rifles led the fighting to recapture Lutsk; for his personal bravery Denikin was awarded the rare diamond-studded Sword of St. George. The Brusilov offensive momentarily crippled the Austro-Hungarian effort and impelled the Germans to reinforce them. Significant for Denikin's future misfortunes was the fact that Romania, heretofore neutral and a liability as a military ally, chose this time to declare war on the Central powers. In September 1916 General Denikin commanded the 8th Army Corps sent to aid Romania, which was threatened with annihilation by two

German armies under Generals Mackensen and von Falkenhayn. Denikin's corps fought valiantly despite tremendous losses as 1916 drew to a close. The Brusilov offensive became, meanwhile, a Russian rout.

Denikin's memoirs break off at this point. The events of the next four years of his life, beyond the scope of the present book, are well known and only a summary need be provided here.

As one military disaster after another decided tsarist Russia's fate, Nicholas distractedly played solitaire at Mogilev while Alexandra toyed with the more exciting and dangerous game of "ministerial leapfrog" at the capital. Duma opposition leaders grew increasingly daring in their verbal attacks on the regime and no one dared silence them. When Rasputin was assassinated, thoughtful men recalled his oft-repeated warning that the throne would fall within months of his death, but still the court seemed paralyzed. Discontent in both the countryside and the cities permeated armies at the front and began the demoralization of the Russian military which, ironically, had finally attained adequate material strength. Unrest accelerated at news of the first revolution of 1917 and Nicholas's abdication. Amid strikes, disorders, and chaos, the Provisional Government contended unsuccessfully for authority with the Petrograd Soviet, most of whose members were determined to take Russia out of the war. Events of the Provisional Government period most significant for Denikin were Order Number One, his appointment to Supreme Headquarters, and the so-called "Kornilov mutiny" which caused his imprisonment.

Order Number One guaranteed civil rights to the soldier without considering the need to maintain military discipline. Supposedly intended only for the Petrograd garrison, it reached front-line troops as well, effectively destroying the remaining discipline of the Russian soldier-recruits and opening floodgates of insurrection which Denikin and his fellow officers were never able to close. Talk of impending peace "without annexations or indemnities" and rumors that land redistribution had already begun prompted peasant-soldiers to head for home.

Although Denikin had long recognized the need for sweeping governmental reforms, he never sanctioned or supported revolution to attain them. Nevertheless he accepted the Provisional Government's leadership, perceiving it as a necessary interim authority until a constituent assembly could be convened. But when the new leaders proved incapable of restoring order, the chaos of the Provisional Government period was reflected in Denikin's career. He was briefly chief of staff to General Alekseev and then commander of the western front during the unpropitious June-July offensive of 1917, Russia's last effort in World War I. Front-line troops pushed the enemy back but rear units refused to advance to consolidate the gains, allowing the Germans to counterattack. Propagandized Russian soldiers refused to stand and defend their positions; instead they killed their officers and fraternized with the enemy or retreated in total disorder.

In July Minister of War A. F. Kerensky named as commander in chief General L. G. Kornilov, an outstanding combat general and a national hero who advocated a harsh program of purge and repression to strengthen the Russian military against the German onslaught. But Kerensky soon came to fear Kornilov, who insisted on a completely free hand in directing operations and appointing senior commanders. (Most threatening to Kerensky's position was the concept implicit in Kornilov's declaration that he would save the country, then hold power until a constituent assembly could decide Russia's political future.) As commander in chief, Kornilov transferred Denikin to command headquarters at Berdichev near Kiev, on the southwest front. En route to his new post Denikin visited Mogilev, where he pledged his support to Kornilov.

Only a month later, in September 1917, Kerensky ordered Denikin arrested and imprisoned at Berdichev along with his chief of staff General S. L. Markov and other generals accused of "attempting an armed uprising against the Provisional Government." General Kornilov and others were similarly imprisoned at Bykhov, the district center near Mogilev. As mobs gathered demanding their deaths, the Berdichev prisoners were shipped by rail to Bykhov to stand trial with the other officers. Kerensky had assumed personal command of the Provisional Government's forces, with young General N. N. Dukhonin as his chief of staff.

In late October (OS) the Bolshevik revolution began. Kerensky vanished and Dukhonin, left in charge by default, ordered the Bykhov prisoners released. They made their separate ways south under various incognitos, having agreed to reassemble in Novocherkassk, the center of the traditionally loyal Don Cossack region. By Christmas 1917, senior officers at Novocherkassk had organized themselves under a tripartite leadership: Kornilov was military commander of the Volunteer Army, Alekseev would handle the civil administration and foreign affairs, while Ataman Kaledin, in whose territory they had assembled, would continue to administer the Don region.

Since Kaledin, only recently elected as ataman, could not maintain order in the Don, the ragtag Volunteer Army headed south in February 1918 for the Kuban region, hoping to obtain food and additional volunteers before confronting the newly formed Red Army. Despite heavy losses the Volunteers captured reserves of ammunition and weapons from the Bolsheviks; large numbers of Kuban Cossacks swelled their slender ranks. But the Bolsheviks had already captured Ekaterinodar, the Kuban capital. General Kornilov was killed by a grenade at his improvised staff headquarters during the unsuccessful attempt to recover Ekaterinodar. General Denikin, as his deputy, inherited command of the White movement with General Alekseev's blessing.

Hearing news of anti-Bolshevik uprisings in the Don region, Denikin decided to abandon the fight in the Kuban area and lead his troops back to the Don. The Whites now learned that the Brest Litovsk negotiations had faltered and that the Germans had invaded South Russia. Denikin characteristically did not hinder Bolshevik resistance to German aggression, only seizing every opportunity to capture needed military supplies stored at railheads.

Bolshevik preoccupation with the Germans allowed the Volunteers their first rest in months and provided their commanders an opportunity to formulate political objectives. Denikin has often been censured, usually by critics who overlook the fact of his wholly military background, for not having publicized a definite political program. Not only was political manipulation alien to his experience, as the present book illustrates so well, but he was hamstrung by the diversity of his followers. To proclaim either a republic or a monarchy would have estranged one half or the other of his Volunteers; Denikin settled, therefore, on a policy more compatible with his own nature — "non-predetermination." He simply called on the army to deliver Russia "united and indivisible" from the Bolsheviks, then to remain nonpartisan, preserving Russia intact for the sole purpose of letting the Russian people decide their own future political course. This program, innocuous as it may appear, presented several problems. Monarchists feared, for example, another period of anarchy should the people be allowed to elect representatives and decide their future. National minorities, some of whom had proclaimed their independence, feared a forced resumption of second-class citizenship as well as subservience to a Great Russian state. Rightist groups favored the interests of the former landowning class while peasants demanded recognition of their rights to expropriated land. Denikin believed that he stood above partisan interests and refused to entangle himself in a web of contradictory promises to which he, unlike the Bolsheviks, would have felt bound.

Foreign governments, former Russian allies, hindered as much as they helped White efforts to liberate Russia by their confused intervention policies based on both selfish economic motives and woeful ignorance of Russian affairs. Further complications arose from the Czech Legion's unpredictable activities as well as from Soviet successes in coopting former tsarist officers into the Red Army, using hostages and military commissars to assure their loyalty.

Although the Volunteers were better trained and organized than the Reds, they lacked military supplies and were initially outnumbered at least ten to one as they launched the second Kuban campaign in June 1918. Denikin's minimum goal was to seize important railway junctions and separate the Reds from their Kuban food supplies. The Whites succeeded in liberating the Kuban by November 1918, but Denikin's closest friend and confidant, General Markov, was killed early in the campaign. In September the full weight of civil administration fell on Denikin's shoulders when the ailing General Alekseev died.

By February 1919 the White troops controlled the entire North Caucasus area and Denikin was a national figure. Ironically, the man who was to replace him a year later, the dashing and aristocratic cavalry commander General Baron Peter N. Wrangel, also attained a ·brilliant reputation in the second Kuban campaign. Nevertheless, the Reds were gaining discipline and experience while the assassination of the imperial family left the White monarchist sector nonplussed and divided. Equally important, the German surrender left the strategic Don region open to Bolshevik invasion.

Recognizing the need for a civilian administration, the Whites organized the Special Council as an advisory body to the chief commander, the title Denikin assumed after Alekseev's death. Denikin was pushed into political as well as military leadership and his time was, therefore, increasingly spent on speechmaking rather than planning strategy. He emerged as an unusually able orator, never flamboyant but quietly persuasive.

In the spring of 1919 Denikin received the title of commander in chief of the Armed Forces of South Russia, reflecting his authority over both the Volunteer Army and the Don army. In May, with some 300,000 Whites under his command, he launched an offensive in the Ukraine against Red forces which outnumbered his three to one. Denikin's advance initially succeeded because of his superior cavalry, British tanks, uprisings in the rear of the Red army, and defections from Reds to Whites. In June he set Moscow as his goal, although he could no longer count on the hoped-for juncture with anti-Bolshevik forces based in Siberia. Many of his senior generals opposed the plan and perhaps they were right. But Denikin's optimism is understandable: the Bolshevik armies were retreating in confusion and he understood the strategy of pressing his advantage.

The Whites took Kursk and Orel and the road to the armaments center of Tula and to Moscow lay open. But the Bolsheviks successfully counterattacked, having restored discipline and somewhat overcome their cavalry deficiency. They stopped Denikin's forces by October 1919, then rolled them back to the Black Sea, indirectly aided by the Poles who had reached a separate peace with Moscow and left the Reds a secure frontier in the west. Typhus and desertions decimated the White ranks, giving the retreat an air of total disaster.

The demoralized White army rapidly disintegrated into factions, most of whom blamed Denikin for their failures. The Armed Forces of South Russia were, however, foredoomed for reasons about which much has been written. They lacked geographical unity as well as political and social homogeneity; they were unable to control foraging, which became outright looting and turned the population against them. An influx of criminals and mercenaries diluted their commitment. Outside support failed to materialize. Guerrilla-type partisans operated in the rear. Their front was too broad to support and their supply lines were overextended. Militarily, their situation was hopeless.

Denikin's personal flaws cannot, of course, be ignored. As his memoirs indicate, he was idealistic to the point of inflexibility. Totally honest and incorruptible, and trusting his generals to maintain the same high principles, he relied on subordinates who concealed from him the pogroms, the exploitation of inhabitants in White-held territory, and the degree of corruption and rapacity prevalent among the White forces. Punishment of rank and file was inconsistent while top officials went unpunished; morale steadily declined as a result.

Denikin's apparent lack of firmness fed the ambitions of his less idealistic rival, Baron Wrangel, who was noted for maintaining discipline in his segment of the White forces. As insurrection spread in the rear, grumbling, petty quarrels, and intrigue proliferated among military leaders. A savior was wanted. Wrangel, now widely respected, seemed the logical person to replace the hapless Denikin, whose military strategy had failed to produce the necessary miracle. By February 1920 Denikin, now recognized by the Whites as Supreme Ruler of Russia, was engaged in bitter recriminations with Wrangel, and when such old and trusted friends as General A. P. Kutepov defied him, he decided to resign. By then Bolshevik forces had crossed the Kuban and forced the precipitous evacuation of wounded and refugees from Novorossiisk. As the Reds bore down on the port city, some troops fled to the Crimea and elsewhere on foot, others were evacuated by allied ships, but many were captured.

Denikin was among the last to leave Novorossiisk for the Crimea, where he abruptly ordered a reorganization of the government of South Russia and the election of a new chief commander. His last order confirmed Wrangel as his successor and in April 1920, at the age of forty-seven, he left Russia forever.

Denikin spent the rest of his life in emigration, principally in France and finally the United States, where he died in 1947. Throughout his remaining years he wrote constantly and spoke whenever possible of the necessity for removing the Bolshevik blight from his homeland.* But he remained his own man, refusing to be dragged into

---

*Denikin's chief publication was his five-volume history of the civil war, *Ocherki russkoi smuty* (Outlines of the Russian Turmoil). For a listing of his other books and arti-

bootless émigré factional quarrels and holding a viewpoint that was consistently anti-German as well as anti-Bolshevik.

Into his mid-seventies Denikin continued to lecture and to write, and the present book, begun in France, was well under way when he died. He had planned to extend these memoirs to the civil war period, at which point his *Ocherki russkoi smuty* begins, but he suffered a fatal heart attack when he had only begun to describe the 1916 Brusilov offensive. The uncompleted manuscript was published posthumously in 1953 as *Put' russkogo ofitsera* (The Path of a Russian Officer) by the Chekhov Publishing House of the East European Fund, an émigré relief organization supported by the Ford Foundation. It now appears in English translation for the first time.

cles, see Dmitry V. Lehovich's comprehensive biography, *White Against Red: The Life of General Anton Denikin* (New York, 1974), based in part on family papers and manuscripts now in the possession of Columbia University. Denikin's civil war archives were earlier entrusted to the Czech Ministry of Foreign Affairs in Prague, where they subsequently fell into German, then Soviet hands.

CONTENTS

    Photographs appear between pages 202 and 203

PART I

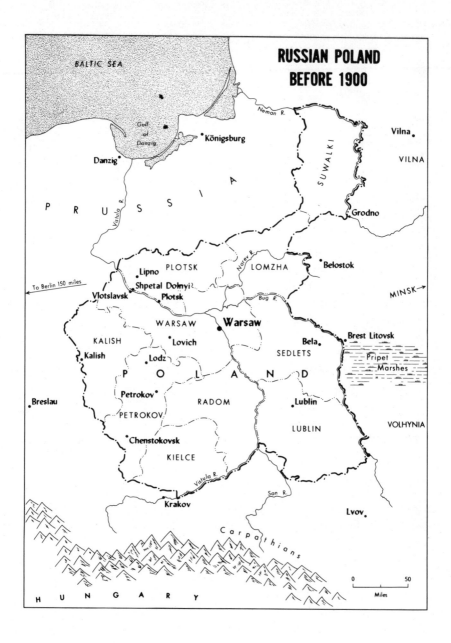

CHAPTER 1 PARENTS

I was born on December 4, 1872, in the Warsaw province village of Shpetal Dolnyi, across the Vistula from the city of Vlotslavsk [Wloclawek].[1] Fate had brought us there because my father served in the Alexandrovskii Brigade of the frontier guards, the staff of which was stationed in Vlotslavsk. My parents remained there after my father's retirement. Of course much of Poland, including the capital, Warsaw, was part of the Russian Empire then.

My father, Ivan Efimovich Denikin, was born in 1807, five years before Napoleon's invasion of Russia, to the family of a bond serf in Saratov province. If my memory does not betray me, he was born in the village of Orekhovka. He died when I was thirteen. From that time to this, sixty years have passed. About my father's previous life (which I know only from his stories) I have retained, therefore, only confused, faint memories.

In his youth Father was a serf. At the age of twenty-seven he was handed over by the estate owner as a recruit.[2] At that time transportation was so backward and the life of a soldier (soldiers served twenty-five years and rarely returned home) was such that, torn away from his native village and family, changing regiments and quarters, Father was continually on the move, first to Hungary, then the Crimea, then Poland. And his family fell apart early, too. Father's parents had died before his military enlistment and his brother and sister were scattered to the winds. He was not even sure where they lived.

Once while Father was still a soldier and his regiment was being transferred through Russia, fate took him to the city where he thought his brother was living (he had, as Father expressed it, "gone out among people earlier than I"). I vaguely recall the tale of how Father delightedly went to the home of his brother, who had friends to dinner that day. And of how his brother's wife brought a knife and

3

fork to the Russian soldier in the kitchen, "not allowing him in the dining room." Father rose and left without saying goodbye. From that time on, the brothers never met again.

Father began his military service during the reign of Emperor Nicholas I (1825–1855). The "time of Nikolai" was a period of drab, harsh life for the soldier, a time of severe discipline and cruel punishment. To endure twenty-two years of such a life was to live through an entirely unique experience. Father's tales about "running the gauntlet," a punishment then practiced, made an especially painful impression on me. Soldiers armed with ramrods stood in two opposing ranks. The ones to be punished ran between the ranks and received blows from everyone. Men were often beaten to death![3] Father spoke of those times with epic calmness, without malice or censure, always ending with the customary refrain, "There was severity in our time, not like nowadays!"

Father entered military service with only a scanty knowledge of reading and writing. In the army he managed to learn a few more things. After twenty-two years, by then a sergeant major, he was allowed to take the "officers' examination," which at that time was relatively uncomplicated and required only a knowledge of reading and writing, the four rules of arithmetic, military regulations and clerical functions, and religious instruction. Father passed the examination and in 1856 became an ensign appointed to service in the Kalishkii and later in the Alexandrovskii Brigade of the frontier guards.[4]

In 1863 the Polish revolt began.[5] The detachment which Father commanded was ordered to the Russian frontier in the vicinity of Petrokov, a district capital. Father was on good terms with the neighboring Polish landowners; they often visited each other. A long time before the revolt the situation on the border had already become exceedingly tense. All kinds of rumors were afloat. Information reached Father that on one of the estates with whose owner he was acquainted there was to be a secret meeting, a gathering of conspirators. Father took a platoon of border guards there and deployed them in concealment near the house with the terse command, "If I do not return in half an hour, attack the house."

Familiar with the arrangement of the house, Father went directly to the meeting room. He recognized many acquaintances there. General tumult ensued. Some of those who did not know Father rushed up to him with the intention of disarming him, but others restrained them. Father addressed those present, saying something like this: "I know why you are here. But I am a soldier and not a spy. When I have to fight you, I shall do it. Don't bear me a grudge for that. But let me say that you plot only stupid things. You will never match Russian strength. You will only carelessly destroy many people. Give it some thought while there is still time." And he left. I have cited only the gist of his speech, being unable to communicate his style adequately here. Generally Father spoke briefly, picturesquely, as common people do, inserting a strong word here and there. His style, in other words, was not suited to the salon.

In cold, dry, terse military terms, Father's Ukase of Discharge mentioned his participation in the defeat of the Miroslavskii band in the forest near the village of Krzhivosondz and the Jung gang in the village of Novaia Ves, as well as the victory over Rachkovskii at the frontier post of Plovka, and so on.

Father seldom spoke of the Crimean and Hungarian campaigns, apparently because he had participated in them only indirectly.[6] But he loved to talk about the Polish campaign, for which he received promotion and decoration. I used to listen with rapt attention as Father described how he drifted about the border region with his detachment, pursuing outlaw bands. Once he entered a little Prussian town and almost caused diplomatic complications.[7] Another time, when he and soldiers of his detachment were steaming themselves in a bathhouse, the horse patrols reported the approach of a band of "mowers" on horseback. Lacking arms, many Polish gangs armed themselves with scythes. Stopping only to throw on their sabers and guns, the frontier guards rushed naked after the scythe-bearers. Terrified passersby fled at the unusual sight of furiously racing creatures, naked, swarthy from the heat and the dirt, half devils and half men.

Father also related other incidents. More than once he had spared the lives of Polish rebels, who were mostly inexperienced young men. I must state that Father was an extremely zealous soldier. He was a severe person, prone to violence, but at the same time he was unusually kind. Many young men were captured, most of them gymnasium and university students. The immediate transfer to "higher instances" of those caught carrying weapons meant deportation for some and even worse for others, since Father's superior, a certain Major Schvarts, was an authoritarian and quite merciless German. So Father often risked the major's ire by ordering his secretly approving squad (none of whom denounced him) to "give the urchins a drubbing with ten switches," mostly as an example, and "let them go."

I have never forgotten an episode which occurred about fifteen years after the insurrection. I was only six or seven years old at the time. It was winter. Father had to go to the city of Lipno in a sleigh as a witness in some judicial matter. I begged to go with him. At one of the way stations we stopped at a roadside inn. Seated at the table was a tall, vigorous fellow in a bearskin coat. He stared at us fixedly for a long time, then suddenly rushed to Father and embraced him. It developed that he was a former rebel, one of the dissuaded "godsons."

The Polish uprising, which began on January 10, 1863, ended in December in full defeat. Subsequently properties were confiscated and numerous captives sent to Siberian settlements. In general, a more rigorous regime was introduced on the border.

Father retired in 1869 with the rank of major. Two years later he contracted a second marriage with Elizaveta Fedorovna Vrzhesinskaia, my mother. Father rarely spoke about his deceased first wife; apparently the marriage had not been a happy one.

My mother was Polish, originally from the city of Strelno in the Prussian-occupied zone, and she came from a family of impoverished small landowners. Fate had brought her to the frontier town of Petrokov, where she supported herself and her elderly father as a seamstress. There she met Father.

When the Russo-Turkish War started (1877–1878), Father was already seventy years old.[8] It was obvious to those of us around him that he was melancholy. He became more taciturn and gruff and seemed to be brooding about something. Finally, without my mother's knowledge, he submitted a petition to reenlist for active service. We learned about it later when the garrison commander sent papers ordering Major Denikin to proceed to Novogeorgievskii fortress, there to form a reserve battalion which would subsequently be sent to the theater of war.

There were tears and reproaches from my mother. "How could you do this without saying a word, Efimovich? My God! An old man like you!" I cried too. But in the depths of my little soul I was proud that "my papa was going to the war." Shortly afterward, however, came the news that the war was over and mobilization had ceased.

CHAPTER 2 CHILDHOOD

There were indications of dire poverty in my childhood. My father received a pension of some thirty-six rubles a month. Five of us had to exist on this meager income during my first seven years. After Grandfather's death, there were only four of us. As a matter of necessity we stayed in the country where living was cheaper and it was possible to breathe more freely. But in my sixth year, when I started to school, we moved to Vlotslavsk.

I well remember our wretched little apartment in a courtyard on Pekarskii Street. There were two rooms, a small dark pantry, and a kitchen. One room served as the parlor for receiving guests. It was also the dining room, the workroom, and everything else. In the other, a dark room, three of us slept. Grandfather slept in the pantry and my nursemaid in the kitchen.

Although she had entered our household as a hired servant, my nanny Apoloniia (commonly called "Polosia") gradually became part of our family. She concentrated on us all the love and devotion of her solitary being and she was never apart from us until her death. I buried her at Zhitomir where I was commanding a regiment.

The pension, of course, was not adequate. Every month before it came, Father had to borrow five or ten rubles from a friend. It was willingly given but this business was painful for Father. He often prepared himself for two days before going to ask for a loan. The first day of the month it was invariably paid off but at the end of the month the story began all over again.

Once a year (but not every year) manna from heaven fell upon us in the form of a bonus, no more than 100 or 150 rubles, from the government (the frontier guard regiments were subordinate to the

Ministry of Finance). Then we would have a veritable feast. We would repay debts and buy supplies, including a "fashionable" dress for Mother and something new to be sewn for me. Father would buy a cheap cloak (alas, civilian garb, which was an excessive burden for him). His military clothing was worn out and new uniforms cost too much. But he was never without a military cap and in his trunk lay his last uniform and his military breeches; he wore them only on great feast days and for personal celebrations. They were carefully preserved, sprinkled with snuff to protect them from moths, "in order not to be ashamed in death," so Father said, "to lie, although in the ground, as a soldier."

We were in such straitened circumstances that against my will I was in the mainstream of all family matters. My parents were friends. My mother was as solicitous for my father as for me. She worked without tiring, straining her eyes, sewing embroidery which brought in a few insignificant *groshki*.[1] Besides, she suffered from migraine, often with convulsions, which did not leave until her old age.

The two of them had their quarrels and differences, of course, and predominantly from two causes. On the day Father received his pension, he always managed to lend some *groshki* to friends poorer than himself, without hope of being repaid. This put Mother, who guarded the wretched nest egg, out of patience. She would pour out reproaches. "What can you be thinking of, Efimich? At this rate, we will soon be starving ourselves." The other cause of their quarrels was the soldierly frankness with which Father treated people. He was so disturbed by falsehoods and slander that he showed his displeasure to acquaintances and eventually they would cease speaking to him. Mother, in anger, often said, "Tell me, to whom is your 'truth' necessary? We must get along with people. Why make enemies for us all?" But Father never made permanent enemies. People liked him and forgave his temper.

In family quarrels Mother always took the active role. Father's only defense was silence. He was silent until Mother calmed herself. Then neutral elements would slip into their conversation. Once, for instance, Mother hurled this rebuke: "Here it is only halfway through the month and your tobacco costs so much." That very day Father gave up smoking. He seemed to grow a little gray and thin; he lost his appetite and quit talking altogether. Toward the end of the week his appearance was so pathetic that Mother and I both tearfully begged him to smoke again. He resisted for one day but on the next he smoked. Everything returned to normal. That was the only time when I took sides in a family argument. Generally I never dared to do so. But in the depths of my childish heart I was nearly always on Father's side.

Mother often complained about our situation. Father never complained and probably for this reason I recall our poor life as somewhat pleasant, without passions or spite, not burdensome. Of course there were disappointments at times, such as a not too well-fitting uniform made from Father's old frock coat. And the few pencils I had were poor and brittle, not factory made like those of others. My mathematics case with drawing instruments which we bought at the rag fair was incomplete and carelessly made. As for skates, I bought them myself in the fourth grade from my first honorarium for tutorial work. And although I still remember how good the steamed "little hearties" (kolbasy sausages) smelled as I stood near the buffet counter in the school corridor during midday break, they were beyond my means. Moreover, I could not swim every summer day in the Vistula because admission to the bathhouse cost three kopecks and my parents would not allow me to swim along the open shore. There were quite a few such minor annoyances.

With swimming there was an easy way out. I sometimes went secretly with a crowd of children to the shore of the Vistula and splashed there for an hour or so. Thus I became one of the best swimmers. Nothing else mattered. I was to be an officer and wear an elegant uniform. I would not only have skates but I would ride horseback and eat "little hearties" every day. But there were times when my little soul was seriously disturbed. For instance, thanks to that messy mathematics instrument case and even though I was a good draftsman, my mathematics teacher once gave me at the end of a quarter an unsatisfactory mark and I fell downward on the scholarly lists.

And still another time: In my sixth or seventh year, barefoot and wearing a dress made of ticking, I was playing with children in the street near the house. My friend from the upper division, a student in the seventh grade named Kapustianskii, came along and as usual caught me up and allowed me to turn flips, which delighted me. The inspector for the realschule happened along at that time. Disgustedly pursing his lips, he stopped and asked Kapustianskii, "Are you not ashamed to play games with a street urchin?"

I had never in God's world suffered such a bitter insult. I ran home in tears and told my father. Father boiled over. He grabbed his cap and left the house muttering, "Ah, the son of a bitch! What if we don't have governesses? I will show him!" He went to the inspector and seared him with such harsh words that the poor man hardly knew how to justify himself.

CHAPTER 3   RUSSIAN-POLISH RELATIONS

Russian-Polish relations affected our family life from outside but within they had no influence whatsoever. Father was a genuine Russian. Although Mother remained Polish, my parents brought me up in true Russian spirit and Orthodoxy. Actually the idea that they "brought me up" is misleading. This assumes that there was some sort of system. There was none. I simply grew as best I could in our limited circumstances, living among adults, hearing much, seeing much, both necessary and unnecessary, assimilating and modifying impressions according to my personal understanding, rarely turning to my elders with questions of a spiritual nature.

Neither Father nor Mother was distinguished by linguistic aptitude. Unfortunately I inherited this characteristic. Father, having served in Poland for forty-three years, was not prejudiced against either the Poles or their language. He understood Polish but did not speak it at all. Mother later managed to learn Russian and to read a great deal of Russian literature but to the end of her days she spoke the language poorly.

At home Father always spoke Russian and Mother Polish while I, not because of instructions but from my own intuition, spoke Russian with Father and Polish with Mother. Later, after I left officers' school and Mother lived almost exclusively in Russia, I spoke to her only in

Russian in order to help her learn. But I did not forget the Polish language.

There was no divergence in my religious training. Father was a person of deep faith. He did not miss a single church service and he always took me to church. When I was nine, I became a devout churchman. I served at the altar with great enthusiasm, rang the bell, sang in the choir, and later on became a lay reader.

By personal inclination I sometimes went with Mother to May Day services in the Polish Roman Catholic church. But I felt at home in our wretched regimental church and viewed the festive service in the imposing Polish Roman Catholic church only as an interesting spectacle.

Enough Polish-Russian differences came in from outside. In our town, on Passion Saturday before Easter, the Roman Catholic priests and the Orthodox cleric visited the houses to consecrate the Paschal table. To us would come both the Catholic priest and the Russian priest, Father Elisei. The latter was familiar with our customs and viewed our situation calmly. But the Catholic priests were different. Sometimes they agreed to come and sometimes they declined. I remember how bitterly such rejection affected my mother and how angry it made my father. One of the priests explained that he did not object to visiting us but simply feared some kind of repression from the Russian rulers.

Once when I was only nine Mother returned from Catholic services unusually upset, with tear-reddened eyes. Father questioned her for a long while but Mother did not wish to talk about it. Finally she told him that at confession the priest would not grant absolution of her sins and would not permit her to make communion, demanding that in the future she bring up her son secretly as Catholic and as Polish. Mother was devastated. Father flew into a rage and started swearing. He went to the priest. There occurred a stormy confrontation at the end of which the perplexed priest asked Father "not to destroy" him. The Russian officials from the Pre-Vistula frontier were at this time (1880) rather harsh men, and a charge of "attempted perversion" might have led to the priest's exile to a Siberian settlement. Of course the matter was not publicized. I do not know how my mother's confessions went after that because my parents never spoke of it again. But the episode made a deep impression on me. From that day forward, from some inner motive, I never visited the Roman Catholic church again.

I must acknowledge that Russian-Polish relations were exacerbated by the absurd, troublesome, and offensive Russification program imposed on the Poles from St. Petersburg and carried out particularly in the district schools.[1] In the Vlotslavsk realschule where I studied from 1882 to 1889, the situation was as follows: Religious instruction was to be delivered by the Catholic priest to Poles in the Russian language. Study of the Polish language was not required, there was no examination in it, but when it was taught, it had to be taught in the Russian language. Our Polish language teacher was a German named Kinel and he spoke even Russian with a heavy accent! Inside the school, within the school fence, even in the students' quarters, speaking Polish was strictly prohibited and those found guilty of it were subject to punishment. St. Petersburg applied a heavy hand. And even the late Warsaw governor-general Gurko, that hero of the Russo-Turkish War whom the Poles regarded as the "oppressor of the Polish heritage," did not once in his devoted reports to the tsar (with whom I became acquainted later) point out abnormalities of "over-Russifying" measures.[2]

Actually strict prohibition was a dead letter. During lessons the priests flung out a few Russian phrases for the sake of appearance. Pupils never spoke Russian among themselves. Only the precise German Kinel vainly attempted to communicate with Russian words the beauties of the Polish language.

I must say, however, that such ludicrous Russification measures pale completely in comparison with the history of the period when merciless and savage measures of Polonization were applied to the Russian territory transferred to Poland by the Riga Agreement of 1921.[3] The Poles began to eradicate all traces of Russian culture and citizenship, to abolish all Russian schools, and especially to persecute the Russian church. Polish became the official language of the administration and of religious instruction, of church sermons, and in some places, of the Divine Liturgy. Then the closing and destruction of Orthodox churches began. In the Warsaw diocese fine examples of Russian architecture were blown up. In a single month in 1937, 114 Orthodox churches were destroyed by government agents to the accompaniment of scoffing abuse of holy relics and the forcible arrest of clergy and Orthodox parishioners. On Holy Easter itself, the Polish primate in his sermon summoned Catholics to struggle against Orthodoxy and "to follow in the footsteps of ardent, single-minded apostles." So one might say that the Poles repaid us with interest. And in the future no bright spot in Russian-Polish relations could be seen.

Let us return, however, to the distant past. I, a ten-year-old urchin, developed a modus vivendi toward schoolmates through personal intuition. With Poles I began to speak Polish; with Russians, of whom there were three or four in every class, I spoke always Russian. Because many of the latter were "Polonized," I often teased them, scoffed at them, and sometimes in serious cases even beat them when the "correlation of forces" permitted it. I recall the moral satisfaction provided me once in the sixth grade when a friend, a serious lad and a good Pole, gave me his hand after one such scene and said, "I respect you because you speak Russian with your own kind."

Besides the Poles and Russians there were Jews in every class, although never more than two or three. Almost half the population of the town was Jewish and they held all the trade in their hands. Many of them were competitive persons but only a few sent their children to high school. The rest confined themselves to *heders*, a special Hebrew, outmoded, Talmudic, medieval sort of school which was permitted by the authorities but not given educational recognition.[4] In our realschule the "Jewish question" simply did not exist. Jews were not regarded as a separate class. Among the pupils they were judged according to their individual morals and true comradely natures.

By the seventh grade, I was already studying away from home, in Lovich [Lowicz] realschule about which I shall tell more later. I was an "elder" in the students' quarters (twelve boys). The job of elder meant a discount, half price for board, which was very pleasant. In return one had to hold inspections and keep internal order, naturally. But the troublesome part was filling out the monthly reports. In one column were to be listed "students discovered conversing in the Polish language." This was oppressive. It amounted simply to a denunciation. At the risk of dismissal from my position, which would be pitifully reflected in our budget, I always entered in that column, "There were no such occurrences."

After three months I was summoned to the director. Director Levshin knew me from the Vlotslavsk school, from which he had been transferred to Lovich, and he liked me. Why, I do not know. It must have been because I studied in an orderly fashion and sang well in the school choir, his pet project.

When I went to his office, he said, "For three months now you have written in the report that there were no students conversing in Polish."

"Yes, Mr. Director."

"I know this is not true."

I was silent.

"You do not seem to understand that these measures protect the interests of the Russian state. We must pacify and Russify this border area. Well, when you are older, you will understand. You may go."

Whether the director really believed in the equity and appropriateness of such methods of "pacification," I do not know. To the end of my student days I continued to enter the ritualistic phrase, "There were no such occurrences," and I was not discharged from my job.

Thus during my eight years in realschule I never experienced frustration with the Poles on nationalistic grounds. More than once during our public outings to the suburbs, when one of the comrades would strike up one of the songs considered revolutionary, "From the Smoke of Dead Fires" or "God, Preserve Poland," the others would hush him, saying, "Stop that! You know there are Russians with us."

But friction came later. I went on to officers' school while the majority of my Polish comrades attended higher technical institutions. Circumstances had changed. Polish was no longer prohibited.[5] We became free people and I demanded "equal rights" when I met former classmates. I conversed with them in Russian, leaving them free to speak their native language. Some were agreeable while others were offended and we parted forever. But such meetings occurred only in the first few years after we left our schools. Later destiny scattered us to the winds and I never met my school friends again.

There was only one exception. In 1937 I had occasion to hear from my dearest school comrade, one with whom I had shared a room. We had studied together and compatibly solved all "world questions." This was Stanislav Karpinskii, the first director of the state bank of independent Poland who for a short time was minister of finance. At the time Karpinskii was retired. Having read my books and obtained my address from one of the publishers, he sent me his book of remembrances and a correspondence grew up between us which lasted until World War II. But what became of him then I do not know.

Karpinskii, born in Russian Poland, was one of those rare Poles who was judicious, lacking preconceived views about Russian-Polish relations. He could clearly see Polish as well as Russian transgressions and he considered reconciliation not only possible but necessary.

CHAPTER 4   LIFE OF THE TOWN

Our townspeople lived quietly and peaceably. There was no social life, no cultural diversion, not even a town library. A few people subscribed to newspapers; if necessary, we could turn to them for information. There were no amusements aside from a theater which now and then featured some passing troupe. For the ten years of my more conscious life in Vlotslavsk, I remember all the "important events" that occurred in the quietness of our lonely place.

For example, there was the time "we" captured a "socialist." Under this common term Vlotslavsk inhabitants lumped together all representatives of this dangerous and unfamiliar inclination who for some reason struggled against the government and were sent to Siberia, but about whom few had a very clear idea. For several days the "socialist," accompanied by two gendarmes, was taken for interrogation to the lieutenant colonel of gendarmes. A throng of urchins always accompanied the procession. And as this kind of event occurred in our town for the first time it stirred interest and much gossip among the residents.

Once the ceiling in the house of a rich merchant fell in, seriously injuring him. Many residents, both acquainted and unacquainted with him, went to visit the ill man, not so much from solicitude as from curiosity to see the fallen ceiling. Of course I visited him too.

Then the director of the local bank appropriated a sum of money and fled abroad. During several days people gathered near the banker's house, gesturing. Probably they were small depositors. And on Pekarskii Street where the bank was located, there was quite a crowd. Probably there was no one in the city who did not go to Pekarskii to see the building with locked doors and the crown seal upon them.

A more serious event occurred in our realschule. The seventh grade, or "supplement" as it was called in official language, was closed to me for the following reason. Previously school had consisted of the normal seven grades. According to established custom, the seventh graders enjoyed special privileges. They went outside school in civilian clothes, visited restaurants where they drank, and walked around the town after curfew. They were impertinent to the teachers and so on. Finally, however, wantonness reached such limits that the director decided to end it. During some sort of altercation between the director and a student of the upper division, the student slapped the director in the face.

This incident aroused and excited the whole town as well as the school. The seventh-grade student was dismissed "with a wolf's ticket," that is, without the right of going to any other school. I remember that the student's action provoked general condemnation, as the director, who was subsequently transferred to some place in central Russia, was a humane and just person. Certainly we, the urchins, condemned the student's behavior. The seventh grade was closed, as the official document expressed it, "forever."

Finally, another event comes to my mind. When I was seven or eight years old, news reached our town that Emperor Alexander II was returning from abroad through the Alexandrovskii frontier and his train would stop in Vlotslavsk for ten minutes. Several local residents were invited to meet the sovereign, my father among them, along with the authorities. Father decided to take me with him. Having been reared in the spirit of a mystical union of Russia with the person of the tsar, I was beside myself with joy.

At home there was tumult. Mother spent all day and night sewing me a pair of plush trousers and a silk shirt. Father put his military uniform in order and rubbed buttons through a special little board with holes until they gleamed.

At the station I noticed that except for me there were no children, and this fact filled me with pride. When the tsar's train arrived, the ruler came to an open window of the car and conversed affably with one of those who had come to greet him. Father froze at attention with one hand lifted to his cap, disregarding me. I did not take my eyes off the ruler.

After the train left, one of our acquaintances turned to my father and said, half jokingly, "Ivan Efimovich, how can your little son be so disrespectful to the sovereign? He did not even remove his cap."

Father was so embarrassed that he blushed. I could already see that it would be impossible to boast to my small friends about meeting the tsar. They would all know about my carelessness and they would laugh at me.

Some time later, all of Russia was shocked by an awful event. On March 1, 1881, Emperor Alexander II was murdered. In our town the Orthodox church was hushed in mourning. In Russian families, as in our own home, people cried. How the event affected the Polish population I was not then in a position to estimate. I remember only that for several days the town was immersed in a painful silence and a feeling of emptiness. By order of the abashed local authorities, a mounted lancer patrol came into the stunned town and the sound of horses' hooves in the singular quiet of the night added to the troubled mood which may be expressed in the words of a Polish poet:

> Quiet everywhere, emptiness everywhere,
> What will happen, what is to be?

CHAPTER 5   SCHOOL

My parents began my education early. When I was four, my mother prepared a surprise for my father's name day. She secretly taught me to read and write in Russian. Triumphantly presented to Father, I unwrapped a little book and began to read to him. "Enough, brother," he said, "you know that by heart. Now see if you can read this." I read something else for him. His joy was immense. It was as if there were two name days in the house.

When we moved from the country into town they took me to the

"German" school because it was located near our house and the regular school was far away. The German school was so called only because the curriculum there included the German language. Among
other things primary schools did not offer the Polish language.

To reflect on that time is depressing except for one "miracle." After
our lessons one day the teacher detained me for some error made
during class hours. It was very unpleasant. I knew that, back home, I
would be scolded for over half an hour, a punishment far worse than
any other. As I waited, I knelt before the school icon and prayed,
"God, grant that they will allow me to go home soon." The moment I
arose the door opened and the teacher came in, saying, "Denikin,
Anton, you may go home."

I was shaken. That episode strengthened my childish faith. But
(forgive my skepticism) it occurs to me now that the teacher might
have happened to glance in the window (it was a one-story building)
and, seeing the tableau of the penitent sinner, might have been
moved to compassion. Besides, many times later when I sinned and
was punished by being detained, I implored God, "Lord, let me be
spanked when I get home, but not scolded!" Yet my supplications
were rarely heard. I went on being scolded, not spanked.

I studied in primary school for two more years and in 1882, at the
age of nine years and eight months, I passed the examination for the
first grade of the Vlotslavsk realschule. There was great joy at home. I
was the hero of the day. I put on my school cap with much the same
feeling as when I later donned my first officer's epaulets. For the first
time in my life my parents took me to a confectioner's shop and
treated me to chocolate and pastries.

At first I was a good pupil. But in the second grade there, I contracted smallpox and then scarlet fever with all the complications. I
lay in bed with fever and delirium. The old-fashioned brigade doctor
who treated me came once, looked me over, made the sign of the
cross, and left without a word to my parents. In despair they rushed
to the city doctor, who soon had me on my feet.

For several months, however, my studies were neglected and I was
behind my classmates, especially in mathematics, which was considered to be the most important subject in realschule. I managed to
drag through the third and fourth grades, but in the fifth I barely
held on until completion. In midyear, my average mark in each

> When a person has persisted in his labors
> What are the things he cannot do!
> Is it thanks to his endurance, or his
> Intellect, or his will, or God's wishes?

By the last phrase, the inspector explained to us, the poet meant good luck. In my composition, however, I had interpreted the words as "And, of course, God's wishes." Not "luck," as "others" think, but literally "God's wishes." I explained that not in vain did the wise Russian proverb teach, "Without God, nothing is possible." For my insolent interpretation of what "others think," my paper was marked with a three and from then until graduation, in spite of all my efforts, I could not score higher than a four.[2]

In the fourth grade my "literary exercises" began. We were required to write and at home I wrote essays by the bundle for my Polish classmates, three or four at a time on a single theme. It was a difficult matter but apparently I did not write poorly. At least, Maziurkevich once addressed a friend having benefited from my work with the words, "Confess, you did not write this. Perhaps you borrowed these essays from an acquaintance, some Warsaw student?" Such a testimony was flattering to the anonymous author and elevated my prestige at school.

I worked gratis at times or else for a trade, for the right to use a good mathematics instrument case or for the loan of an electrical machine, the limit of my ambitions! In my thirteenth and fourteenth years I wrote verses. They were excessively pessimistic in character, such as this:

> Why do I continue to live
> Without shelter, without welcome?
> No, it is better to die
> Since my song is all sung.

I sent my verses to the journal *Niva* and feverishly awaited an answer. But the rascals did not reply. At the age of fifteen, however, it occurred to me that not only to write but to read verses was nonsense. I later valued the charm of Pushkin, Lermontov, and other poets. But then immediately after reading Gustave Aymard and Jules Verne, I precociously went to Leo Tolstoy's *Anna Karenina*, literature which was strictly prohibited at the time for youngsters.[3]

At sixteen and seventeen (sixth and seventh grades) our circle was already rather knowledgeable. We read about and deliberated social problems in a topsy-turvy fashion, without sequence or guidance. We analyzed literary productions on our own and were interested in science and novel technical inventions. Only on political questions did we spend little time. Possibly this was because in the minds and souls of my Polish friends one idea dominated and stifled everything else: Poland is not dead. And it was inconvenient to discuss such a subject with me present.

We were more passionately occupied with the subject of religion than with any other. Not confessions of faith particularly, but questions about the existence of God. Sleepless nights, authentically sincere torment, passionate quarrels occurred as we studied the teachings of the Bible along with Renan and other "godless" literature. It was useless to ask our school religious instructors about our misgivings. Our old priest Father Elisei was not sound on the knowledge of God, and the Lovich religious instructor, when my seventh-grade friend Dubrovskii once turned to him, instead of an answer gave him a two in religious instruction and threatened to fail him on the final examination. Poles could not risk talking with their Polish priest for fear that he would denounce them to the school authorities. Did he not promptly present lists of those avoiding confession? The parents of the "guilty" would be summoned to the director for extremely disagreeable explanations and the guilty ones were penalized one mark for poor conduct.

Many years later when I was studying at the General Staff Academy, professor of psychology A. I. Vvedenskii told us in one of his lectures, "The existence of God is to be assumed but not proved. During my first course in the university, I heard a lecture on theology. The lecturer spent an entire hour proving to us the existence of God by points, one, two, three. When a friend and I left the auditorium (he was a believing person), he said to me sadly, 'Well, brother, apparently God's case is a bad one if one is obliged to have recourse to such evidence as that.'"

The reason I mention Vvedenskii is this: In the sixth grade a Polish friend of mine, contrary to the rules, went to confession not at school but to some young priest. He confessed to his lack of faith. The priest listened and told him, "I pray you, my son, to fulfill a request of mine which will not trouble you and will not bind you to anything."

"Certainly."

"In moments of such doubt, pray to the Creator, 'God, if You exist, help me to know You.'"

My friend left the confessional deeply stirred.

I too went through all stages of hesitation and misgiving in one night, literally in a single night, in the seventh grade and I came to the final and irrevocable decision, "Man, a three-dimensional being, is unable to understand the higher laws of existence and creation. I reject the animal-like psychology of the Old Testament but I completely accept Christianity and Orthodoxy." It was as if a mountain had fallen from my shoulders! By this belief I have lived. And in this belief I will end my years.

CHAPTER 6 TEACHERS

Who were our teachers in school? Recollecting my school years in my memory, I try to find outstanding examples among the teaching staff of my time and I cannot.[1] There were good and bad people, learned and unlearned, honest and greedy, upright and biased, but almost always they were just functionaries. Serving out their time, giving instruction according to the manual, assigning "from this to that" — that was all they did. How it affected us was of no consequence. So we grew by ourselves independently of any school influence. Some were taught by their families and some by their schoolmates the unwritten moral laws about comradeship or relations with their elders, laws which, though unlike the official ones, were not all bad. As illustration, anecdotes must suffice.

There was a teacher of German who atrociously murdered the Russian language. We could not understand him nor he us. In halting speech he once tried for several hours to convince us that the greatest poet of the world was Klopstok.[2] We became so sick of his Klopstok that the very name came to be a cry of invective with us.

He was replaced by another teacher, K., who was a corrupt bribetaker. K. often used to throw rebukes such as this at a student: "You are not improving in this subject. It will be necessary for you to take private lessons from me." His terms were well known. The price was twenty-five rubles a month for half-hour lessons two or three times a week. Good marks for the year and on the examination were guaranteed. Cheap! K. made me such a proposition once. I answered, "We have no money to pay for lessons. Anyway, I know enough to get a three."

In the border regions the instruction in Russian literature with its emphasis on Russification, not only as education but as pure propaganda, should have set an example. But our teachers invested their subjects with such tediousness, such conventionalism, that it is a wonder that they did not kill in Poles as well as in us Russians all inclination to study. They could not, however, extinguish our natural interest in the living word, a thirst for self-education.

In Lovich four subjects in applied mathematics were taught by B., a sickly person who was semi-paralyzed. By nature or because of his illness, he was evil and irritable. He seldom came to school and never explained a lesson. He merely assigned reading and then asked questions. Then without compassion he scattered ones and twos among us. He returned our homework notebooks without a single correction. Obviously they had not been checked but only signed, with one stroke of the pen, by his wife. The head of the school knew all this but closed his eyes to it because the teacher was only two or three years short of his full pension.

At last our class rebelled. We decided to voice our dissatisfaction and I was commissioned to do this. As a Pythagoras, I was subject to less danger from the teacher's wrath.

When B. arrived in class, I addressed him, "Today we are unable to answer your questions. No one has explained anything to us and we do not understand the assignment."

B. shouted at us. He called us fools because we could not understand "such simple things." He still did not explain but began as usual to ask questions. But he put no marks down that day.

The father of one of my friends, Narbut, who had been unjustly barred from an examination, complained to the trustee of the Warsaw educational district. In his complaint he painted a picture of the eccentric teacher B. The complaint was not acted upon but B. was dismissed from administering final examinations and a professor was sent out from Warsaw University to conduct them. Contrary to expectations the examinations went well so B. remained to serve out his time.

This is how written examinations were handled at the end of the year. Teachers from the entire district sent to the trustee confidential plans for examinations or exercises in their subjects. The trustee selected a basic theme and provided copies for all the students at once, sending them to various schools in sealed envelopes which were to be opened only at the examination hour. The completed examinations were returned to the district where on their basis the head appraised the quality of instruction. For two years examinations in "application of algebra to geometry" proved unsatisfactory and our teacher of pure mathematics, G., was called in for a reprimand. G. therefore told one of my classmates with whose family he was on friendly terms, "Although this is a government offense, I will give you my examination plan for the class. The only stipulation is that Ya. not be told about it. I do not trust him."

I must confess that in accordance with our unwritten schoolboy code, we regarded this unexpected aid not as a crime but as a means of self-defense. Moreover it was given not just to favorites but to the entire class. Our school moral code regarded copying and crib sheets in the same way, as well as all other schoolboy deceits, as long as they were not contrary to the interests of the group as a whole.

It was out of the question to tell Ya., who lived in the same quarters with me, about the test, of course. But G. was mistaken about him. He was an orderly person and a loyal friend. I was commissioned by the class to work with him so that, without explaining the reason, I could force him to work out solutions to those exercises which we expected would be on the examination.

Now another question arose: Did we have the moral right to use such an advantage if the Warsaw seventh graders did not have the same benefits? Many of them might fail. The class decided that this was dishonest. We sent a secret envoy to Warsaw to meet there with our friends, the Warsaw seventh graders. Taking Hannibal's oath with them to preserve secrecy, he gave them the exercises — and returned happily.[3]

The day for the examination arrived. They placed us at separate tables. The commissioner opened the envelope and the teacher wrote the text of the exercises on the board. Oh, dear! This was a different exercise and furthermore, at first glance, extremely difficult. I read the problem again. What rubbish! It made no sense. I read it once more. I exchanged glances with the other Pythagorases. With their eyes and gestures they also displayed perplexity. I rose and gave my stamped sheet to the monitor, saying, "The problem is stated incorrectly."

Others followed me. The educational commissioners already were doubtfully whispering among themselves. They went into a huddle with the director. It developed finally that the district council functionary had omitted one line in transcribing the exercise, thanks to which the meaning was lost.

Quickly the commissioners returned and opened the reserve envelope. Hurrah! G.'s exercise. Needless to say, students in our school as well as those in Warsaw performed brilliantly in the examination on the "application of algebra to geometry" and G. received praise from the district head.

Examinations in religious instruction were amusing. We knew the subject poorly. To save face, the religious instruction priest usually assigned questions in advance to those who were graduating and each prepared answers for himself. Each boy was responsible for this assignment and his mark came from them, not from the examination. They proceeded as follows: "Before answering the examination question, I find it necessary to explain . . ." (and the boy would explain the question he had studied in advance). The representatives of the inspection commission listened inattentively and it all passed off as prearranged.

Father Elisei summoned us, the four departing Orthodox students, and said, "I have heard that the Roman priest cheats on the examination. It is unthinkable that we Orthodox should lose face before Roman Catholics. I will ask you, therefore, to copy this . . ." And he showed each of us his plan for the fake examination.

"Now following this," he said, "as if by accident I will give one more question. I will ask one of you, 'Do you know what two holy days are imminent at present?' You answer and explain the significance of the holidays. Another I will ask, 'Do you know what saint's memory is honored today in the holy church?' You will answer. 'And what was remarkable about his death?' You will answer, 'He was sawed apart by his tormentors with a wood saw.' And I will ask you . . ."

I was given the question on the two holidays so all went well. But my poor friend who was assigned the tale about the wood saw understood the insinuation beneath the mocking, piercing glance of the inspector. He blushed, panted, and could not answer. But let us leave that subject.

The exception to teachers such as these was our teacher of pure mathematics, Alexander Zinovevich Epifanov. A Muscovite, an Old Believer, a populist, a sometime Tolstoyite, he came to our town with his young wife immediately after graduation from the Moscow Technical Academy. At once they attracted the attention of all residents because they did not keep servants. And when neighbors observed that Mrs. Professor herself washed the linens and dried them in the yard and that Mr. Professor took out the pail to the cesspool (there being no aqueduct and canal system at that time), there was no end to the amazement and censure.[4] Moreover, when workers brought Mr. Professor's furniture and he, after helping them set it in place, asked them to dine with himself and his wife, everyone in town had different opinions of the event. Some said he was "nutty." Others shook their heads and pronounced the little-understood word "socialist." And the wife of the lieutenant colonel of gendarmes reported in confidence to my mother that secret surveillance had been established over Epifanov.

Epifanov never engaged in subversive activities and in fact never even mentioned politics in conversations with his students. But his influence on us was profound. As a teacher, he made his way into our lives, tried to find causes for delinquency and failure, gave advice, protected us from the excessive wrath of inspectors, and knew how to chastise and to forgive so that we all appreciated the justice of his decisions.

Once four of us went to his home for some kind of clarification. He received us amiably, gave us tea, and invited us to come in the evenings "whenever troubling questions pop into your heads." We went often. He did not moralize or impose his own opinions in either literary or simply worldly subjects but held free discussions with us, which was especially flattering. Imperceptibly he influenced our understanding of good, of truth, of duty, and of relations with others. Alexander Zinovevich Epifanov sowed many good seeds in youthful souls.

One evening a teaching assistant inspecting the students' quarters did not find me and the others at home and discovered that we had gone to the Epifanovs'. The school head immediately ordered us to discontinue these visits.

Epifanov did not remain in Vlotslavsk long. He was transferred, not at his own request, to Lovich. The authorities in Lovich did not appreciate him either. After stormy protests from him against the denunciation system they protected, he was transferred at a lower salary to Zamost where there was then some preparatory gymnasium or trade school. I know nothing about his life after that.

CHAPTER 7   FATHER'S DEATH

Father did not teach or instruct me. That was not in his character. But everything he told me about himself and about people was imbued with such sincere serenity, such straightforward integrity, such clear protest against all dishonest individuals, and such stoical behavior in all misfortunes that those conversations were deeply implanted in my soul.

In spite of his age he was healthy and robust. I recall that once we were in town and met a fifteen-year-old who stood crying beside a heavy sack of meal. He had put the sack down from his shoulders in order to rest and then was unable to take it up again. Father lifted the sack dusty with meal and thus contracted a serious rupture. That was the first illness or injury of his life, unless one considers the wounds to his hands dealt by Polish "mowers" in hand-to-hand combat, so deep that scars remained. Father considered the wounds minor and they were not even entered on his service list.

Only in the last years of his life did Father begin to suffer pains in his stomach. He would not see a doctor, never having been accustomed to one. Besides, they were too expensive for us. For several years he used some kind of home remedy. In the spring of 1885, Father could not get out of bed because of severe pains and incurable hiccups. The doctor diagnosed it as cancer of the stomach. Mother did not leave the sickbed. At night they made me sleep in a neighboring room. Father began often and calmly to speak of his impending death, causing searing pain in my heart. I have never forgotten his final farewell:

"Soon I am going to die. I leave you, dear, and your mother in poverty. But you must not grieve. God will not forsake you. Only be an upright person, support Mother, and everything else will take care of itself. I have lived long enough. I thank the Creator for everything. My only regret is that I will not live to see your officer's epaulets."

The days of the Great Fast came. Father often prayed aloud, "Lord, let me die together with Thee." On Good Friday I was in the shrouded church to sing, as usual, in the choir. A boy we knew came to me saying, "Your mother says that you are to come home." I ran all the way home. But Father was already dead. His wish to die on Good Friday was fulfilled. Was it self-willed or the grace of God?

On the third day of Easter Father was buried. Musicians from the 1st Rifle Battalion played the funeral march; a hundred frontier guards conducted the coffin to the grave with a rifle salvo salute; the grave was covered with earth. Mother and I, unfortunate and miserable that day as never before, returned to our orphaned home.[1]

With Father gone our material circumstances seemed catastrophic. Mother began to receive a pension of only twenty rubles a month. It occurred to me, although I was still young and not skilled in the science, to tutor two young second graders. For two lessons I received twelve rubles a month. I had no inclination for teaching and this employment bothered me terribly, particularly in winter when darkness fell so early. I would return from school at four o'clock, eat quickly, and run to one lesson, then to the opposite end of town for the other. Thus it was already night before I could prepare my own lessons. There was no leisure for childish play or for Gustave Aymard. I lived for holidays as for manna from the sky.

We led a miserable existence for two more years before it became unbearable. In a family council (Mother, Nanny, and I), we decided to ask permission to rent quarters to students. I went with Mother to Director Levshin. He gave us permission to keep eight students. The normal price was twenty rubles per person. Because of my school reputation as a Pythagoras, the director designated me the "elder" in the apartment. After that, although we were not wealthy, at least the unremitting poverty which had hung over us for so many years ended.

At that time a sharp alteration in our family status occurred. My school successes, a kind of seriousness brought on me by Father's death and his dying admonition to support Mother, and my participation in earning our bread were some of the causes. But on the other hand, poor Mother was so lonely that she instinctively sought someone to lean on, even if that someone was a fifteen-year-old son. All this plainly made me an equal member of the family. Never again was I chastised or scolded. Mother shared her experiences with me and sometimes even asked my advice concerning our uncomplicated household economy.

Later, when I was an officer, Mother came to live with me. She died in 1916 in Kiev, when I was in the war, commanding an army corps.

CHAPTER 8   CHOICE OF A CAREER

During my first year, according to the ancient custom, my parents practiced divination on some family holiday or other. They placed on a tray a cross, a toy saber, a wineglass, and a little book. Whatever I first touched was supposed to predestine my career. When they brought them to me, I first was drawn to the saber but afterward I played with the wineglass. And I showed no interest in anything else. Telling me about it later, Father laughed and said, "Well, I think it is poor business. My son is to be a bully and a drunkard!"

The foretelling was true in one way but not in the other. The saber, as a matter of fact, actually predicted my life's career, but I have not

avoided bookish wisdom. Neither did I become a drunkard although
I have not altogether avoided spirits. I was drunk, however, only once
in my life and that was on the day that I was promoted to officer.

Father's tales and my childish play ("war" with saber and rifle) all
built toward an agreeable decision. As a boy I used to disappear for
hours to the exercise area of the 1st Rifle Battalion and walk to the
water troughs and horse baths with the Lithuanian lancers. They
allowed me to shoot in target practice with the frontier guards. I
would walk three versts [about two miles] to the target-shooting area
of the sharpshooter company and make my way to the scorekeeper's
hole concealed in front of the targets. The bullets whistling over our
heads were terrifying but always interesting and awe-inspiring to a
small boy, eliciting envy for the soldier's life. Walking back along the
road with the riflemen, I accompanied them in soldiers' songs, such
as:

> The glorious blare of trumpets
> From the Danube, from the river . . .

In short, I grew up in a military environment. I made acquaintances among the officers and still more friends among the soldiers.
From the soldiers I sometimes bought military cartridges with some
chance five-kopeck note which might come my way or with money
obtained from selling old school notebooks. I would unload the cartridges to get gunpowder to shoot in Father's ancient pistol or I would
blow up mislaid field charges.

I saw my future officer's life as a regime of perfect delights and
uninterrupted merriment. Two cornets from the 5th Lancer Regiment lived in our house.[1] I often watched them galloping at drills,
and in their apartment smoke always drifted to the beams when their
friends gathered. Through their open window I could hear the merry
shouts and singing. Although it frightened me too, I was especially
intrigued when one of the cornets would sit on the windowsill and
lower himself by his feet, still holding his wineglass. He would noisily
greet acquaintances approaching along the street. I thought: He is on
the third floor, he may fall any minute and hurt himself!

Twenty-five years later during the Japanese War, I had the opportunity to reminisce with the object of my youthful admiration. The
former cornet was then General Rennenkampf, the famous leader of

the Eastern detachment of the Manchurian Army and I was his chief of staff.

By the time I reached the higher grades in school, my free time had virtually disappeared and I had other interests as well so my "military exercises" almost ceased. But I loved gymnastics and thrived on the military regime which was introduced into school programs in 1889.[2] In any case, when I completed realschule, although my high marks in mathematics offered the possibility of going to any technical institution I chose, there was no discussion about my future. I chose a military career.[3]

CHAPTER 9   IN MILITARY SCHOOL

In the late 1880s there were two types of schools that supplied the Russian army with officers. There were the military schools, homogeneous in terms of both education and cultural level because they were filled with lads who were graduates of the cadet corps (secondary educational institutions with military training). There were also the junker schools to which young men came "from aside," that is, from all categories and all classes of civilian secondary schools. The majority entering the latter had not completed their secondary education, a fact which gave these schools their second-rate character. Military schools furnished officers to all branches of the army, but the junker schools prepared only for the infantry and cavalry in the ranks midway between officers and sergeants. Only later were junker school graduates promoted to officer.

In the 1880s the ratio of graduates from military and junker schools was 26 percent and 74 percent respectively. After application of progressive reforms before World War I, by 1911 both schools became "military."[1] Then the Russian officer personnel conceded nothing in qualifications to German officers and were higher than the French in quality.

In 1888 a third type of school was created, the so-called "Moscow Junker School with a military school curriculum." The program and regulations were identical with those of the military schools, and volunteer enlisted men who applied there were accepted so long as they had completed courses in legitimate secondary or higher civilian educational institutions. That type of school proved so necessary that the "Moscow School" was soon crowded; therefore, a similar program was also made available in the Kiev Junker School, where I enrolled in the fall of 1890 after preliminary registration in the 1st Rifle Regiment quartered in Plotsk.

There were ninety of us. For class assignments we were divided into three sections with individual staffs of teachers, but in all other respects (schedules, provisions, equipment, front line instruction) we were molded in the same way as were junkers in the junker program. But our great superiority at graduation gave us an involuntary sense of pride.

Our school was housed in an ancient fortress with vaulted wall niches. Windows faced the street and cannon embrasures overlooked the field toward the Dnieper River. A new life began for us, locked inside four walls from which the world was prohibited and accessible only on furlough days. The schedule of our daily routine was strict and punctilious to the hour and the minute. Day and night, work and leisure, even our intimate functions were performed under the bombardment of glances from dozens of strangers.

For people accustomed to freedom such as gymnasiasts and students, this half-free existence was new and strange. Some junkers were dejected initially and sauntered forlornly around their uncomfortable quarters repenting their choice of a career. I personally, having been associated from childhood with the military life, was not uncomfortable in the junker regime. But with the rest, in the quiet nights of the fragrant southern spring, I often spent hours in the open embrasures languidly contemplating the field, meditating on freedom. Some became so bold that, risking certain expulsion from school, they would descend on knotted sheets through the embrasures down to a vacant place. Then they would go through the field to the Dnieper shore and wander there by the hour. Just before dawn, by a prearranged signal, a whistle, they were summoned by fellow conspirators left upstairs. In case of an inspection by the officer of the day, stuffed figures rested quietly in the beds of the disobedient absent ones.

Leaves (normally one day a week) were exceedingly valuable to us and loss of leave for bad conduct or an unsatisfactory mark was a painful experience. Those who had forfeited leave therefore sometimes went secretly into the city. They returned through classrooms on the lower floor. There junkers usually prepared lessons every evening. I came to misfortune once. Returning from an unauthorized leave, I rapped discreetly on the window of our section. My friends heard. One placed himself at his post by the glass doors, another opened the window into which I threw my bayonet, cap, and cloak. Then I jumped in the window and instantly pretended to be absorbed in a book. But I was left with the problem of transferring my outdoor clothing to our quarters. Most difficult of all was the cloak. I threw it over my shoulders and proceeded with caution toward my company. Unfortunately I walked into the path of the officer of the day.

"Why are you wearing a cloak?"

"I had a bit of a chill, Captain, sir."

The captain had suspicion in his glance. Maybe once or twice in his life he too had been forced to pretend he had a "chill."

"Have you been to the infirmary?"

"I refuse to give in to it, Captain, sir."

He walked on and I escaped expulsion from school.

Junkers had to return from legitimate leaves by evening roll call. To be late, even if only by a minute, meant God preserve you. There was no widespread drunkenness in school. But junkers often returned from town slightly tipsy. This always caused complications, for to be found drunk could mean cashiering from school. For "smelling of wine" the penalty was arrest and "third section for conduct," which adversely affected a junker's standing, especially with regard to graduation.[2] If the junker were unable to report to the officer of the day without stumbling, then he was obliged to take heroic measures which involved grave risk. Instead of the drinker, one of his friends would report, provided that the officer of the day did not know their faces. Such substitutions did not always succeed.

Once false Junker K. reported to Captain Levutskii: "Captain, sir, Junker P. reporting . . . " Under Levutskii's fixed stare, his voice trembled and his eyes began to waver. Levutskii understood the situation. He barked, "Bring Junker P. to me as soon as he sobers up." In the morning both junkers, terrified, placed themselves before Levutskii. The captain addressed himself to P.: "Well, sir, my dear fellow, obviously you are not entirely a bad sort or Junker K. would not have risked his career on the day before his leave. I do not wish to ruin you. Get out!" And he did not report it to the head of the school.

Cadet psychology accepted punishment for drunkenness, considering it somewhat oppressive but unavoidable. But the offense of "smelling of wine" was incomprehensible, especially since we were eighteen to twenty-three years old and some in the junker course were even thirty. In the army at that time, on military celebrations, drams of vodka were issued by the crown. Besides, our school administrators were not exactly puritans.

Of course, military discipline, in the sense of carrying out direct orders and rendering the respect due to rank, was held in great esteem. But our junker tradition had made some unique modifications. Deceit in general, and in particular harming others, was considered dishonest. But to deceive teachers in recitation or examinations was permitted. Junker circles fully approved absence without leave or use of the bayonet in hand-to-hand struggle with "freebooters" in some strange suburb of Kiev, when it was necessary to rescue friends or to "uphold junker honor." Any audacious action in which junkers forgot to fear risk was considered right. But on the other hand, punishment for such acts, although it elicited compassion, was respected as legitimate. Especially firmly upheld was the tradition of comradeship, particularly in one of its manifestations, not to tattle. When one of my comrades struck an informer and was transferred for this to the "third section," not only his comrades but some of the superiors tried to rescue him from his misfortune and even persecuted the struck one.

As for rations and salary, we in the junker course lived almost in a soldierly situation. We ate modestly because our per diem allowance (about twenty-five kopecks) was only ten kopecks more than that of the soldier. We also received the imperial uniform and linens of the soldier, of poor quality at that time. Most junkers relied on a small sum of money from home (Mother sent me five rubles a month). But junkers without homes or from very poor families had to subsist on the crown stipend, which consisted then of 22.5 kopecks a month for privates or 33.3 for corporals. This was not enough to buy tobacco or a toothbrush or postage stamps, but they endured their situation stoically.

Of course, living conditions in a school distinguished by austere simplicity and frugality were a good introduction to a subaltern officer's life. It is necessary to note that in the early 1890s a young officer received about fifty rubles a month. Although the salary was to increase twice before the revolution, an officer's living standard always remained at a low level. Therefore, when during revolutionary meetings Bolshevik orators classified officers as bourgeoisie, a hateful and detrimental term, this was not accurate. In the main the Russian officer corps belonged to the category of laboring proletariat intelligentsia.

The military education stood rather high in all those schools. Military training soon transformed former gymnasiasts, seminarians, and students into proper junkers, creating that special bearing which remained with most men until death and allowed one to distinguish a military man even in civilian dress. We passed through soldier training sequentially, the first year as students, the second as instructors of young junkers. To promote success, we boasted and companies competed with one another. Understandably, therefore, we all experienced bitter insult when the commander of the military district, the famous General M. Dragomirov, took a single glance at the school and, finding complete confusion in the ranks, banished us from the drill ground. The problem was that, according to the program, there were only platoon drills going on but Dragomirov, not knowing, expected battalion drills. The misunderstanding was soon cleared up. On the other hand, all of us sighed with joy when the general warmly praised us on a maneuver. We participated in a "first" for the Russian army, an exercise with live cartridges, firing artillery over the heads of the infantry. Until that innovation by Dragomirov, infantry was not deployed in front of batteries in the enormous sector of artillery fire, which entirely distorted the representation of actual combat. Artillerymen were obviously nervous and projectiles sometimes fell dangerously close to us. In junker ranks, however, this caused not the slightest confusion and the drill generally went brilliantly.

During classwork there was always quiet and order. Only in French language class did the junkers behave without constraint. Military subjects and corollary courses were on a sound basis, although too theoretical. Later, during the military renaissance following the Japanese War, programs were altered for the better.[3] They gave knowledge of civilian subjects, but did not elevate general education, which was supposedly completed in secondary schools. General subjects included religious instruction, two foreign languages, chemistry, mechanics, analytics, and Russian literature. It was characteristic that, probably from the fear of spreading "pernicious ideas," only ancient literature was taught.

If three-fourths of the junkers' energy and labor went toward mastering science, then, just as in my realschule, one-fourth went to pranks. Cribs, particularly for chemical formulas and for ballistics, were written on cuffs or on paper pulled out from the sleeve on rubber bands. Recitation in religious instruction came straight from the manual. For a written test in the Russian language we prepared notes beforehand and distributed them. Each junker prepared one exercise, allotted in sequence numbered by parts. And during the examination, accompanied by notes, they seated themselves in order by cribs. And so on.

I studied well and rarely had recourse to such legerdemain except in French recitation. My classmate Nesterenko, who had a good mastery of languages, usually delivered the recitation for three, twice changing clothes. In someone else's uniform, now with sunken cheeks, then with candy in his mouth to alter his voice, he had a deeply comical appearance. The French teacher never remembered a face. Nesterenko would translate French slowly and deliberately for me, at about an eight or nine mark.[4] But once he forgot and read the French text with such a good accent that the French teacher pricked up his ears and fell silent. Nesterenko expected to be told when to stop but the order did not come so he translated and translated.

The Frenchman, now wise to the affair, solemnly took us both in hand and began to lead us to the inspector of classes. "Your Excellency, do not ruin us," we cried. And all of the recitation class chorused: "Do not ruin them." The Frenchman took us only as far as the door and then let us go.

Such customs proved especially tenacious. Reading reminiscences by a junker who was there eight years later, I found that he described his junker pranks exactly as I remembered mine, with only slight "technical improvements."

One way or another we completed school with sufficient specialized knowledge for entry into the service. But neither school program nor instructors nor authorities bothered to broaden our views of the world nor to answer all the spiritual questions of such young men. Russian life was tempestuous then but the so-called "damnable questions" including politics, governmental decisions, and social questions remained beyond us.

I must say that nowhere were university youth engaged in such stormy and active participation in the political life of the country as they were in Russia. Party circles, participation in revolutionary organizations, student strikes for political motives, meetings, "resolutions," "going to the people" about whom, alas, the youth knew so little (*Nov'* of Turgenev and others) — all this filled student life.[5] In one account of the St. Petersburg Technological Institute, the following data emerged about student participation in political life: "Representing party organizations, 80 percent; without party affiliation, 20 percent; considering themselves 'leftists,' 71 percent; 'rightists,' 5 percent."

Underground literature of the time, composing in many cases the spiritual nourishment of progressive-minded youth, deepened the alienation of students from nationalism, disturbed the mind, and hardened the heart. Left out in this respect, the junker was alienated from the student, who in the main looked on the military sphere as something strange and hostile.

Military schools guarded their charges from spiritual disease and from immature political involvement. But as I have already said, it failed to help them meet the questions which had begun to rock Russian life. The deficit had to be made up by self-education. Many did catch up but the majority did not find the time.

At our school the authorities gave orders, saw that orders were executed, and stood guard over regulations. And no more. Outside working hours, we had no contact with school officials. Nonetheless all the surrounding atmosphere — the living wordless reminder about duty, the strictly regulated life, perpetual work, discipline, junker tradition — educated not only scholastically but also wisely. All of this to a certain degree made up for inadequacies in school, creating a military consciousness and a military psychology which were preserved in later life and provided stability during both peace and war in the days of deep shocks, great temptation.

The military environment remade all the heterogeneous social, propertied, and spiritual elements which passed through military school. A student at St. Petersburg University, N. Lepeshinskii, the brother of a famous Social Democrat who afterward made his career as a Bolshevik, was expelled from the university for revolutionary activity without the right to attend any educational institution — in other words with a "wolf ticket." [6] Lepeshinskii burned his documents and took examinations for a secondary educational institution, pretending to have been previously taught at home. On receiving a certificate, he entered the Moscow junker school.

After several months in this school, where Lepeshinskii studied and conducted himself excellently, he was summoned to the inspector of classes, Captain Lobachevskii. "Is this actually you?" Lepeshinskii turned pale. On the table lay the proscription list periodically dispatched from the Ministry for Public Instruction and on it, underlined in red, was his family name.

"Yes, Captain, sir."

Lobachevskii looked him steadily in the eye and said, "Now go!" And it was never mentioned again.

Truly, Lobachevskii must have had great faith in the "immunity" of the military school. Lepeshinskii and I served together in the 2nd Artillery Brigade. Except for his extreme skepticism, nothing revealed his past because he served his country zealously. In the Japanese War he fought valiantly until cut down by hostile fire.

I have dwelt on these questions because our military way of life later had two significant historical consequences. As a result of insufficient information about local political currents and especially about social questions, Russian officers were at a loss on the day of the first revolution and conversion of the country to a representative regime. And in the year of the second revolution the majority of officers were unarmed and helpless before the unrestrained revolutionary propaganda, unable even to answer soldier semi-intelligentsia trained in revolutionary underground activity.

As to the second consequence, a man of the socialist camp who was hardly inclined to idealize the military said, "The intelligentsia scorned sport as they did work and consequently were unable to defend themselves from physical abuse. Despising the military regimen as a school for war, they aspired to escape or to curtail the sole possibility for them to acquire physical qualifications, that of military service. Only the officer corps received different schooling and therefore it alone was capable of bearing arms to defend its national ideal in the epoch of civil war."[7] Without these two prefaces one cannot understand the course of the Russian revolution and civil war, 1917–1920.

CHAPTER 10   GRADUATION
AS AN OFFICER

Before the last camp roll call at the completion of the two-year course, we performed a "funeral" with appropriate solemnity. We buried "science" (textbooks) and a graduating junker, with his full consent of course. Behind the coffin (an unhinged door) we walked solemnly in procession as the relatives, while in front were the "clergy" dressed in vestments of quilts and sheets. The clergy proclaimed a eulogy, the choir sang, and the school orchestra followed with a funeral march. We carried lighted candles and burned incense which was really cheap smoking tobacco. The procession, all classmates in rank order, continued until the unexpected appearance of the officer of the day put the entire company to flight, including the "late lamented."

None of us imputed a sacrilegious meaning to this "funeral." The majority of the participants were believing people who regarded the traditional "ritual" as a prank but did not at all scoff at sacred things. In the same way it is not sacrilege in the Russian tradition to represent in song, such as children's Christmas carols, heavenly forces in twofold earthly and familiar appearance.

The cadets had composed songs in which the personalities of their superiors were only lightly disguised. They had analyzed with precision the characters of their chiefs, observed their weaknesses, and dispensed well-earned nicknames. For one there was a eulogy, for another evil accusations. These songs had often been sung secretly to classmates but now they were sung openly to graduates, even the entire company in the line returning from studies. The authorities did not react.

Before going to the last camp roll call an action important to junkers occurred, that of choosing our future posts. On a list according to longevity were sergeant majors, then student noncommissioned officers; last came junkers according to marks.

At the beginning of the first year an unpleasant thing had occurred to me. I had applied myself to the junker program without any preconceptions and had made quite a few friends among the junkers. But all of a sudden those friends began to avoid me and the junker chief (above all it was a junker course) began to persecute me, using his authority for chastisement in a way not employed with others, constantly reporting me to the officer of the day. I could not understand why. Finally one of my junker friends explained to me confidentially that the junker chiefs of our company (the 1st) had agreed to punish me for an insult to the entire program. Allegedly, during evening class-preparation, when a junker had come into our section, I had said, "I cannot tolerate it when these blockheads come here."

The junker was mistaken. The incident actually occurred; however, it was not I who had made the remark but Silin, a junker from the 2nd Company. Silin, a person of integrity, went immediately to the 1st Company and confessed to the sergeant major that he had said it. The persecution ceased at once. Relations with friends were restored but my conduct record was hopelessly ruined. Until the end of the year I remained in the secondary ranks for insubordination and regardless of good marks was not promoted to student noncommissioned officer. The second year passed without punishment and my graduating marks averaged 10.4. They promoted me at last and thus guaranteed a good position.

On the junker exchange openings were quoted as follows: Guards (1 vacancy), field artillery (5 to 6 vacancies), military engineers (5 to 6 vacancies), and the rest were in the infantry. Our sergeant major took the single vacancy in the Guards. For later graduates there were more but Guards' vacancies were scarce then. Although no formal regulations existed, according to tradition only the hereditary nobility were promoted to the Guards.[1] Misunderstandings occurred when junkers not of the nobility and not warned in advance chose Guards' vacancies. Some notorious cases went as far as the sovereign. But the emperor could not or would not violate tradition. The young officers, humiliated, were removed from the Guards regiment and received other appointments.

I chose a vacancy in the 2nd Artillery Brigade quartered in the town of Bela in Sedlets province, which later went to Poland by the Riga Agreement of 1921. I remember feeling a certain sense of loss after choosing a position. Aside from objective conditions and individual tastes, there was something final and providential in this choice of our life's path, a crisis of destiny. That choice predetermined for many men the arrangement of their personal lives, their official success or failure, even life or death. Persons at the end of the roll were left only staff positions with famous historical names. Some were relegated to barracks in open fields far from towns, some were sent to the Caucasus or quartered in hopeless Siberian wastes. In some of those forlorn places, outside the regimental cemetery lay special cemeteries for "those who committed suicide." Most of them were quite young officers who could not adjust to the sadness, the primitive conditions, and the lonely ways of their new lives.

Fate scattered us to the winds, to our various camps. Of my schoolfellows in the Kiev graduating class of 1892, only two achieved outstanding military careers, Pavel Sytin and Silvestr Stankevich. Pavel Sytin completed the military school course and went into the artillery as a second lieutenant. Later he graduated from the General Staff Academy and returned to the lines. By the end of World War I he was the commanding general of an artillery brigade. At the start of the revolution, this intractable demagogue and "revolutionary" snatched his fortune from the bloody calamity. And he was successful. He was one of the first to enter the service of the Bolsheviks, named originally (though not for long) as commander in chief of the Red southern front. He led that Red horde against the Don and my Volunteer Army in the winter of 1918.[2]

When Silvestr Stankevich completed the junker course, he went as an ensign bearer to the infantry. He received his first George's Cross in the Chinese campaign of 1900, commanding a company of Siberian riflemen in the famous feat of taking the Taku forts.[3] In World War I he commanded a regiment and later a brigade in the 4th Rifle "Iron" Division which I commanded, and he performed courageously in all its glorious battles. In 1916 he took over the Iron Division from me. When the army broke up, since he was of Polish descent, he had an opportunity to occupy a high post in the Polish army, but he did not wish to desert his adopted land. He fought skillfully and valiantly against the Bolsheviks at the head of the Dobrovolskii Division in the Donets basin against Pavel Sytin's troops. There he died. The two men illustrate the tragic bifurcation of the Old Russian army. Two paths, two consciences.

Promotion day approached. We felt as though we were the center of creation. The impending event was so important, such a sharp break in our lives, that the waiting obscured all other interests. We knew that the promotion ceremony in St. Petersburg was to be very solemn; a brilliant parade would take place at Krasnoe Selo in the Highest Presence. The sovereign himself would congratulate those promoted. How it would be for us, however, was uncertain. This would be the first graduation of officers in Kiev.

On August 4 the rumor suddenly spread through the camp that the promotions had already occurred in St. Petersburg. On the basis of this several junkers had received congratulatory telegrams. Agitation and bitterness. Had we been forgotten? Actually it was a misunderstanding. Toward evening of the next day we heard the resounding voice of the duty junker, "Officers must assume formation in the foreyard." We ran headlong to the entrance, buckling our belts on the way. The school head entered, read a telegram congratulating us on our promotions, and said several cordial words designed to prepare us for our journey to a new life. And that was all.

We were confused, even stunned. How simple, how prosaic it seemed for such an extraordinary event. But the feeling of annoyance soon dissipated and a sudden groundswell of joy engulfed us, penetrating every pore of our transformed beings. We hastily threw on our new officers' uniforms and rushed into town. We went to relatives, acquaintances, anyone who merely happened to be in town. We mingled with the noisy throngs in the teeming streets, plunging ourselves into the heretofore unreal and forbidden life we imagined to be full of lights, joy, and merriment.

That evening, smoke hung about the rafters of all the entertainment establishments in Kiev. We wandered in groups from one place to another, taking our boisterous merriment with us. Most of the school officers were along. Wine flowed freely as we improvised songs and exchanged reminiscences. Our heads were in a drunken fog but our hearts were so overwhelmed with emotions that we felt we could take all the world in our arms and kiss it. Later the people, the little tables, the stages all melted into one many-sided, many-colored spot and swam off.

In Old Russia there were two occasions when carefree, drunken merriment was acceptable in the eyes of society and of those preserving order. These were occasions acknowledged to carry immunity from the usual rules. One was the day of promotion to officer. The other was an annual university holiday, "Tatiana's Day," when old professors and ex-students of all ages and positions forgot their years, gray hair, and ailing livers and joined the young students wandering from one restaurant to another. They drank endlessly, kissed, sang the "Gaudeamus," and in an excess of emotion and booze swore "loyalty oaths" to disregard any police prohibitions.

Two days after our holiday, they shipped us from Kiev to all the corners of Russia for a twenty-eight-day leave, after which our new lives began.

PART II

"I have been informed that several participants in the past campaign have expressed extreme dissatisfaction with my lectures. I humbly beseech these individuals to make their opinions public. I am prepared to prove my every word with documents, frequently handwritten by the person who expressed the opinion."

No one spoke. But apparently the question put by the ruler received a negative answer, since the history project was again shelved. It was not published until 1905.

Speaking of the negative aspects of the academy, I must at the same time with all sincerity express my honest appreciation of our alma mater, in spite of its deficits and despite all the trials about which I write. Although the courses offered were frequently unessential and unnecessary, outdated in regard to the applied arts of war, still they immeasurably extended our horizons, provided direction and criteria to our knowledge of military affairs, and equipped those who seriously wanted to continue working and studying in their future lives. Because the best teacher of all is still life.

It had been recently decided that the academy would be a multipurpose institution. It then functioned as a special school for training General Staff officers but also as a military university. From the academy came twice as many officers as were then needed for the General Staff, so those who did not receive staff positions were returned to their regiments "to elevate the military educational level of the army."

The military university idea failed. It was almost impossible for an officer otherwise unprivileged to enter the broad path of a peacetime military career except through the narrow gate of the General Staff. Suffice it to say that at the time of World War I the high command included an overwhelming majority of officers graduated from the General Staff Academy. Twenty-five percent of them were regimental commanders, 68 to 77 percent were commanders of infantry and cavalry divisions, 62 percent were corps commanders. Academy graduates not among the top fifty in their class were not promoted to the General Staff, sometimes because of a fractional deficit in their final marks, and they returned to the ranks in a dejected mood. They bore the stamp of an unlucky person in the eyes of line officers and their futures were cloudy. This circumstance plus the inadequate salary provided by the St. Petersburg contract (eighty-one rubles a

month) as well as the competition raging in academic life gave existence the character of an authentic struggle for survival.

It was during my academic years that I first had an opportunity to
see Emperor Nicholas II and his family. I saw them in various set-
tings. The first time was at the opening of the officers' Assembly of
the Guards, Army, and Fleet, which was founded by order of Emperor Alexander III. The enormous hall was overflowing. Present
were Emperor Nicholas II, the grand dukes, high-ranking generals,
and many ordinary officers. Our professor, Colonel Zolotarev, was on
the podium and his speech was dedicated to the history of the reign of
Alexander III. While Zolotarev spoke about the domestic policies of
Alexander III (which were, of course, extremely conservative), those
in the hall listened in strained silence. But then his lecture moved to
external policies. Sketching in sharp detail the "pro-German policies
of the predecessor of Alexander III which were so humiliating to
Russian dignity, so extremely detrimental to the interests of Russia,"
Zolotarev attributed great merit to the late tsar who established the
watchword, "Russia for Russians," and who urged "renunciation of all
obligations to the Hohenzollerns and restoration of our freedom of
action in regard to other western powers."[1]

The first rows began stirring. I could hear dull whispers of disap-
proval; chairs moved demonstratively and sarcastic smiles appeared.
The higher dignitaries on the whole showed their indignation at the
lecturer's address. I was astonished. How could high-ranking people
of quality support such obvious Germanophile views and behave so
ungracefully in the presence of the ruler? When Zolotarev finished,
however, the ruler went to him and in cordial words thanked him for
the "impartial and truthful characterization" of his father's activities.

At the Winter Palace balls were given periodically for the current
circle of high-born persons and officials. But the ball which opened
the season was more accessible. Often fifteen hundred guests attended. The court protocol section invited, among other guests, some
officers of the St. Petersburg garrison and of the academies. The
General Staff Academy received twenty invitations, one of which fell
to me. Two of my friends and I stuck together. Provincials that we
were, the ball seemed to us to be an unheard-of fairyland with the
grandiose and imposing ballroom, the brilliant military and civilian
uniforms, the ladies' gowns, and all the peculiar court ritual. But even

so we were not made to feel uncomfortable by the ritual or the dispar-
ity of our circumstances.

Court officials, swiftly gliding along the parquet floors, with practiced motions cleared a vast circle in the center of the grand hall.
They opened curtains and from an adjoining room, to the strains of a
polonaise, the tsar, the tsarina, and members of the tsarist family
approached two by two. They traversed the living walls of the circle,
affably nodding to the guests. Subsequently the tsar and tsarina were
seated in an adjacent room where they observed the dancing and
conversed with individuals invited into their parlor. Dancing went on
inside the circle. According to court etiquette all guests stood. There
were no chairs in the hall.

Since dancing did not particularly interest us, we moved closer to
the parlor and kept a curious eye on happenings there. Not only was
court life interesting but also the sequence of the guests. We recognized that if, for example, an ambassador of one power was invited in
for conversation, then another would not be; also, that if one was
invited in ahead of another, this signified something in the nuances of
foreign policy. And that, since one of the Russian ministers whose
position was said to be insecure was conveyed to the parlor, it meant
he had nothing more to fear.

At intervals, while keeping an eye on the parlor, we sampled the
tsarist champagne according to our capacities, going from one refreshment buffet to another. At that time the palace served champagne with a French label. But soon after, at Emperor Nicholas's
initiative, Abrau-Diurso came into vogue from a vineyard near
Novorossiisk which was not at all inferior to French wine. And this
fashion spread to all of Russia to the detriment of French exports.

After the dancing, all the invited guests went to an upper floor
where supper was served in a series of halls. At the tsar's table and in
adjoining rooms certain individuals were placed here or there according to a list; the rest were disposed freely without regard to rank.
Before the conclusion of supper, during coffee, the ruler walked
through the halls, pausing from time to time in front of the little
tables to converse with one or another of the guests.

The accessibility of the Winter Palace surprised me. When we entered the palace, the sentries allowed us to pass without even checking
our credentials. I became apprehensive because I had experienced a

last-minute crisis. While dressing at home, I had noticed that my epaulets were not sufficiently shiny so I borrowed some from my neighbor, an artilleryman. They were new but in my haste I did not notice that his bore a different number (mine was two).

The Winter Palace was still more accessible every year on November 26, the holiday for the Order of St. George, when everyone in St. Petersburg listed as a knight of the order was invited to a Te Deum and to an imperial luncheon.[2] An imperial presentation was held in the palace. Between ranks of officers lining the path from the imperial apartments to the palace church came a procession of veterans from the Sevastopol campaign, the Turkish War, and the Caucasus and Turkestan expeditions.[3] Russia's history was embodied in those individuals who had witnessed her military glories. At the end of the procession walked the tsar and both tsarinas, passing only three or four steps from our ranks.[4]

All officers had access to this imperial presentation but there was never a troublesome occurrence. Obviously, an assassination attempt would have been simple but the militant revolutionaries could not get in. Actually, after the 1825 Decembrist insurrection, there was only one case (in the mid-1880s) of a more or less significant officers' plot against the regime. That was the so-called Rykachev affair. Later incidents of officers participating in revolutionary movements were isolated and not serious.

In my time at the academy, as in the army, there was no apparent interest in active political work. I never knew of the existence of political groups in the academy or anything about our officers participating in conspiratorial organizations. Long before our graduation, in the days of the Rykachev affair, the head of the academy at the time, General Dragomirov, was conversing on this subject with academicians and told them, "I will speak to you as persons of conviction. You are free to enter whatever political party you choose. But before you enter, take off your uniform. It is impossible to serve both the tsar and his enemies at the same time." This tradition no doubt was followed by subsequent generations of academicians.

The various academic courses, in addition to serious reading and conversations with St. Petersburg intelligentsia of various opinions, significantly broadened my views. I became acquainted accidentally with underground publications which for some reason circulated under the conventional designation of "literature." It was chiefly propagandistic and served to educate a wide circle of our university youth. What sincere emotion, what genuine warmth the youth brought to this work! And how many lives, what promising young talents were distorted in the underground!

On one occasion two female acquaintances, two students, came to me and said emotionally, "For God's sake, help us. We are expecting a raid. Would it be possible for you to hide some literature for a few days?"

"Certainly, but with the stipulation that I may look it over personally."

"Please do."

That evening they dragged in three bulky suitcases. I familiarized myself with this sterile, misguided literature which composed in many cases the sole spiritual nourishment of outstanding young people. I think that the authors or the distributors of that propaganda, if some are still alive, would feel awkward reading it now. The watchword was destruction; nothing was said of building, there was only malice and endless hatred. At that time authority gave sufficient cause for censure and condemnation, but the literature was often host to conscious untruths. In matters involving labor and the peasants, demagoguery played upon base emotions without regard to state interests. This literature refused to concede the necessity of the army as protector of the state and misunderstood or ignored the army's customs and life. Those were anonymous pamphlets. But a former officer, the author of *Sevastopol Tales* and *War and Peace*, the philosopher of Yasnaya Polyana — Leo Tolstoy himself — wrote brochures such as "Pis'mo k fel'dfebeliu" (Letter to a Sergeant Major), "Soldatskaia pamiatka" (A Soldier's Memorial), and "Ne ubii" (Do Not Kill) in which he called upon the army to mutiny, reiterating: Officers are murderers. Governments with their taxes, their soldiers, their prisons and gallows, and their impostor-priests are the greatest enemies of Christianity.[5]

Later I read illegal journals published abroad and smuggled into Russia. They made the same negative impression on me. Struve's *Osvobozhdenie*, the journal with the idea "fight for a constitution" as its basic tenet, played a part in the preparation of the first revolution (1905); Amfiteatrov's *Krasnaia znamia* was particularly notable for its crude demagoguery.[6] In the latter journal one could read such revelations as this: What is the first thing necessary to make a victorious socialist revolution? The answer is: Relying on the peasantry and laboring masses, to proclaim and make the military class obsolete. "Revolutionary democracy" thus tried to prepare a gloomy fate for Russia in the face of well-armed Pan-German and Pan-Asiatic (Japanese) expansion and encroachment. As for the "socialist revolution" and the "military class," history has already shown us how this turned out.

My political creed was formed in the academic years. I never sympathized with the *Narodniki* (whose heirs were the Socialist Revolutionaries) and their terror and incitement of the peasants to riot, nor with Marxism and its elevation of materialistic over spiritual values and the destruction of human personality. I espoused Russian liberalism in its ideological essence without any sort of party dogmatism. In broad generalization this attachment led me to three theses: (1) constitutional monarchy; (2) radical reform; and (3) a peaceful path to restoration of the country.

The first year of academic study ended badly for me. I passed Professor Geisman's examination in the history of military science easily and went on to Baskakov. There I was asked about the battle of Wagram.[7] After listening for a time, Baskakov interrupted me.

"Begin with conditions in the area at exactly twelve o'clock."

I could not recall any crisis at that time and became confused. Baskakov was not satisfied with my approach to the events and he repeated irritably, "Exactly at twelve o'clock."

Finally looking, as always, indifferently and contemptuously at his hearer, he asked, "Perhaps you need an hour to think?"

"It would be utterly useless, Colonel, sir."

At the conclusion of the examination, the commission deliberated for a long time. Torment. At last Geisman entered with a list and read out the marks. In conclusion he said, "The commission's opinion concerning Lieutenants Ivanov and Denikin was to add a half mark to both. Thus Lieutenant Ivanov was given 7 and Lieutenant Denikin 6½."

Assessment of our knowledge was a matter for the professors' consciences, but the "addition" was only malicious mockery. Promotion to the second course required nothing less than a mark of seven. I blushed, however, and said, "I thank the commission very much for its generosity." I had failed. At the academy one could not repeat the first year so it meant expulsion for me.

I digress now to a later time. After several years I got my revenge. In the war with Japan, in 1905 when the Mukden battle began, General Mishchenko was being treated for an injury and for a time General Grekov commanded his Horse Guards. His chief of staff was the professor, Colonel Baskakov. At the time I was chief of staff of one of General Mishchenko's divisions. We had already fought and had acquired some experience. Baskakov was a novice in war and had obviously lost his composure. He arrived at my observation post to ask, "What do you think? What does this movement of the Japanese mean?"

"They are obviously beginning a general attack by encircling the right flank of our army."

"I fully agree with you."

Baskakov arrived three or four more times to inquire what I thought until one time when we came under heavy machine-gun fire while he was there. After that his visits ceased. I must confess to a human weakness. I received great satisfaction from those meetings as retribution for the "twelve o'clock" of Wagram and for the business of the half mark.

But that half mark was my downfall. To return to the brigade after such humiliation was not desirable. In despair I searched for an answer: resignation, transfer to the Amur district border guards, becoming an instructor in Persia? Finally I took the prudent decision to start all over again. I returned to the brigade and after three months again took the examinations for the first course. I did well that time, fourteenth out of 150 (two subjects which helped me were mathematics in which I scored 11.5 and Russian composition, 12). Had it not been for the episode which I will describe in the next chapter, I would have completed the academy happily.

CHAPTER 13   GRADUATION FROM THE ACADEMY

Minister of War Kuropatkin decided to make a change in the academy. General Leer was discharged and a former professor and close friend of Kuropatkin, General Sukhotin, was named head of the academy.[1] That appointment proved to be a complete fiasco. In order to be brief, I will not delve into the specialized circle of scientific academic life. By nature overbearing and churlish with his men, General Sukhotin made an absurd entrance into the academy. He cast public aspersions on Leer, on "his" school, and on "his" students, although his own teaching proved as outmoded and as far from reality as that of his predecessor. He destroyed but he did not build. His brief (about three years) administration of the academy was the dimmest period of its history.

In the spring of 1899 the last of Leer's pupils completed the third course during the time of Sukhotin. According to the Fundamental Laws, lists were drawn up and published of those completing the course, arranged according to seniority in marks.[2] Marks were averaged in two ways: (1) the average for the two-year theoretical course, and (2) the average for three dissertations. About fifty officers, I among them, then a second captain of artillery, were appointed to the General Staff Corps while fifty others (with lower marks) were to return to their units. We, the winning ones, were invited to the academy in Sukhotin's name to be congratulated for achievement; then we were to start our practical work, two weeks of training for the General Staff. We wound up our affairs in St. Petersburg and prepared for departure.

But a surprise awaited us at the academy. The list of officers named to the General Staff had been taken down and in its place was substituted another one, put together on an entirely different basis from that prescribed by law. The total for the final marks was now based on an average of four elements: the average for the two-year theoretical course plus the separate score of each of the three dissertations. The new list represented a complete shuffle. Several officers were dropped from the list altogether and replaced by others. Everyone at the academy was agitated. I passed onto the new list but I was still upset about it.

Our sense of foreboding was justified. Several days later the second list was also rescinded. The new coefficient was of dubious value. For the new total, seniority was composed of five separate coefficients: the mark from the field trips, already computed once in the total marks, plus the four previously used. The field trips, which came at the end of the second year's instruction, were decisive for several officers and the new third list represented a different sequence by which new victims, contrary to regulations, fell from the ranks.

According to tradition, any officer present at the farewell dinner who had received a fraction less than the passing mark for the third course (a ten) could petition the chief for advancement. The request was almost always granted and the officer received a higher mark, which we called a "charity" mark. Looking at the third list, I saw that four officers who had actually received such charity marks were included in the list, and four others who were on the first lawful list had been deprived of their rights.[3] I was one of these four!

It appeared that everything was finished for me. Several days later the academic authorities made new modifications in the total marks; these constituted a fourth list, which proved to be final. I did not appear on that list, nor did the three other officers similarly deprived of their rights.

The lobby and refreshment room of the academy presented an unusual spectacle during those days. Weary from work, tense, uncertain what the next day would bring, we all excitedly discussed the misfortune which had befallen us. A wicked will had played with our destinies, scoffing at law and human dignity. Soon we learned that Sukhotin, without consulting or even notifying the chief of staff to whom the academy was then subordinate, had unceremoniously gone to the minister of war to recommend "academic reforms" and had brought them back with endorsement.

Several times we met, the four of us thrown overboard, to discuss our position. We complained to our academic authorities without result. One of us tried to meet with the war minister but he was not allowed to see him without permission from academic authorities. Another of us appealed to General Ridiger, a personal acquaintance who was head of chancery of the War Ministry and a worthy professor at the academy. Ridiger knew all about the affair but he could not help. "Neither I nor the head of the General Staff can do anything. This nest of wasps has completely surrounded our war minister. My nerves have gone to pieces. I am ill and I am going on vacation."

In my opinion there remained only one thing to do, to take recourse to the legal and prudent means of the Disciplinary Regulation and enter a complaint. Because a violation of our laws occurred by decision of the war minister, a complaint about it must be presented directly to his superior, that is, to the ruler. I proposed this to my comrades in misfortune but they were afraid. So I presented a complaint to the Highest Name. In military existence, to penetrate right through the atmosphere of subservience to anything approaching the very summit of the hierarchical ladder seemed impossible. I confess that it was not without apprehension that I dropped the complaint envelope into the box suspended in the designated building, the box which was labeled "Chancery Petitions to be Presented to the Highest Name." The die was cast.

This episode made a ripple not only in the academy but in the highest bureaucratic circles of St. Petersburg. The chief of staff, the chancery of the War Ministry, and the professors looked upon the incident as a way of fighting Sukhotin. It seemed that whatever happened Sukhotin would not remain undisturbed. Most of the conflict went on above us and the fate of one small officer, locked into it unwillingly and accidentally, was exposed to shocks from omnipotent authority.

My tribulations began. No day passed during which I was not summoned to the academy for interrogation, conducted in a biased and slanted way. They seemed to be summoning me for the purpose of trying to elicit some imprudent word or action in order to cashier me from the academy and be done with all the unpleasant business. They accused and threatened me with trial for the entirely foolish and improvident "crime" (found nowhere in the regulations) of entering a complaint without the permission of that individual about whom the complaint was composed.

The war minister, on learning of the complaint, ordered an academic conference for consideration of the matter. The conference came to the decision that "the assessment of the knowledge of graduates introduced by the head of the academy is unlawful and unjust with regard to those who have already completed the course and objectionable if it is applied to future graduates."

I soon received another notice to come to the academy. Also invited were my three comrades in misfortune. Colonel Moshnin, the director of our course, greeted us and said, "Well, gentlemen, I congratulate you. The war minister has agreed to appoint you to vacancies on the General Staff. Only, Second Captain, you must withdraw your complaint and the rest of you gentlemen must intercede for yourselves in, you know, pitiful terms. Something like this: 'We have no rights, we know that, but taking into account the years we have spent and the work we have done, we beg the kindness of the chiefs.'"

In retrospect I think that Moshnin was endeavoring to obtain our testimony that we had made a "false complaint." But at the time I did not analyze his motives. Blood rushed to my head. "I will not beg for kindness. I seek only that which belongs to me by right."

"In that case, we have nothing further to discuss. I warn you, however, that you will end up badly. You may go, gentlemen."

Putting his arms on the shoulders of my three comrades, Moshnin led them upstairs to an empty auditorium. He gave them paper and seated them at a table. They began to write their piteous petitions.

After the conversation with Moshnin, I became more troubled in spirit and the persecution increased. Moshnin had made a direct statement to the students at the academy: "The fate of Denikin is a foregone conclusion. He will be expelled from the service."

In order to moderate the severity of the academic authorities, I decided to go to the chancery petition director's reception to ask about accelerating the investigation about the war minister. I calculated that after the matter went to another court they would relieve my persecution.

Many people were in the reception room, most of them widows, the rest pensioned service people, all with pathetic afflictions and needs, people in quest of moral right having recourse to their last refuge from deafened truth and official lies. Among them was another artillery captain. He talked nervously with the officer of the day, showing that agitation which afterward he revealed to me. His wandering eyes and incoherent speech clearly disclosed some serious mental illness. Bowing nearly double, he told me in an excited whisper that he possessed an important state secret about high-ranking individuals (he mentioned their names). They knew this, he said, and had tried to extort it from him. They were persecuting and tormenting him, he said, and now he was bringing it all to the tsar. I was relieved to take leave of my neighbor when my turn came.

The setting of the reception astonished me. The director stood at one end of a long writing table as if he had placed himself in opposition to me. A courier was visible, half turned from the door, suspiciously keeping an eye on my movements. The director began to ask me strange questions. It was one of two things: either they imagined I was that eccentric captain of the waiting room or else they thought that an officer venturing to make a complaint about the minister of war must be a lunatic. I decided to explain.

"Pardon me, Your Excellency, but it seems to me that there is some misapprehension here. At the reception today you had two artillerymen. One is obviously deranged but the one before you is quite sane."

The director laughed and sat down in his armchair. He asked me to sit down too, the door closed, and the courier disappeared. Listening attentively to my tale, the director expressed the hypothesis that the law had been violated in order to take into the General Staff some "wet nurses' sons." I denied this. The four officers unexpectedly put on the list, I said, were confused as to the reason. But perhaps he was right. Certainly such rumors were going about the academy.

"How may I assist you?"

"I ask only that the inquiry about the war minister be made as soon as possible."

"Ordinarily we have a rather longish procedure, but I promise you that in two or three days your request will be honored."

Because Moshnin had threatened to expel me from the service, I then turned to the chief of the artillery administration, General Altfater, who assured me that I would remain in artillery ranks in any case. He promised to make a full report to the head of the artillery, Grand Duke Mikhail Nikolaevich.

The request to the chancery for a reply from the war minister had results. The academy left me alone and the matter went to the General Staff. General Maltsev, the man appointed to investigate my transgressions, enjoyed infinite respect in the General Staff. Because of this I was generally treated courteously in the General Staff and was well informed about the side issues of my affair. I knew that

General Maltsev's report proceeded from the view that graduation from the academy had been conducted illegally and that the action which I had taken had not been a violation. The answer drafted to my chancery petition was being written by lawyers on the General Staff and in the War Ministry but their opinions did not satisfy Kuropatkin, who had already torn up two proposed replies, saying exasperatedly, "In this version there seeps through the lines the opinion that perhaps I was wrong."

It dragged on week after week. The usual date for graduation from the academy was already long passed. Our credit was exhausted and our pay had been discontinued, at least the supplementary wages and money for quarters from St. Petersburg. Many officers were in actual need, particularly family men. Authorities of other academies persistently approached Sukhotin to know when the incident would be resolved since it delayed the presentation of officers from all four academies (General Staff, Artillery, Engineering, and Juridical) to the emperor.

At last the War Ministry composed and dispatched an answer to the chancery of petitions. On the day of His Highness's reception, an edict was read about the promotion of graduating officers "to the following ranks for distinguished success in their studies." To my astonishment I was named for promotion to captain.

By custom, on the day before presentation to the ruler, the graduating officers were presented to the minister of war in one of the halls of the academy. General Kuropatkin reviewed us, greeting and holding a short conversation with each one. Coming to me, he inhaled deeply and said in an uneven voice, "Captain, it is difficult for me to speak to you. I will say only one thing. You have taken steps of which none of your comrades will approve."

I said nothing. The war minister was poorly informed. He did not know the touching attention and interest which the officers showed the disgraced captain. He did not know that for the first time in the academy's existence, at the public banquet for the graduates, sharp protest against the academic regime and in particular against the new director was expressed that year. I was silent and I waited.

A special train was sent for the graduating officers of the four academies and the individual directors. Several times at the station I noticed searching and hostile glances turned on me from the academic heads. They did not speak to me but apparent on their faces was uneasiness and anxiety that there should be no scandal at the triumphant reception.

In the palace we were arranged in a single row along a series of halls according to the final (illegal) list of seniority. Upon Kuropatkin's arrival and after his conversation with Sukhotin, Colonel Moshnin came to us and extricated my three comrades in misfortune from the ranks below me and transferred them to the higher ranks of those appointed to the General Staff. He divided us at intervals of two paces. Not having earned inclusion, I remained in the lower flank of officers. Everything was set.

But General Altfater fulfilled his promise. Grand Duke Mikhail Nikolaevich was present at the reception. He came to me before the reception and, expressing sympathy, said that he had spoken with the ruler and had given him all the details of my case. We waited for a long time. At last, by rows, we heard the quiet command, "Gentlemen officers!"

Moors drew up in frozen stance before the doors through which the emperor was to appear. General Kuropatkin, standing opposite us, humbly bowed his head. The ruler arrived. By nature a timid person, he obviously experienced no small amount of agitation during such a large reception, in this case several hundred officers to each of whom he was expected to say something courteous. His attitude was apparent in his kind but melancholy eyes, his fatigued pauses in conversation, and his nervous play with the straps hanging from his epaulets.

He approached me at last. I felt choking, oppressive gazes upon me. Kuropatkin, Sukhotin, and Moshnin all stared at me menacingly. I called out my rank and family name. I heard the voice of the ruler asking, "Well, and where do you expect to be appointed?"

"I do not know. I await the decision of Your Imperial Majesty."

The ruler turned and glanced questioningly at Minister of War General Kuropatkin who bowed in a servile manner and announced, "That officer, Your Majesty, was excluded from the General Staff because of his character."

The ruler turned back to me, nervously putting his straps in order, and asked me two more insignificant questions — how long I had been in the service and where my brigade was stationed. Then he nodded courteously and moved on. I saw how the faces of my superiors shone. They were so obviously overjoyed that several people of the court retinue standing nearby smiled. But from that long-awaited conversation I left with a dull sinking in my soul and disenchantment with the "true will of the monarch."

I was to have occupied a staff position in the Warsaw military district and later to return to my 2nd Artillery Brigade. But the Warsaw staff, administered then by General Puzyirevskii, proved a boon to my fate. General Puzyirevskii appointed me to a vacant office of chief of staff and, having sent a flattering testimonial to St. Petersburg about me, three times interceded concerning my transfer to the General Staff. To the first two intercessions, no answer at all arrived. To the third came the reply, "The war minister has prohibited any sort of intercession concerning Captain Denikin."

After some time an answer came from the chancery petition: "After hearing a report from the war minister about your complaint, His Imperial Majesty has sanctioned an order that the matter be dropped." Nevertheless, by judgment of the reviewing officers, attention was quickly turned to all the officers who had successfully concluded the third course at the academy. Notwithstanding their marks they were all appointed to the General Staff. All, that is, except me.

There was nothing else to anticipate and nowhere else to turn. The head of the Warsaw district tried to persuade me to stay with him. But my indefinite circumstances weighed heavily on my mind. I did not wish to continue living with false hopes and to float between two shores, not appointed to the General Staff, yet removed from the lines. In the spring of 1900 I returned to my brigade.

PART III

CHAPTER 14 IN THE BRIGADE
ONCE MORE

In the brigade I found circumstances changed at the top. The new commander, General Zavatskii, was a distinguished front line commander and an experienced teacher of troops. He began by shutting himself in his study with his adjutant, Lieutenant Ivanov, a sensible person. They conversed for three hours and Zavatskii became acquainted with General L.'s sad legacy. Afterward, gradually and without fanfare, Zavatskii began to restore order to the damaged brigade life.

The commander often attended our mess for his meals and he enjoyed talking with us. He was just as courteous with second lieutenants as with colonels. Somehow in a conversation he remarked, "According to my standards, training can only be conducted by officers. And if the officers are inadequate, it is better to abandon the entire operation."

Odd scenes began to occur in the brigade. One morning a lieutenant of the 3rd Battery slept through his duties and General Zavatskii substituted and instructed for him without saying a word to the battery commander. Another day he was in the 5th Battery, advising the gunners. Once he unexpectedly served as instructor of firing in the 1st Battery, then soothed the battery commander who, having heard about the brigade commander's appearance, had hastily dressed and run to the range. "It is nothing. It was no inconvenience for me. I was free this morning." Two weeks later even the most dissolute second captain who occasionally played cards all night and forgot the road back to the battery, began to appear regularly at his post.

In addition, gambling soon ceased. Zavatskii summoned us and lectured on the demoralizing influence of gambling. In severe and authoritative tones he ordered that gambling cease. Everyone of us understood that it was not just an empty threat when he said, "I will never permit myself to certify a battery officer who engages in games of chance." Card games, which had flourished openly and insolently in the officers' club, were transferred for a time to the bachelor quarters behind curtained windows. After a while they disappeared altogether.

Knowing and demanding good work, the general actually entered into the brigade way of life. There was nothing, not even the most minute detail, which in five years did not receive Zavatskii's uplifting influence. Beginning with the physical arrangements of the camp, the brigade assembly, and the soldiers' shop, he built baths in the Bela garrison for the first time. He arranged for youths to complete their education and eradicated the "landlord psychology," a survival of the past which still held in thrall some battery commanders who regarded the battery as their personal property.

The arresting of officers, which had previously seemed necessary to maintain order in the service, was no longer practiced. I must explain that in the Russian army as in all others, confinement of officers to the guardhouse for insignificant offenses was largely left to the discretion of the superior officer. This consecrated, historic tradition of discipline was, in the main, a disgraceful method and had no counterpart in the civil bureaucracy. In the first twenty-five years of my service, I knew among the high command of the army only one person who broke with this tradition. He was General Meves, commander of the 20th Corps, who died three years before the Japanese War. He strove to convey to officers a knightly notion of their calling and moral appearance. General Meves saw such punishment as "highly insulting to the individual, a disgrace to our profession." He only believed in a reprimand by the superior and the influence of comrades. "If such measures do not suffice," he said, "then the man is not suitable officer material and should be dismissed."

Meves actually was not an innovator, for there existed a forgotten old order from the harsh Russian Middle Ages issued by the founder of our regular army, Tsar Peter the Great: "No officer shall be arrested without court martial except for treasonous matters . . ." Like Meves, General Zavatskii adhered to such views. He never imposed disciplinary punishment upon officers. Instead he invited the guilty one to his study. One of my comrades invited for such a conversation said, not without foundation: "My prospects are not enviable. It would be better to sit in the guardhouse. That fellow possesses an amazing aptitude for proving to you in the course of an hour, in irreproachably correct form, that you are a parasite for not holding equally correct views of the officer's obligations."

In such a calm and healthy atmosphere I served two years under Zavatskii. I was designated senior officer and assistant to the director in charge of the 3rd Battery premises, Lieutenant Colonel Pokrovskii, a distinguished commander, an excellent artilleryman (I mean in firing guns), and an experienced administrator. In the five years I had spent outside the brigade I had naturally lost a little artillery skill. But in drills I quickly occupied my proper place and in the area of tactics and maneuvers was considered the brigade authority. It was only military accounting that I did not understand at all. I therefore arranged with Pokrovskii that he would temporarily keep the management of the battery in his hands, instructing me so that I would be able progressively to take it over from him. I studied diligently and not without success. In scope and in accounting, battery management was on a small scale analogous to the basic management of a regiment so my experience greatly benefited me in future service. Among General Staff officers in high command posts, with some rare exceptions, competence in military economics was unusual and was handled willy-nilly by their commissaries. In general I brought away a great deal of useful knowledge from the school of Zavatskii and Pokrovskii.

Neither my academic experience nor my "expulsion" from the General Staff impaired my knowledge or prestige in the eyes of my comrades. On the contrary they regarded me with sympathy and respect. Once this was revealed to me in a touching way. A captain of the General Staff arrived from staff corps. He was my junior in rank and had sat only one desk away from me at the academy. He was to conduct a tactical examination of the officers. To several officers, including me, he gave the most elementary exercises. Indignant at such tactlessness, the division commander ordered me not to appear at the evening assembly where the results of the examination would be given. As for the touring captain, after the results were read our young officers showed him so much contempt that the man did not know what to do. Another proof of my comrades' sympathy was the fact that they elected me a member of our brigade court of honor and president of our management committee of the mess.

The atmosphere of Bela, that lonely place, did not bother me too much. Except for gatherings of the brigade officers, my personal social life in the main was restricted to a circle of colleagues and two or three city families of the intelligentsia. One of these was the family of V. S. and E. A. Chizh, the parents of my future wife, and I was content with them. Apart from duties and friendships, there still remained sufficient time for studies and for literary work. While still at the academy I had written a tale about brigade life which was published in the military journal *Razvedchik* in 1898. The tale itself was a trifling thing but I experienced great emotion, as probably all neophyte writers great and small do when their first production enters the world. Since then I had published sketches from my military experiences in *Varshavskii dnevnik*, the sole Russian-language organ serving Russian Poland. I wrote under the pseudonym "I. Nochin," which did not keep my identity secret. I wrote tales of the familiar, including one mischievous story which shook the quiet workings of Bela life. Here, briefly, are its contents.

There lived in Bela a "millionaire," Pizhits by name. He made his money from various leases and contracts with the army — building barracks, repairs, heating, and so forth. Also in Bela lived a certain Finkelstein, a competitor of Pizhits whom Pizhits completely ruined. Finkelstein cherished a lively hatred for Pizhits and, every time he could, tried to harm him. He fed information and denunciations to all Pizhits's clients without result. Pizhits had an "in" with staff circles and with the governor. Consequently, by legal and illegal means, he became exclusive contractor to all the province.

Pizhits had a son, Leizer, whose time came to enlist. Pizhits made "gifts" of money to members of the Bela military council and was assured that his son would be rejected, although he had no physical defects. On examination day Leizer answered the doctor so correctly and made his eyes look so glazed that the council unanimously pronounced him myopic and unfit for service. That evening at the local club over vodka, the doctor revealed his secret to a friend: "Very simple. When I held the glass in my right hand, he said 'I can see.' In the left hand, 'I cannot see.'"

The general commission in Warsaw required further inspection of the ailing eye. Pizhits knew, however, that the chairman of this commission was not averse to a gift of money either. So he betook himself to Warsaw. Pizhits was announced to the chairman of the commission. For a long and unseemly time the visitor haggled, speaking so insolently to the chairman that the latter finally showed him the door. Finkelstein (for this was actually Finkelstein and not Pizhits) then dashed headlong through the reception room and disappeared.

Next day, when the real Pizhits appeared at the chairman's quarters, the lackey returned after announcing him and told the astonished Pizhits that he had orders not to allow him to cross the threshold. A few days later a young soldier, Leizer Pizhits, was sent off to one of the regiments beyond the Urals.

My story, with imaginary names of course, was full of factual and comical details. One must know the life of a lonely place in the outlying districts in order to imagine the alarm with which my story was received there. The governor was furious. The military head was hastily transferred to another city.[1] The doctor's wife refused to speak to me. Pizhits did not leave his house for two weeks. But Finkelstein, walking along the main street of town, thrust copies of the newspaper at all acquaintances saying, "Have you read it? This was written about Pizhits!"

That is how we lived, worked, and amused ourselves in that lonely spot, Bela.

Little by little my recollections of academy episodes have lost their sting and only somewhere deeply implanted is the importunate realization: Through such impassable bramble woods is the path to truth.

On a gloomy fall evening spent in solitude and thought, I wrote a private letter to "Alexei Nikolaevich Kuropatkin." It began like this: "'It is difficult for me to speak to you.' You addressed these words to me, Your Excellency, on the occasion of the officers' graduation from the academy. And for me it was also difficult to speak with you. But two years have passed. Fears have subsided, the heart has grown calm, and I am now able to relate to you the truth about what occurred."

Then briefly I set down the information which is already history to you, the reader. I did not expect a reply but wished simply to unburden my soul. Several months went by. On the eve of 1902 I received an unexpected telegram from fellow officers in Warsaw addressed to "Appointee to General Staff Captain Denikin," containing their sincere congratulations. The furlough with which I greeted the New Year was unique.

Later I learned from St. Petersburg how all this had occurred. The war minister had left for Turkestan when I wrote to him. On his return to the capital he immediately sent my letter to the academy for settlement. By then Sukhotin had received another appointment and was gone. An academy conference recognized in the contents of my letter the whole truth of the matter. And General Kuropatkin, in his next audience with the ruler, expressed regret that he had "behaved incorrectly" and requested an order to transfer me to the General Staff. Taking leave of the brigade, I left for Warsaw in a few days for my new post.

CHAPTER 15   THE RUSSIAN SOLDIER

In the summer of 1902 I was transferred to the General Staff and assigned a staff position in the 2nd Infantry Division, then stationed in Brest Litovsk. I was not there long before I was given command of a company with which to prove myself. Then in the fall I returned to Warsaw where I took command of a squadron of the 183rd Pultusskii Regiment.

By that time I had actually served five years in the artillery and had supervised training sections in various branches of the army as well as handling the instruction of soldiers. Now all aspects of the soldier's life passed before my eyes. That year was my time of greatest proximity to the soldier, that soldier whose fighting qualities remained unchanged in Turkey, in Japan, and in World Wars I and II. The Russian soldier could rise to his greatest heights or sink deeply as it happened in the revolution of 1917 or the first period of World War II. That high and low phenomenon, often incomprehensible to himself, is an absolute enigma to foreigners. I wish, therefore, to say a few words about the way of life of the soldier in the Old Russian army.

Reflecting the population distribution of Russia, the army was composed of 80 percent peasants, 10 percent workers, and 10 percent from the remaining classes. The army, in other words, was essentially peasant. Due to the freedom from military obligation of many non-Russian peoples and to a disproportionate evasion of conscription and other causes, the main burden of the levy fell upon the purely Russian population. Heterogeneous elements, however, lived in harmony in the barracks atmosphere. There was greater tolerance for different races and religions in Russia than elsewhere. Racial discrimination in the Russian barracks was nowhere comparable to that of our former enemies. In Old Austria, for example, the predominant Swabian and Magyar elements regarded Slavic soldiers as representatives of a lower race. And Germany not only ridiculed the Poles but had mostly Prussian officers as commanders in the south who referred to the South German soldiers as *"zhids"* with unconcealed contempt.[1]

Our soldiers lived in a harsh and austere setting. At the time of which I am speaking wooden bunks, sometimes sections of trestle beds, stood along the barracks walls. On them were straw mattresses and straw pillows without pillowcases, nothing more. For a covering the soldiers used their cloaks, which were filthy after drill and wet after rain. Company commanders dreamed about blankets for the troops but the crown did not provide them. Blankets were sometimes bought from the regimental housekeeping budget or by voluntary contributions of money which soldiers received from home. Personally I did not allow such deductions. Not until 1905 was a reform introduced which provided the troops with bed linens and blankets.

Uniforms for the Old Russian army had one glaring defect. They were the same for all latitudes, whether for Arkhangelsk or for the Crimea. Until the Japanese War, we could not rely upon an allotment of warm clothing. A thin cloak protected the Russian soldier in both summer and the Russian winter. To relieve this situation, some branches of the service, as finances permitted, instituted such innovations as cloth jackets made from threadbare cloaks in the infantry and short fur coats in the cavalry (richer because they saved by grazing their horses).[2]

The soldier's food was characterized by extreme frugality. Here is a typical day's menu: morning, tea with dark bread (three pounds of bread per day); lunch, *borshch* or soup with half a pound of meat or fish (after 1905 three-fourths of a pound), plus porridge; for supper, thin gruel prepared with suet. In terms of calories and suitability, the food was entirely adequate and in any case was more nourishing than the food which the peasants had at home. And there were few abuses in economy on the soldier's food. The soldier's stomach was the object of special solicitude by superiors of all ranks. Inspection of the soldiers' food was a traditional ceremony performed by the highest commanders, not excluding the ruler himself, who would visit the barracks at lunch or at the supper hour.

Until the 1860s, that is, until the time of Alexander II's Great Reforms, corporal punishment and beatings, as in all European armies, were the basic method of educating the troops.[3] But resistance to physical punishment was widespread in the country, in the schools, and in the family. From the 1860s until the first revolution, corporal punishment was permitted for soldiers only if the punishment was to exceed, by judicial decree, the "category of fines." I would like to point out that by law the Russian army dispensed with this survival of the Middle Ages earlier than did other armies because even in the English army corporal punishment was not abolished until 1880 while it persisted in the English fleet until 1906.

Generally Russian military laws concerning punishment of the soldier were matchlessly humane, more so than in other first-rate armies of more "civilized" peoples. In the German army, for example, exceptional cruelty and roughness was the rule. There were cases of smashed teeth and broken eardrums; as punishment soldiers were forced to eat straw or literally to lick dust from boots. This was evident not only from the press but from official orders. In 1909 alone military judges handed down 583 decrees concerning the harsh dealings of superiors with soldiers.

In the Austrian army the basic punishment was "suspension," a ceremony in which a soldier, his hands bound behind him, was suspended so that he could touch the ground only with the tip of his big toe. The fellow was held in that position for several hours, usually of course in a fainting condition. Or he would be placed in shackles, chained with right hand to left foot and kept in that bent position for six hours. Such punishments persisted until 1918, that is, until the breakup of the Austrian army.

Such "civilization" was a far cry from ours. We had laws governing punishment and arrest, laws which regulated assignments to work out of turn, denial of leave, or demotion to lower responsibilities. I do not deny that there was severity in our army. And I do not say that there were not cases of insult and stupidity or that no beatings occurred. But especially after the late 1880s these were only isolated incidents in barracks life — clandestine, condemned, and prosecuted when uncovered. On the other hand, by far the largest portion of officers were sincerely solicitous, accessible, and anxious about the needs of the soldier. In the Russian military occurred many examples of self-sacrifice when our men risked their lives behind enemy wire obstructions, crawling and dragging the wounded without regard for rank.

Among the Russian prisoners taken by the Japanese was a wounded captain from the Kaspiskii Regiment named Lebedev. The Japanese considered it possible to save his leg from amputation by skin graft. Twenty Russian soldiers in the hospital, prisoners all, volunteered their services. The duty fell upon Rifleman Ivan Kanatov, who allowed the doctors to cut out a piece of his flesh without using chloroform. This incident made quite an impression on the Japanese and, when it became known, upon our people as well. Of course similar events occurred under conditions of friendly comradeship, on marches and in battles, as well as in the straits of enemy captivity.

The alienation which existed between the Russian intelligentsia and the people was reflected in the relations of officers with the men, of course, but to a much lesser degree by virtue of the special conditions of the military way of life. It took exceptional circumstances to change these relations so sharply afterward.

Military science was a mystery to our peasant-soldier because of the absence of pre-conscription education. Before World War I, 40 percent of the conscripts were illiterate. The imperial government had a long-range plan for gradual progress in universal primary education which was to have been completed by 1922.[4] The army introduced general training in reading and writing in 1902 and bridged the gap somewhat. After that, every year 200,000 reserves left the army having learned to read and write. But illiterate or not, soldiers, thanks to that natural skill or adaptability common to all native Russians, generally adjusted easily to the most complex aspects of camp and military life.

As I have already mentioned, Russian society, liberals as well as socialists, from ignorance of military life and from ideals of pacifism and antimilitarism, spoke of the army with indifference and even contempt. They expressed their sentiments with such epithets as "war mongers" and "militarists." But good or evil, the army embodied the very essence of national defense. In 1902 and 1903 the army was certainly put to the test when some areas virtually burst into flame with disorders. The troops, bound by strict regulations and trained for pacification, were supplied with arms.[5] They and their well-intentioned commanders were more than once exposed to grievous and undeserved abuse from mobs. It is perhaps astonishing that there was so little reflection in the army of the ferment which gripped the masses, spread by revolutionary propaganda and socialist dissatisfaction. Soldiers performed their duties smoothly.

In our area, in the town of Radom, a revolutionary mob attacked a company of the Mogilevskii Regiment. The company was preparing to fire when their commander, Colonel Bulatov, arrived on the scene. He stopped them with the words, "Do not fire! Don't you see that there are women and children there?" He went unarmed into the crowd and was murdered on the spot by a young worker.

In summary, the soldier of the Old Russian army was brave, skillful, uncommonly tenacious, dependable, and perfectly disciplined. That is, until waves of revolution swept away discipline as well as the army.[6]

Our regiment did not take any part in the suppression of disorders. Despite the volatile conditions there were no disturbances in Warsaw at that time. They began later.[7] Instead, my regiment was assigned from time to time to guard the Warsaw fortress.

Among the areas of the fortress which we guarded was the notorious "Tenth Pavilion," in which important and dangerous political criminals were detained. Fantastic rumors circulated among the Warsaw Poles in regard to the pavilion; for example, it was said that the Russian government systematically poisoned the prisoners confined there. My instruction sheet for the watch on duty contained a paragraph providing for tasting twice a day the food served in the pavilion. The rumors were absurd, of course. Actually the food served to the prisoners was no worse than that in any officers' club.

During duty hours I often used to look inside the building, but there was nothing to see except for a long L-shaped corridor with rows of doors opening onto it and little windows in them. It was very hot, even in winter, and deathly silent. My men guarded only the entrances and exits of the pavilion. We were not permitted to go along the corridor. Secret police served there.

Occupying one of those cells was the future marshal and dictator of Poland, Joseph Pilsudski. In 1887, before his twentieth birthday, Pilsudski had already been deported to Siberia for five years for his indirect participation in the attempt on the life of Emperor Alexander III. The main role in that attempt was played by Lenin's brother, Aleksandr Ulianov, who was executed for his part in the affair.

Political criminals, to the extent that they were presumed dangerous, were exiled to Siberian towns or remote settlements. Many were sent to the northern frontiers, with its severe climate and lack of even the barest comfort. There in Siberia Pilsudski had been given a small subsidy which permitted him to live and to work at an occupation thought suitable for him. On his return from exile, Pilsudski entered a revolutionary organization, the Polish Socialist Party (P. P. S.) which, in keeping with its Marxist inclination, had as its main purpose the raising of popular insurrection in Poland. Pilsudski rose to prominence in the party, becoming editor of the underground *Rabochei gazeta* (Workers' Gazette). But in 1900, in spite of a counterfeit passport, he was discovered by the police, and he and his wife were seized in the clandestine printing office. He was placed in the Tenth Pavilion. The Warsaw authorities planned to hand him over to a military court which probably would have sentenced him to hard labor, but St. Petersburg rescinded this decision and lessened the penalty to administrative exile to a Siberian colony.[8]

Pilsudski's friends then devised a plan for his freedom. It was known that escape from the Warsaw fortress was impossible. In order to obtain his transfer to another place, it was decided that Pilsudski should feign mental illness. No small amount of assistance was provided by an official of the fortress staff, Sedelnikov, who instructed the prisoner as to methods.

Pilsudski demonstrated his "illness" by falling into a rage at the sight of a military uniform passing his cell window. This supposedly blinded his reason. He also refused to eat the food offered to him on the grounds that it was poisoned, so he was fed on boiled eggs. After a time a Warsaw psychiatrist, Shabashnikov, was brought in to examine Pilsudski, whether from charity or by complicity in the plot, I do not know. At any rate, Shabashnikov confirmed that the prisoner's condition was indeed serious, requiring clinical treatment. Therefore, after an eight-month confinement in the fortress, military authorities dispatched Pilsudski to St. Petersburg's Nikolaevskii Hospital for the mentally ill, from which he managed to escape without any particular difficulty and to leave the country with his wife.[9] Her freedom had been obtained earlier under the provision that a wife is not accountable for the acts of her husband. Pilsudski later returned illegally to Russian Poland, took part in forming the "battle organization" of the party, and in 1905 began his terrorist activities, including the robbery of the treasury.[10]

Old Russian authority had many faults, not the least of which was its suppression of the cultural-national aspirations of non-Russian ethnic groups. But when one compares the "bloody tsarist regime" (as the Bolsheviks and their foreign fellow travelers call it) with its political opposition — not only the Bolshevik regime but also Pilsudski himself when he became dictator of Poland — it seems extremely humane.

My year as company commander passed without adventure. I could see clearly some deficiencies in our system of military training and even wrote upon the theme. But actually, in my modest and subordinate role as company commander, I could accomplish little. I will not expand on this except to cite one example intelligible to nonspecialists. Rapid-fire artillery and machine guns had already been introduced in the army, and warnings were sounded in the military press about potential waste on the battlefield. Yet all our artillery units were still sent out, foolishly, into open positions; in the Warsaw area our front-line infantry still marched shoulder to shoulder in dense columns, firing by ranks, moving in step into the area of actual fire!

We paid for that negligence in the first months of the Japanese War. And that war was moving nearer every day. I surrendered command of my company in the fall of 1903, on the eve of war. But the proximity of hostilities was not in the least reflected in the lives or mood of the troops. I am not only referring to Warsaw frontier troops who were not intended to be moved from the Austro-German front, but nowhere was there any special technical training, nor any moral or spiritual preparation of soldiers and officers for the approaching war. We commanders, both high and low, by orders from above, could tell our subordinates nothing. We had to keep SILENT!

CHAPTER 16   **BEFORE THE JAPANESE WAR**

We were silent. Yet how could we have talked with the soldier, tried to provoke his interest, raise his morale, when we ourselves knew nothing at all about what was taking place in the Far East? Neither the command staff nor the officer corps nor the General Staff, beyond an exceedingly narrow circle of individuals closest to the Ministry of Foreign Affairs, knew anything. Nor did Russian society know. At the beginning of 1903, however, talk circulated that Vice Admiral Abaza and retired Staff Captain Bezobrazov (who to the surprise of all would shortly be promoted to the high post of State Secretary to His Majesty), in the company of the most highly placed individuals, had acquired concessions to exploit forests in Northern Korea.[1] They were installing military detachments there to protect woodcutters. That one adventuristic episode, to which rumor attributed exceptionally greedy motives, prevented society from seeing the real motives of the complicated historical drama ripening in the Far East.

The Council of Ministers did not represent a unified government with initiative and collegial responsibility. Decisions of tremendous importance to the state were frequently made in St. Petersburg without broad deliberation. Sometimes such decisions were even contrary to the opinions of government councils; they were made on the rec-ommendation of such and such a minister, sometimes quite an irresponsible individual. Dealings of secret diplomats such as Abaza were often placed before government members as an accomplished fact and the country was kept in complete ignorance.

Deplorable results occurred. "At this time in Japan, all the people, from members of the High Privy Council to the lowest porter, personally understood the meaning of the impending war," it was later said in an official history of the war. "Feelings of hostility and vengeance toward the Russian people had accumulated for years; everyone was talking about future war with Russia. But to all of us the enterprise in the Far East proved completely unexpected. Its significance was understood only very slightly. Everything which might have explained the meaning of the imminent conflict, its purpose and the designs of the government, was suppressed and it was stated in print that everything was all right. As a result, at the very moment when general unity between authorities and the masses was essential, there was an abyss difficult to remove."

I will review in general outline the chronological events. Japanese expansion on the continent, although only political and financial, had Korea as its first objective as early as 1882. Because of this a lasting conflict resulted between Japan and China, culminating in 1894 in war with China, which suffered a complete rout.[2] According to the peace treaty of Shimonoseki, China had to cede to Japan Formosa and the Liaotung peninsula (with Port Arthur) and to pledge payment of a large indemnity.[3] But because of the intervention of Russia, Germany, and France, Japan was forced to give up Liaotung.[4] Korea was recognized as an independent state at that time.

With French assistance, Russia made a large loan to China for the payment of the first installment of the indemnity and gave a guaranty for the next payment. In return for this exceedingly helpful service, by an agreement signed in 1896 by Minister of Finance Witte with Li Hung-chang, China granted Russia the right to build a branch line of the Trans-Siberian Railway to link the Trans-Baikal area in a straight line with Vladivostok across Manchurian territory through Harbin.[5] After thirty-six years China could buy the railroad or, in eighty years, it would be transferred to China gratis. This agreement was mutually advantageous, providing an opportunity to populate the sparsely settled and untamed expanse of Northern Manchuria. It appeared to be a natural defensive union between Russia and China and not a predetermined occupation of the region. The military security of the railroad right-of-way was to be under Russian jurisdiction, not extending to the native population but limited only to the narrow strip expropriated along the railway line. This arrangement was observed for four years, until the Boxer Rebellion.

After 1895 Japanese expansion in Korea increased. Japan brought military divisions into Korea along with many thousands of colonists. Japan took over commerce, mail, telegraph, and railroad building, then arranged a palace revolution. The contemptuous attitude of the Japanese toward the Korean people and the introduction of a cruel regime kindled revolution. The Korean king appealed to Russia for assistance so Russia sent military instructors and financial advisers to Korea.[6] Although Japan and Russia had made an agreement in 1896 concerning the division of influence in Korea, the predominant influence there remained Russian.

At the end of 1897 an event occurred as a result of systematic German provocation. Emperor Wilhelm had exerted every effort to involve Russia in the Far Eastern conflict with the aim of weakening us and thus allowing Germany to have a free hand in the West. On a frivolous pretext, the Germans seized Kiaochow. According to Witte's testimony, this was done with the knowledge of Russian Foreign Minister Muraviev.[7] And over the protests of Witte and other ministers, Russia, which had only recently defended the sovereignty of her "friend" China, not only did not protest Germany's act but herself seized the Kwantung peninsula, returned to the Port Arthur fortress, and opened Dairen (Dalny), a commercial port, for foreign trade.

This act cannot be justified. Certainly free passage to an ice-free port of the Pacific Ocean was of vital interest for our empire with its immense Asiatic territory and its sea boundaries ice-locked a large part of the year and half-closed strategically by the Japanese islands. But the forcible way by which this task was accomplished corresponded with neither the interests nor the dignity of Russia.

Finally on March 15, 1898, the Chinese government agreed to lease the Kwantung ports to Russia for a twenty-five-year term and we were permitted to build the South Manchurian rail branch through Mukden to Port Arthur.

Russian advancement created hostility toward us in China but a veritable tempest in Japan, in whose plans Manchuria figured second only to Korea as a target for expansion. It also caused dissatisfaction in England and America, which were threatened with the loss of the Manchurian market. This complex political situation, with the new problems related to securing passage to southern ports, and finally aversion to war with Japan, led the Russian government to surrender its influence in Korea. Russian advisers and military instructors were withdrawn and Japan took over solidly in Korea, in essence occupying it. This situation created a serious threat to our Pre-Amur borders, as well as to the Siberian main line and free sea communications with the Far East through the Korean Straits.

In 1900 the Boxer movement began in China against the "foreign devils."[8] This movement, in which motives both rapacious and nationalistic were intermingled, was a reaction against the China policy of foreign powers. It was expressed in the assassinations of foreign diplomats, merchants, and residents, and in destruction of foreign commercial and cultural institutions. Because the Chinese government had neither the strength nor the inclination to resist this movement (and in fact sympathized with its supporters), by an agreement of the interested powers, international troops were brought into China commanded at least nominally by German Field Marshal Waldersee.[9]

The revolt was suppressed. Having occupied Manchuria in the course of the war, Russia pledged to withdraw her troops in three stages, "provided there is no hindrance in the form of acts by other powers." The first stage of evacuation was effected, but further withdrawal was suspended at the beginning of 1903 because of St. Petersburg "secret diplomacy" on the one hand and on the other the aggressive acts by Japan which set China against Russia and deliberately upset the Russo-Chinese agreement. Japan impudently demanded (!) an explanation and offered China military assistance against Russia.

During 1903 lingering, boring, insincere negotiations dragged on between St. Petersburg and Tokyo. I will not dwell on details but will only note the essential position of each side. Japan demanded a completely free hand in Korea and sought participation in the solution of the "Manchurian problem" as a country "having broad and substantial rights and interests there." Among other things, Japan demanded the right to build a railroad from Korea to join the South Manchurian line and extend beyond it to Shanghai-Huan-Nu-Chzhun. The construction of the Japanese railroad, pursued above all other strategic aims, signified hostility toward China as much as toward Russia.

The Russian government did not permit Japan to interfere in her treaty relations with China, merely assuring the Japanese that "Russia will not hinder Japan nor any other government (having in mind England and the United States) from using to advantage the rights acquired in Manchuria in accordance with their Chinese treaties." Leaving Korea entirely to Japanese occupation, Russia demanded only a guaranty that Korean territory would not be exploited for strategic advantage and that no military goods would be produced which might menace shipping through the Korean Straits. And for the security of its almost indefensible Pre-Amur frontiers, to which the border of Korea was adjacent, Russia proposed to establish a neutral zone to the north of the 39th parallel into which neither side could introduce troops. Thanks to this measure, the Abaza-Bezobrazov timber concessions along the Yalu would lose their menacing character. Moreover, as a result of the persistence of ministers Witte and Kuropatkin, the sovereign ordered on April 5, 1903, that all military personnel be withdrawn from the concession territory, leaving it a purely commercial area open to the participation of foreign capital.

In the thick of these negotiations, to the surprise of everyone including the government, on July 30, 1903, the sovereign established a viceroyalty in the Far East, including in it the Pre-Amur governor-generalship, the Kwantung area, and Russian institutions and troops in Manchuria. Admiral Alekseev was named viceroy and, as direct representative of the sovereign, was given charge of all Far Eastern affairs.[10] The ministers of war and foreign affairs thus had little right to interfere.[11] That resolute champion of a peaceful solution to Far Eastern problems, Witte, was removed from the post of minister of finance. Kuropatkin submitted his resignation but he was retained, receiving only a prolonged vacation. It is interesting to note that Kuropatkin displayed hesitation in this case. At the beginning of 1903 he had not allowed the evacuation of Manchuria but by the end of the year, in a report to the sovereign (November 26, 1903), he proposed to return Port Arthur and Dairen to China and to sell to China the South Manchurian branch of the railroad in exchange for special rights in Northern Manchuria. The solution was a radical one. And there is no doubt that if we had left Southern Manchuria, it would have fallen into Japanese hands, thereby strengthening to an incredible extent the Japanese strategic position vis-à-vis the Russian Far East.

Pushed into his post by palace intrigue, neither fleet commander nor regimental leader nor diplomat, Admiral Alekseev found himself under the strong influence of behind-the-scene political maneuvers by Abaza and Bezobrazov, who gave to the negotiations a more irritating and demanding character than that of the ministers. The pernicious role this system of dual politics played may perhaps be judged by a remarkable episode in the Russo-Japanese diplomatic conversations.

On January 28, 1903, by command of the sovereign, a special conference was held under the chairmanship of Grand Duke Aleksei Aleksandrovich, who met with three ministers (those of foreign affairs, war, and navy) and Abaza to deliberate Japan's latest offer. The conference decided to concede as much as possible and even to give up the idea of a "neutral zone" in Northern Korea. Abaza alone professed different views but asked nothing more than the delimitation of the neutral zones by the Yalu-Dzianskii watershed. Two days before the conference presented its report to the sovereign, Abaza, after a personal report to the throne, summoned Japanese Ambassador Kurino and informed him of his own version of the decision. Minister of Foreign Affairs Lamsdorff recognized Abaza's prank a long time after the opening of military activities and in his report to the sovereign called it "quite incredible," diplomatic language not permitting stronger expression. Two days after Abaza's trick, imperial sanction was given to the opinion of the minister of foreign affairs and the conference. In our final proposal to Japan, Russia allowed the intrusion of Japan into the Manchurian railway from Korea, giving up guaranties and neutral zones, and leaving Japan a completely free hand in Korea.

But by that time concessions by the official leaders of Russian politics could not improve the situation nor could behind-the-scene counteraction aggravate it. Japan, having set in motion its entire military mechanism, had already decided on armed conflict and hastened to strike before Russia could reinforce. The final Russian offer was dispatched by telegram to our ambassador in Tokyo on February 4, with copies the same day to Paris and London. Its contents were therefore made known that same day to the Japanese government by our ambassador in Tokyo as well as by Kaiashi, the Japanese ambassador to London, who telegraphed Tokyo on February 4 that the English government considered the Russian concessions as great as possible and that it felt that Japanese refusal to agree to them could incite all foreign powers to withdraw their aid to Japan.[12] But no peaceful solution to the problem entered the designs of the Japanese government. Transmission of the answering telegram to our ambassador in Tokyo was delayed until the seventh of February, but on the sixth, through their envoy in St. Petersburg, they directed a note to the Russian government which, after the actual seizure of Korea by Japan, resounded with intolerable hypocrisy.

"His Majesty, the Emperor of Japan," the note read, "considers the independence and territorial inviolability of Korea essential to his proper tranquillity and security and is unable to regard with indifference any act tending toward making Korea's position insecure." The note concluded with the words, "The Imperial government reserves the right to take such independent action as is consistent with its best interests in the safekeeping of its rights and privileges."

That day, February 6, Japan surprised ships of the Russian volunteer fleet (commercial), which was then in eastern waters. Admiral Togo's fleet put to sea and on the night of February 8–9, without a declaration of war, attacked the Russian squadron at Port Arthur, removing from the lines two armor-clads and one cruiser and blockading the squadron.[13]

Now, since the events of World War II have shaken the world, the causes of the outbreak of the Russo-Japanese War must be reexamined in an objective manner. Certainly more direct and friendly relations of the Russian government toward China and the elimination of behind-the-scene activities by dark forces might have delayed a crisis. But only delayed it. Japan had already proclaimed the Pan-Asiatic idea, an idea which had taken possession of the leadership of this young nation, so lately come forward into the world arena of power, and had permeated the masses of Japanese people. Although in later years the Japanese parties of Minseito and Seiyukai lost their position of power to the war group (Black Dragon Society), which was entirely different in methods, scope, and direction of expansion, all of them similarly referred to the "historic mission" of Japan.[14]

Russia was destined to confront the first serious pressure of Japanese world expansion. Of course, in seeking the Kwantung ports as outlets, the Russian government was guilty of violating Chinese sovereignty. In moral-political aspects, all the great powers were far from innocent in their dealings with China, using as they did its weakness and backwardness as a means to territorial usurpation and economic exploitation.[15] The practice of foreign concessions and settlements was far removed from their statements of idyllic friendship. But subsequent events have shown that Russia, by ordering the occupation of Manchuria, was an immeasurably less dangerous presence there for foreign powers (in consideration of their rights of negotiation) and for China than Japan would have been. This was not understood then, however. China, although taking no active part, maintained a hostile position with respect to Russia.

In 1902 England entered a union with Japan, pledging to provide military assistance if Japan, in defense of its interests in China, should become involved in conflict with another power and with the latter were joined more than one or several powers.[16] In other words, Japan gained security against an anti-Japanese coalition. England promised (and actually rendered) extensive material aid to Japan, playing a substantial role in the creation of the Japanese fleet. The English universally provoked Japan against Russia, and after we occupied Port Arthur, their chief commander, General Wolseley, declared that "in case of war, the British army will be in full readiness."

In its struggle against Russia and for a foothold on the Asiatic mainland, Japan also found support in the United States. American political leaders and a large portion of the press were on its side. Visiting in New York, Japanese Prince Fushima was received quite courteously and was assured that "the United States shares not only commercial but also political interests with Japan." Japan was promised broad economic aid.

Without such a guaranty from the United States and especially from England, Japan would not have entered the war in 1904. These nations forged weapons for their natural enemy and created that "great power," Japan. And the historical boomerang which smote the

Russians at Port Arthur in its reverse flight crossed all of China and struck a blow at Singapore and Pearl Harbor.

As a result of the war and the victory by the yellow race over the white, Japan moved forward to the rank of a first-class power, thereby inflaming the imagination of that nation and definitely determining the path of Japanese imperialism afterward found so clearly forecast in the so-called Tanaka memorial.[17] In that document, a report to the emperor in July 1927 by the former premier and chief of the Seiyukai party, then head of a special commission, were these remarkable lines: "In accordance with the will of Meiji, our first step consisted of the conquest of Formosa and the second, annexation of Korea. Now we must take the third step, conquest of Manchuria, Mongolia, and China. When that has been accomplished, the rest of Asia will lie at our feet. The race of Yamato may then go forward to conquer the World." And since the United States has raised objections to our conquest of China, then "we must subdue it."[18]

We were unprepared for war in 1904, both politically and militarily. The need to strengthen our military potential in the Far East was hindered by our western posture, one of distrust toward Germany. In 1900 War Minister Kuropatkin considered our western frontier to be in "a state of danger unprecedented in the history of Russia" and demanded the strengthening of our military position there, without dispersion of forces and resources in "foreign adventures."[19]

In the entire Far East territory at the beginning of 1904 we had in all 208 pieces of ordnance, 108 battalions, and 66 mounted squadrons, altogether about 100,000 officers and men. Reinforcements had to be supplied from Russia, over an immense distance, filtered through the inadequate capacity of the Siberian main line, which was three pairs of trains a day. From a purely military point of view, would it be better to go through Port Arthur? If we decided on this step, we would then have to concentrate strong forces in the Pre-Amur regions and in Kwantung.

It was highly significant that we underestimated the military strength of Japan. That blunder was common to the military staffs of all the great powers. All military espionage agents in Japan operated in the dark because of the difficulty of the language, the extreme suspiciousness, the prudence of the Japanese command, and, finally, because of the character of the Japanese people, who lack that vicious element which in other nations enters into foreign espionage. Our errors were grave. We considered that with maximum effort Japan was capable of raising 348,000 men under arms and could send no more than 253,000 to the theater of military activity. But Japan actually called up 2,727,000 men, of whom 1,185,000 were used for war, that is, three times as many as our estimate. We did not take into account the fact that there were thirteen Japanese reserve units which had received sufficient training and equipment to go to war immediately as fighting divisions. And there were other errors as well.

Our intelligence about the Japanese fleet was more precise. In Far Eastern waters in 1904 our armor-clad squadron was the equal of Japan's, but it consisted of vessels of diverse systems. Our mine and cruiser vessels conceded to Japan both quality and quantity.

We were insufficiently acquainted with the quality and spirit of the Japanese army. Until 1895 Russian military literature and service organs ignored it. Only after that time, and particularly after 1901, did attention increase. The "Collected Materials about Asia," the only source of information about the Japanese army, was a secret and confidential government publication. The available information, moreover, was contradictory, ranging from precautions and flattering remarks about the Japanese army to a humiliating assessment by our military agent, Colonel Vannovskii, who regarded the armed might of Japan as a bluff and its army as of operetta quality. This was the army about which General Kuropatkin reported to the sovereign after the first battle: "We are dealing with quite serious opposition, excellently prepared, possessing extensive and well-perfected strength and resources, numerically strong, utterly courageous, and excellently commanded."

Despite our underestimation of Japanese armed might, the plan of war adopted by General Kuropatkin in 1901 during his term as war minister was distinguished by unusual caution, providing for stable security in Vladivostok and Port Arthur, concentration of main forces in the region of Mukden-Liaoyuan-Khaichen, and a gradual retreat to Harbin, while awaiting arrival of the best troops. This a priori plan weighed heavily on all decisions made by General Kuropatkin, depriving him of daring, hindering utilization of propitious chances for a march into action, and leading from retreat to retreat.

Under these circumstances, war could not have been popular in

Russian society or with the people. This was so not only because all the complicated troubles preceding it were kept secret but also because few people in Russian society, including scientific circles and the press, were interested in the Far East. As Witte wrote, "In regard to China, Korea, and Japan, our society and even high state officials were wholly ignorant." When war began, the sole stimulus to reviving emotions of patriotism on the part of many people, therefore, was the affront to national pride, the treachery, the sneak attack on Port Arthur.

Rightist society, never prone to criticize government activity, responded with patriotic manifestations. Liberals, however, referred to the war variously, this one with patriotic alarm, that one with indifference. Later they all used military failure as an excuse to heap scorn on an unpopular government. Leftist society showed a defeatist spirit. Brochures published by the Socialist Revolutionaries under the title *"K ofitseram russkoi armii"* (To Officers of the Russian Army) said: "All your victories threaten Russia with the misery of consolidating 'order' while every blow brings nearer the hour of liberation. It is no wonder that Russians rejoice in the success of our enemy . . ." But in the end people gathered calmly in appointed places and mobilization proceeded in an orderly fashion. The army went to war without an uprising, only performing its duty.

The opening of the war found me in Poland. After commanding a company, I had been transferred to the staff of the 2nd Cavalry Corps, quartered in Warsaw. The Poles greeted the declaration of war with pained silence, with an external calmness behind which was concealed ill will and a secret hope for changed conditions for Poland.[20] Moving and emotional, however, were some demonstrations in Warsaw by small groups of Russians carrying standards and singing, *"Spasi, Gospodi, liudi Tvoia"* (Save, Lord, Thy People). They walked in procession along the Warsaw streets among the silent, malevolent crowds.

The Polish Socialist Party (P. P. S.) responded to the call to arms with malice and hatred toward Russia and hopes for a Japanese victory. The moderate party, the Popular Democrats led by Dmowski, warned the citizenry against active dissent which might prove disastrous.[21] They considered that the war would not affect the European countries but might still lead to internal changes agreeable for people under Russian authority. They recommended to the Poles that they "marshal forces and unify" for active work in the future.

This point of view prevailed. There was no attempt toward a popular uprising in Poland. Terrorist acts came exclusively from the numerically small P. P. S., especially after late 1905 when Joseph Pilsudski became head of the battle organization of the party. This party was the only one among all Russian revolutionary organizations which, with great risk but in the name of Poland, attempted to enter into treaty relations with the Japanese staff. In May 1904 Pilsudski went to Tokyo with an offer to form a Polish legion for the Japanese army. He proposed to organize espionage for Japan and to blow up bridges in Siberia. In return he asked Japan for arms, equipment, and money for the Polish revolt. He also asked that at the conclusion of peace with Russia Japan should demand a clause guaranteeing Polish independence.[22]

How little support the P. P. S. enjoyed among the people is apparent from this incident: Pilsudski, appealing for a military uprising, tried by every means not to apply the party stamp to it, but demonstrated "an ardent patriotic spirit." He even mentioned the Chenstokovskii Mother of God.[23] The Japanese treated Pilsudski very courteously but refused all his requests. It was decided only to assign Polish prisoners to a particular command and to allow them anti-Russian propagandists. The Japanese did not give money, only paying for return train fare for Pilsudski. I emphasize this side of Pilsudski's activities because his hatred toward Russia from youth prevailed over the impulse for national expediency. Later on, his implacable attitude led to events singularly tragic for the national anti-Bolshevik movement in Russia as well as for the fate of Poland itself.

The P. P. S. efforts to unify the revolutionary organizations of Finland, the Pre-Baltic, the Caucasus, and other frontier territories against Russia were not crowned with success either. In the Trans-Caucasus, at the outbreak of war, a series of patriotic manifestations were created by Muslims, and Sheik Ul-Islam circulated an appeal to his subjects "to give up possessions and life if necessary."[24] Even Finland, although boycotting at this time a decree designed to impose military obligations on Finnish citizens, made the decent gesture. The Finnish senate sent a telegram to the sovereign affirming their "steadfast devotion to the sovereign of Great Russia" and assigned one million marks for war use. Centrifugal forces did not complicate the difficult position of Russia in 1904.

CHAPTER 17 TO THE WAR

The outbreak of the war found me ailing. Not long before, during winter maneuvers, my horse had fallen on me. Then she dragged me, one foot still stuck in the stirrup, down a hill. As a result I had strained ligaments, bruises, one toe dislocated and another crushed, and so forth. I was forced to stay in bed. When the announcement about the war came, I immediately sent a petition to the district staff to assign me to the active army. Acting on absence of orders from above, the staff refused. To my second request the staff asked, "Do you know the English language?" I replied, "I do not know English, but I know how to fight as well as those who speak it." Nothing happened.

I was nervous and could not keep quiet. At last my immediate superior, General Bezradetskii, sent a confidential telegram along with my request to the General Staff in St. Petersburg. Several days later, to my great joy, an order came instructing Captain Denikin to report to the Trans-Amur Region Frontier Guards. I did not consider waiting until I had recovered. I decided to get to the Siberian express somehow — during the long journey (sixteen days) my foot would heal. I named February 17 as the departure date.

At the Warsaw club, officers of the General Staff prepared a farewell party, a glass of wine for the road, and they presented me with a gift, a good revolver. The eldest of those present, assistant district commander General Puzyrevskii, spoke several warm words emphasizing my ardor for war, not having fully recovered.

In case of my death I left a will of unusual contents with my staff. Since I had no possessions, I included only a list of my small debts, their task being to liquidate them by sale of my literary materials. And I asked friends to look after my mother. My mother accepted the news of my impending departure for war as something completely natural and inevitable. She showed no emotion, tried to keep a merry face, and did not shed a single tear at our farewell in the Warsaw station. But after my departure, so she later confessed, she wept in abundance, both she and my old nurse.

I reached Moscow without mishap and secured a place on the Siberian express. There I met several friends from the General Staff also bound for the Far East. While still in the station I learned from my fellow travelers that Admiral Makarov, just appointed as the commander of the Pacific fleet, would be riding on our train, as well as General Rennenkampf, head of the Trans-Baikal Cossack Division.

At that time, the destruction of our squadron at Port Arthur was painfully reflected in the mood of our navy and of all Russia as well. People received Admiral Makarov's appointment with deep satisfaction and renewed hope. His merits were many and widely known. His military service list began with the Russo-Turkish War of 1877–1878. Russia had then been unable to restore the Black Sea fleet but Makarov, in an adapted commercial steamer, the *Grand Duke Konstantine*, and accompanied by four mine cutters, sank transports carrying entire regiments of infantry and swooped into Turkish ports. Later, with a detachment of sailors, he took part in the Akhal-Tekinskii campaign with the renowned General Skobelev.

He was indebted to no one for his career, which he had spent entirely at sea in various capacities. He had published several important scientific oceanographic studies about the Black Sea and the Arctic and Pacific oceans for which he had been awarded a prize by the Academy of Science, and he had made innovations in naval tactics which he described in a treatise. Finally, he had designed the icebreaker *Ermak*, considered in Russia as the beginning of the navigational struggle with ice. All this increased his popularity and there was no one in Russia who did not know the name of Makarov and his *Ermak*. Courageous, knowledgeable, upright, and energetic, he was an appropriate choice to elevate the prestige of Saint Andrew's banner in Pacific waters.[1]

Admiral Makarov and his staff traveled in a separate car. We heard something about the work going on there from members of his staff. For several hours every day the admiral was occupied with a plan for reorganizing the navy and with setting up instructions for maneuvers and battles. Sometimes General Rennenkampf was invited there for consultation.

Several times during the trip the admiral came into the public salon car where Rennenkampf presented us land officers to him. I do not recall the conversations at that time but they were rarely of a profound nature. I remember well, however, Makarov's appearance — the characteristic Russian face with a full beard and kind intelligent eyes — and that fascination which the admiral's personality always produced in anyone who talked with him, as well as the confidence in him which was involuntarily engendered in us.

General Rennenkampf, the second celebrity, was from another sphere. He had acquired a name and wide reputation in military circles during the Chinese campaign of 1900, for which he received two George's Crosses. Military men referred to him as the "hero of the Chinese war," a cynical epithet since they believed that the war had not been a genuine one.[2] But Rennenkampf's cavalry raid deserved general acclaim for its cleverness and daring.

It began at the end of July 1900 after the engagement at Aigun (near Blagoveshchensk). With a small detachment from three companies, Rennenkampf defeated the Chinese in fortified positions along the mountain ridge of Malo Khingan. Then, outstripping his infantry, he and four and a half Cossack squadrons and batteries covered four hundred kilometers in three weeks with continuous skirmishes. He captured the large Manchurian city of Tsitsihar with a sudden swoop. From that location the higher command was able to direct systematic attacks on Girin. They assembled large forces (three regiments of infantry, six regiments of cavalry, and sixty-four guns) under the command of the famous General Kaulbars. But without waiting for the divisions to assemble, General Rennenkampf took ten Cossack squadrons and batteries and on August 24 moved forward along the Sungari valley. On the twenty-ninth he captured Bodune where fifteen hundred Boxers, taken unaware, surrendered to him. On September 8 he took Kaun-Chzhen-tsi. Leaving five Cossack squadrons there, he covered 130 kilometers in twenty-four hours, dashing into Girin. The incomparable speed and suddenness of Rennenkampf's swoop caused the Chinese to overestimate the strength of his forces to such an extent that Girin, the second largest city of Manchuria, surrendered, its large garrison handing over its weapons. Rennenkampf's handful of Cossacks, lost among masses of Chinese for a period of several days before reinforcements arrived, were in a unique position.

We were in constant contact with General Rennenkampf during the journey, in private conversations and at gatherings during which some of us gave reports on themes related to the theater of war, to cavalry tactics, or to the Japanese army. Rennenkampf reminisced for us about his campaign and very modestly mentioned his personal participation. We organized congenial and comradely banquets in the dining car which, as later in General Rennenkampf's division, never exceeded the bounds of military propriety. '

The general was invariably present at improvised "literary evenings," during which three war correspondents traveling on our train read the articles they sent to their papers from points along the road. The scope of our impressions, from talks with each other, from conversations with ranking assistants of the military echelons, and from superficial observations of station life along the great Siberian road, was limited. And the correspondents in the main wrote only about matters already known to us. The individual approach of each of them to the subject was, however, curious.

The correspondent for *Birzhevaia vedomost* (Market Report), a second lieutenant of supply, wrote boringly and uninterestingly. But from *Novoe vremia* came the journalist and talented artist Kravchenko. He drew an excellent portrait of Rennenkampf, generously provided us with his travel sketches, and in general enjoyed wide popularity among the train passengers. His articles were interesting, warm, and unusually accurate. From *Russkii invalid*, the official organ of the War Ministry, came Under Captain of Cossacks P. N. Krasnov. This was my first acquaintance with a person who later played a role in the history of the Russian civil war. He was commander of the corps directed by Kerensky against the Bolsheviks in defense of the Provisional Government and was prominent as Don hetman for the initial period of the civil war in Southern Russia. Finally, as an émigré, particularly during World War II, he was an articulate spokesman for the Germanophile point of view. Fate destined me to confront him later in the course of my anti-Bolshevik struggle and national construction.

Krasnov's articles showed talent but they distorted facts. Every time he sacrificed vital truth to departmental interests and fantasy, Krasnov would confusingly interrupt his reading for a moment and say, "Here, if you please, gentlemen, is poetic license, for a more dramatic effect . . ." The element of poetic license to the detriment of truth ran throughout all of Krasnov's life. He was a prolific writer, producing volumes of novels, but the thread of invention was woven through his relations with authorities as hetman in Southern Russia in 1918 and 1919, through his later narratives about the battles of the Don, and, what was especially tragic, through his inspired appeals to the Cossacks to fight under the standard of Hitler.

We all became well acquainted during the two-week journey on the train, and later, from orders and newspapers, I followed the fate of my fellow travelers. Admiral Makarov and the ranking members of his staff were killed. On March 8 he arrived in Port Arthur, where he displayed exuberant activity, reorganizing the techniques and tactics of naval defense and above all raising the morale of the fleet. But merciless fate stepped in. On April 12 the armor-clad *Petropavlovsk*, Admiral Makarov's flagship, was exploded by a mine and went to the bottom in two minutes, drowning the hopes of Russia. General Rennenkampf was wounded in a later battle; one of his staff was killed and two wounded. Kravchenko was killed at Port Arthur. The majority of the rest were also either killed or wounded. Obviously our train was marked for a sad fate.

On our arrival at Omsk we learned that General Kuropatkin had been named commander of the Manchurian army. This information pleased the people, but many persons closely associated with him in the service spoke negatively of his appointment, predicting a bad end. The well-known military authority General Dragomirov spoke especially sharply. "Like Cassandra," he wrote, "I have often spoken unpleasant truths to point out that the attractive appearance of a venture does not guarantee its success. Skillfully concealed incompetence was evident to me even then, when most people still did not suspect." However, the majority of prognosticators began to talk in this way only after the fact. Over Kuropatkin still floated the halo of the legendary General Skobelev, for whom he had been chief of staff. His work as troop commander and administrator of the Trans-Caspian district was valued by everyone. He acquired his ministerial post by personal merit, without any patronage. Wide circles of the military, the public, and the press, when asked their choice for commander of the army, named Kuropatkin. Before the war Kuropatkin had been retired and in disfavor. By appointing him commander, the sovereign was only catering to the mood of the public.

Yet it is difficult to say on whom the sovereign's choice might have rested. General M. I. Dragomirov enjoyed great authority in the army but he was already seriously ill. In general there was a severe crisis in the Russian high command in the years immediately following 1900. It is important to recognize that in the selection of Kuropatkin not only the sovereign but Russia itself erred.

The journey came to an end. We had fairly flown along the great Siberian road but nevertheless, even such rapid glances as had been ours conveyed to us impressions of gigantic railroad construction, of the riches of Siberia, and of the unique and stolid arrangement of Siberian life. Everything was novel and interesting. Unfortunately my injured foot restricted my opportunities for observation. Not until Irkutsk, still limping slightly, was I able to walk along the platform. By the time we reached Harbin on March 5, however, my foot was almost healed.

CHAPTER 18   # THE TRANS-AMUR REGION FRONTIER GUARDS

The security of the Manchurian railroad had been entrusted to frontier guards created for the purpose, first from trappers who were fulfilling their obligatory terms of service and later predominantly from Cossacks and officer-volunteers. The guards were subordinate to Minister of Finance Witte, enjoying both his patronage and a higher salary scale than the army. Under the strange living conditions in that severe country, especially before the railroad opened, they sometimes experienced privation, sometimes great temptation, but always danger. These guards were of a unique type, bold, restless, familiar with the country, often going on drinking sprees but always ready to attack the enemy without weighing his strength. At the beginning of the Japanese War, the frontier guards, given the new name of Trans-Amur Region Frontier Guards, were already trained in the basic elements and they were placed under the command of the Manchurian army. But the cadres and traditions remained the same.

Over the vast expanse of the eastern (Trans-Baikal, Harbin–Vladivostok) and southern (Harbin–Port Arthur) branches of the Manchurian road were deployed four brigades of frontier guards, generally calculated at 24,000 infantry and cavalry and 26 pieces of ordnance. These troops were dispersed like a thin filament along the line, scaled to an average of eleven men per kilometer of road. One may easily understand how important the neutrality of China was, therefore, for the rear of our Manchurian army.

On my appearance at the district staff, I was assigned to a newly established position as chief of staff to the 3rd Trans-Amur Brigade. This meant that as a captain I jumped an unusual two steps in the hierarchical ladder and received as well a substantial salary increase which allowed me to retire my remaining debts in Warsaw in only a few months and to care for my mother. But aside from that, the post was disappointing. The 3rd Brigade was stationed at the Khanda-okhets station, guarding the road between Harbin and Vladivostok. After working with all my might to get into the war with Japan, I had been stuck in a third-rate theater where only skirmishes with Chinese bandits could be expected. I was diverted to the staff which was to await a movement of the Japanese from Korea to the Pre-Amur border toward Vladivostok, in which event our brigade would go automatically to the scene of action. This possibility seemed improbable to me. I regarded my appointment, therefore, as temporary and still resolved to go to the Japanese front at the first opportunity.

Questions of construction, battles, and reconnaissance came under my jurisdiction. The charming commander of the brigade, Colonel Palchevskii, indoctrinated me into brigade affairs and subsequently left me broad initiative. I went with him three times on a tour of the almost 500-kilometer line, becoming acquainted with the personnel of each post. With the mounted division I rode hundreds of kilometers through the country, thoroughly studying the region as well as the way of life of the people and becoming acquainted with the Chinese troops stationed outside the zone of expropriation to keep internal order.

Half the frontier guards were in reserve at the stations while the rest took turns on the road. At the more important danger points stood "road barracks," like miniature medieval castles surrounded by high stone walls with round bastions and rows of slanted embrasures with tightly closed gates. Between these barracks were posts consisting of mud huts for four to six persons, surrounded by entrenchments. The duty was demanding and dangerous. One day each unit patrolled for eight hours, the next they stood guard at the post for eight hours. A special procedure was necessary in order to determine whether those who approached were peaceable Chinese or enemies. Simple workers, bandits, and Chinese soldiers all dressed exactly alike. Chinese soldiers displayed few perceptible distinctions because their commanders usually kept for themselves the money allotted to them for equipping their men. The first time I rode along the line on a section car with the brigade commander, I saw before me three Chinese with guns, crossing the railroad. I asked, "Who are these people?"

"Chinese soldiers," he replied.

"But how can you tell?"

"Well, chiefly because they do not shoot at us," answered the brigade commander, smiling.

Bandits seldom attacked the defensive barracks on our line. But there were incidents when they massacred those at the posts. The history of the brigade was full of episodes of valor and ingenuity on the part of individual men. Not a week passed that there was not an attempt on the railway. But these were homemade attacks by brawlers or those seeking vengeance. In other words, Japanese hands were not apparent in these attempts as was the case on the southern branch.

Acquaintance with the border led me to a sad conclusion. The unusual conservatism of the Manchurian and Chinese way of life predisposed their relationships with external cultures. The people were primitive, ignorant, unenterprising, and submissive to their authorities who, from the petty ranks to the provincial governors, were sovereign administrators of the people's destiny, and they were greedy and cruel. Because of extremely low pay and no concept of the dignity of human labor, these workers by enslaving agreements came to a servile dependence on the entrepreneur. They had a primitive and rapacious way of exploiting the land and its interior. I saw burned-out meadows and forest, their way of preparing the land for breaking and sowing. In the mines of the Mudanzian valley, I saw tools from past centuries such as shovels and wooden troughs for washing gold. As I rode along the great road, I would see a swamp unexpectedly blocking the way. Long rows of Chinese bullock carts were stopped. The Chinese hitched all the oxen in turn to each oxcart and went through, or unloaded the oxcarts and crossed the swamp several times with light loads. According to the testimony of old inhabitants, such methods had been used for many years and no one had thought of draining the swamp.

Many Manchurians virtually lived in *khanshin* factories, which simultaneously served as centers of trade and public information. In the Azhekhunskii region adjacent to us, for example, the annual consumption of *khanshin*, a very strong Chinese vodka, was a whole bucket per inhabitant! The Chinese and Manchurians drank *khanshin*, poisoned themselves with opium, and were addicted to taking chances on numerous lotteries, as well as playing a kind of roulette and other games in gambling dens.

But the main hardship of the border was that bandits were an integral part of the people's way of life. The governor of Girin asserted that there were eighty thousand of them in his territory alone. Into the bandit gangs went all those who were outcasts from the social order by necessity, persecution, or crime; those who were unable to accustom themselves to the death noose of cruel or unjust authority tightening over the lower people; and finally everyone who preferred an easy, carefree, though restless and dangerous existence to oppressive, laborious life. Into the bandit gangs walked workers ruined by bureaucrats, the gambler who had lost all he had, the "boy" who had robbed his master, erring soldiers, or simply lovers of adventure. Soldiers who were bored by bandit life returned to their former trades or hired out as mercenaries in other districts.

These bandits elected their own chiefs, who enjoyed absolute authority. The chiefs divided spheres of activity among themselves and I never heard of confrontations among different bands. The bandits imposed a tax on bars, lotteries, and wealthy Chinese. They robbed contractors and made a general requisition in population centers.

Raids occurred, though rarely, on small villages occupied by small Russian garrisons. While one part of the band diverted the garrison, another seized those marked as hostages in order to collect ransom for them. At the conclusion of the operation, all the band hastily retreated. If frontier guards succeeded in cutting off the bandits' retreat, they would fight furiously to the last man.

Neither the Chinese administration nor the numerically small Chinese troops took the fight to the bandits. Apparently a silent agreement existed: "If you do not trouble us, we will not trouble you." The people, defenseless in the face of the terrorizing brigands and battles in their locales, saw this situation as one predestined by fate, inevitable. Once our horse patrol, following the tracks of outlaws, approached a Chinese village. We searched the huts and questioned the inhabitants. They testified that no bandits had been seen and that they had heard nothing about them. As the horse patrol left, we suddenly heard gunfire from one of the houses. Two frontier guards fell dead. The horse patrol wheeled, attacked the house, and killed all the bandits. It seemed that these bandits had pillaged, in sequence, all the houses of the villages in the course of several hours.

Brigands captured in our section were handed over to Chinese authorities at the nearest population center. There they were interrogated and sentenced by Chinese judges. But there was not a single case of bandits, though they were beaten with bamboo canes, who would name their companions. Actually they were exposed to public execution, drawing crowds of onlookers. I was never present at the executions, but I heard from our officers that the bandits went to their deaths calm and indifferent. At the station in Imianpo I saw the famous bandit chief Iandziria, captured by frontier guards, being dispatched to a Chinese court. He sang and made jokes, apparently clever ones, drawing smiles from the crowd of Chinese alongside the car. On seeing me, he smiled, saying in broken Russian, "Hullo! Captain, cut off my head quickly."

Although all of Manchuria was under martial law and military occupation, our brigade was not to be involved in the administration of the country outside the railroad zone. In districts which did not become theaters of war the population continued to live just as they had before the war and the occupation. In regions containing occupation troops, several encounters occurred with the populace over questions of quarters or requisitions because of our ignorance of the local Chinese administrative structure. Generally two factors marred our relations with the Chinese population. I wrote about them several times in the press during my service. They constituted then, and probably still do, an abscess in the colonial and concessionaire practices of governments. One was the greed of many entrepreneurs and contractors who unscrupulously exploited Chinese labor. And the second was our slavish dependence on interpreters. In our brigade, for instance, only one officer spoke Chinese tolerably well, although several had served in Manchuria from the first days of the road building. We were obliged to use Chinese who understood a little Russian. We also used old frontier guards who managed to jabber, badly but quickly, in Chinese. Most of these interpreters represented a rather vicious element, on whose consciences were extortion and the death of more than one Chinese.

Nevertheless the occupation had positive aspects. The great demand for labor, the opening of a huge market for the goods of native landowners who were paid entirely in Russian currency thus alleviated dealing and exports. All this increased the prosperity of the country.

Our General Staff never ceased to be alarmed about the question of Chinese neutrality. Opposite the right flank and rear of the Manchurian army stood the ten thousand troops of General Ma and the fifty thousand of Yuan Shih-kai.[1] In Northern Manchuria small detachments of Chinese soldiers, bandits, and native militia represented no serious threat, of course, but they were fully prepared for partisan war which would cut through the slender web of our two brigades deployed between the Trans-Baikal and Vladivostok, endangering the transport of our army from Russia. As is known, China maintained neutrality. Apparently the Russian occupation was not too onerous to the Chinese population and the Chinese government understood clearly the menace to the country which the Japanese represented.

Around Easter I was promoted to lieutenant colonel. But all the positive factors, such as interesting conditions in the Trans-Amur region and good relations with my commander and colleagues, could not hold me in Khandaokhets. I applied to the head of the district at Harbin, General Chichagov, requesting a transfer to the active army and I received a definite refusal. In August I decided to go to Liao-yuan to the staff of the Manchurian army. I presented myself to the chief of staff, General Sakharov, with whom I was well acquainted from my service in the Warsaw district. General Sakharov explained to me that the Trans-Amur district was subordinate to the army command only in an operational connection, and for that reason he could not dispose of individual personnel. I went back in a state of depression from which I was rescued only by chance. A captain of the General Staff, V., asked to leave the front for less strenuous duties because of his physical condition. They offered him to General Chichagov in exchange for me. Chichagov agreed and in mid-October I finally left for the south, sent off with a small comradely banquet and the good wishes of the commander and of the staff, of whom I retain the best of memories.

When I entered the staff of the Manchurian army, the officer supervising my appointment suggested to me, "We have received a telegram that Colonel Rossiiskii, chief of staff for General Rennenkampf's Trans-Baikal Division, has been gravely injured and evacuated. Do you wish to go there? I must warn you that this staff is in a serious situation. Heads don't stay on the shoulders long there."

"No matter. God is not without mercy. I accept the appointment with pleasure."

Against the dark background of Manchurian failures and retreats, among several older chiefs, army men pronounced the name of General Rennenkampf as one enjoying preeminence and a well-deserved military reputation. My joy on receiving the appointment, therefore, was understandable. I was ready in half an hour. I was assigned a mounted orderly, Starkov, a courageous and resourceful frontier guard originally from the Don Cossacks. He accompanied me through all the campaigns to the end of the war and was rewarded by General Rennenkampf by promotion to sergeant of Cossacks and award of the soldier's George's Cross. My orderly, leading a pack-horse, came to camp with a bedroll in which we placed all my simple belongings. Then I leaped to the saddle and we moved along the path toward General Rennenkampf's eastern detachment, somewhere in the mountains.

CHAPTER 19 FROM TIURENCHEN TO THE SHA-HO

The administrative organization of the Far Eastern troop structure was irregular in origin. There was no single commander. General Kuropatkin commanded the Manchurian army. Over him theoretically was the viceroy, Admiral Alekseev. The two men held divergent views as to how the war should be managed and frequently complained about their differences to the war minister as well as to the sovereign himself. Distant St. Petersburg was, of course, in no position to analyze the local situation and make conventional recommendations. Nor did Kuropatkin carry out the recommendations of St. Petersburg. He clung stubbornly to the idea of avoiding decisive battles until superior forces could be accumulated.

Witte, on taking leave of Kuropatkin, gave him among other things this droll advice: "When you arrive in Mukden, as the first order of business arrest Alekseev and send him in your railroad car to St. Petersburg with a telegram to the sovereign. There he will be either executed or embraced."

By the first of April 1904 the Manchurian army was deployed with its main force toward Liaoyuan, having moved advance guards south to the Inkoi region and east to the Yalu River. The latter position was separated from the main force by more than two hundred kilometers and a mountain pass difficult to traverse.

Having confined our squadron to Port Arthur, the Japanese proceeded without hindrance to disembark men on the mainland. In early April the 1st Army of Kuroki was concentrated on the Yalu River, where it encountered General Zasulich's eastern outposts. Our unsuccessful arrangement of advance guards and our tardy withdrawal led to a great loss (2,700) in a battle near Tiurenchen, where the Japanese had a five-to-one margin of superiority.[1] This first failure on land was painfully reflected in the morale of the country as well as of the army.

The Japanese continued to disembark on Kwantung. In mid-June the 2nd Army of Oku moved to the South Manchurian railroad and

Nogi's 3rd Army prepared for an operation against Port Arthur. Before long our forts were cut off from the outside world.

Viceroy Alekseev demanded a strike against Oku's army to relieve the blockade of Port Arthur, but Kuropatkin decided to leave the forts to their own destinies, at least until reinforcements arrived from Russia. Telegrams flew to St. Petersburg. The sovereign took Alekseev's side and subsequently ordered a force of no less than forty-eight battalions to go to the relief of Port Arthur. Kuropatkin carried out the order only to this extent: He sent the corps of General Shtakelberg (thirty-two battalions) on a limited mission to divert as many Japanese troops as possible from Port Arthur. Kuropatkin sent them off with his customary words of caution: "Do not become involved in any decisive action with superior forces of the enemy."

Oku brought little more strength to the affair than we did. From June 13 to 15 a battle raged near Vafangou, an indecisive battle without apparent preponderance on either side. Shtakelberg retreated to Tashichao unpursued by the Japanese, who, as it turned out, suffered from exhaustion as well as a general lack of provisions and supplies due to a washed-out road. Vafangou was the second blow to the morale of our army.

The viceroy, influenced by his staff, persistently urged Kuropatkin to take action. He now demanded that we hold the Japanese in the south while the eastern detachment attacked Kuroki, whose front was in the mountains to the southeast of Liaoyuan. General Count Keller made a token attack in that direction but it failed because of a tactical blunder. Although his experience in the lines was limited, Count Keller was a noble fellow. In what was probably a unique case, he had the manliness to state in his report, "The enemy surpassed us only in their ability to act." He blamed the failure on his lack of skill. In the next battle he was killed.

On July 22 General Kuropatkin at last found it feasible to direct a decisive strike at Kuroki. He reinforced the eastern detachment with two corps recently arrived from Russia, then went to their position and took command. The southern detachment, commanded by General Zarubaev, which guarded the approach to Liaoyuan along the railroad, was ordered not to enter into decisive battle with superior Japanese forces. On July 23 General Oku attacked Zarubaev near Tashichao with an almost equal force (48 battalions and 258 guns against our 45 battalions and 122 guns). Our artillery, though weaker, was able to gain a concealed position from which they commanded the conflict. All attacks of the Japanese were repulsed; the Japanese were clearly fatigued. The morale of our troops was excellent. The reserves had not yet been expended. Yet on the night of July 25 Zarubaev withdrew to Khaichen.

"There was no justification for retreat," reported the viceroy to the sovereign. Zarubaev never heard the last of that episode. I must point out, however, that in the last battle near Liaoyuan General Zarubaev fought brilliantly. The failure near Tashichao had two important consequences. We were forced to evacuate Inkoi, and the Japanese occupied an area near the branch railway line from the port which significantly facilitated the transport of supplies to their army. The second result was Kuropatkin's subsequent refusal to order a strike against Kuroki.

Toward the end of August the Russian army, by now outnumbering the Japanese, was camped before strongly fortified Liaoyuan. Feeling universally condemned for his "withdrawal" strategy, Kuropatkin enunciated a phrase which sped through the army and lifted morale, "I will not retreat from Liaoyuan."

On August 30 three Japanese armies (Kuroki, Nodzu, and Oku) began to attack our forward positions at Liaoyuan. The battle lasted for two days. There was a moment about which a spectator, the English military observer General Hamilton, later wrote, "Kuroki's staff was terrified; the Japanese withdrew. A little more effort and the Russians might have split Kuroki's army in two, and thrown his transport into disarray."[2] But on the night of September 1, by order of Kuropatkin, the army was assigned to the main position.

General Zarubaev's three corps occupied the central position, the fortifications of Liaoyuan. From this position he repulsed for sixty hours all attacks by Oku and Nodzu, inflicting heavy losses on them. Colonel F. Gertsch, the Swiss military observer, wrote about those battles in his campaign diary: "The Liaoyuan garrison fought with amazing tenacity, not because of high spirits (the Russians knew nothing but defeats) but only from a sense of duty."[3]

The detachment placed to the west of Liaoyuan went on the offensive and held firm, although it suffered heavy losses. A successful battle occurred on the eastern front, in the Sinkvantun position, and

Kuropatkin organized a counterattack by the three corps under his personal command to encircle Kuroki's eastern army. But from the very beginning of the aggressive outburst of the "attacking axe," the *leitmotif* of Kuropatkin's strategy was obvious: "If the position at Sinkvantun proves impossible to hold, do not become involved in stubborn battle but fall back to the next position." And when General Orlov's detachment, situated on the left flank, was diverted, the outflanked corps was ordered not to move forward.

In this survey of the most general outlines of the campaign, I cannot dwell on the activities of individual leaders and troops. Certainly they made no fewer errors in that engagement than in others, and these errors influenced command decisions. But the decision to retreat, issued even before the battle, sapped in advance the psychological aggressive impulse and lent an air of uncertainty to the leaders' plans for action. Under such circumstances, on the eastern front all engagements were particularly bloody. Concerning the Sinkvantun battle, Hamilton wrote, "The Japanese acknowledged that for several hours victory or defeat was in the balance between the two sides." On September 3, early in the morning, Kuropatkin informed Zarubaev that operations were entirely satisfactory on the eastern front. Immediately transmitted to all fortifications, the information stimulated joy. Cries of "Hurrah!" thundered from every position. But at seven o'clock the same morning, in the thick of battle, an order was received to effect a general and speedy withdrawal. The order specified that roads were to be destroyed, bridges blown up, and supplies burned. In half an hour another order followed, to hold up evacuation of the fortifications until dusk. The second order reached some fortifications but not all. Confusion set in. Our premature explosions and fires hindered the defenders of Liaoyuan and delighted the Japanese.

What could have happened in such a short time to alter the entire situation so radically? General Kuropatkin explained his decision this way. Two corps of the eastern detachment had come to the end of their last position and Kuroki had undertaken a flanking movement on the Iantaiskii mines and toward Mukden. From all sides came alarming reports. But Kuroki's feeble forces were unable to threaten outflanking seriously, especially since an entire corps remained untouched in Mukden.

Our situation in Liaoyuan, as it turned out, was far from desperate. The Japanese army was in disorder and had lost the impulse for further attack. The Japanese commander considered his position exceedingly grave. And "when the Russians retreated," wrote Hamilton, "all the Japanese experienced heartfelt thankfulness." In the Liaoyuan campaign we lost 18,000 men and the Japanese 23,500. Our army fell back to the Sha-ho.

After Liaoyuan St. Petersburg decided to dispatch another two and a half corps to the Manchurian theater of war, as well as cavalry. To be on the safe side, by October we achieved more than equality of forces: 195,000 bayonets and 758 guns against 150,000 and 648 respectively. Kuropatkin decided to begin the attack known in history as the "Battle of the Sha-ho" in early October.[4] In order to counter the slander about his withdrawals, he said in his order, "The time has come for us to compel the Japanese to obey our will because the forces of the Manchurian Army are now sufficient for all-out action." The troops welcomed the order with enthusiasm.

General Shtakelberg's eastern detachment led the main blow against the right flank of Kuroki's army, which was a third as large but occupied an exceedingly strong mountain position. Our western detachment, commanded by General Bilderling, was to hold off the armies of Oku and Nodzu. Strong reserves remained at the disposition of the commander, three and a half corps for the center and right flank.

The attack began auspiciously. The Japanese forward units were thrown back, and General Rennenkampf's detachment outflanked Kuroki in the valley of the Taitszikhe River, driving toward Bensikhu. But instead of continuing our swift movement on all fronts, not waiting for the Japanese to recover their wits, on October 9 the eastern detachment received this order: "Prepare to attack the main enemy position but no more." On October 10 Shtakelberg ordered a day of rest! Only on October 11 did merciless, bloody attacks begin in the extraordinarily difficult mountainous region, attacks which had to contend with high, steep mountains. October 11 and 12 were spent in these unrewarding labors.

Meanwhile Marshal Oiyama, having left Kuroki to his fate, returned to the counterattack on October 10, joining the armies of Nodzu and Oku against our western detachment and center. The center held firm, but almost all of General Kuropatkin's reserves were diverted there. The western detachment was obliged to withdraw several *versts*.

The attack by the eastern division stopped. The reasons for failure were various: first, directing the main blow at the mountain when in the west there was level terrain to which our troops were accustomed; next, the inadmissible delay in attacking; and finally the headstrong, costly frontal assaults on the formidable mountain near Lautkhalaz, with massive losses, instead of developing Rennenkampf's encircling movement. But there was no absence of valor among the Russian troops. In that campaign, as in preceding ones, history recorded a series of the bravest exploits by separate units and individuals. For example, there was General Putilov's brigade of the 5th Siberian Division who led an attack on a *sopka* named "Putilovskii" in his honor;[5] despite the loss of 15 officers and 532 soldiers dead, and 79 officers and 2,308 soldiers wounded, they took and held the *sopka*, interring there 1,500 Japanese "with military honors."

Gradually decelerating, the Sha-ho campaign ended on October 17. Our losses were 41,000, those of the Japanese almost the same. The Japanese counterattack ground down even before ours. Almost simultaneously, both sides gave up further prolongation of the operation.

PART IV

CHAPTER 20　IN GENERAL
RENNENKAMPF'S
DETACHMENT

On October 28 I was transferred to General Rennenkampf's detachment as chief of staff of the Trans-Baikal Cossack Division and the detachment staff as well. The detachment mainly consisted of three regiments of the 71st Infantry Division and three regiments of the Trans-Baikal Cossack Division, with artillery. It was deployed in three groups, the central group being sent to Tsinkhechen to cover the left flank of the Manchurian army.

For more than two weeks it was quiet in the detachment. There was only the insignificant and tedious work of guarding and reconnaissance in that region where massive mountains with their curves and folds made observation extremely difficult, where footpaths meandered through deserted passes from which bullets often rained down from an invisible foe.

In the Tsinkhechen area part of the detachment was housed in Chinese huts and outbuildings, the rest in dugouts. They dug pits to one *arshin* [28 inches] in depth, set poles, and thatched the roof with kaoliang strewn with layers of earth.[1] The walls, ceilings, floors, and doors were all made of kaoliang. All day the primitive stone chimney smoked, its flue made of kerosene jugs towering above the roof. In such mud huts people lived all through the icy fall and Manchurian winter, when the Reaumur thermometer registered twenty-five degrees below zero [−24.25 degrees F.].

General Rennenkampf was quartered in a small section of our Chinese hut. The staff huddled together in one hut with two long rows of *kan* [low stoves] covered with double mats of bast, constantly warm, on which we slept, sat, wrote, and usually even ate because the small table squeezed between the two rows of *kan* was unable to accommodate everyone.

The extreme difficulty of victualing the regiment was complicated by lengthy transport through mountain passes. Bread was often unavailable and we were provided with baked pancakes. Our salvation was the abundance of local cattle. The officers' table was scarcely distinguishable from that of the soldiers. Only now and then, when some daring merchant ventured to come to our detachment (charging double for the risk), if he had not been robbed along the road, we had a drinking spree for two or three days.

We were able to dispense with all red tape. The administrative and bookkeeping unit was far away across the mountain pass. There they wrote, printed, and kept accounts but only occasionally did anyone come to me with a report. In our field staff there was no printing machine or mimeograph, only the pocket field book which served for all orders, instructions, and reports.

General Rennenkampf was a natural soldier. He was personally brave, unafraid of responsibility, well versed in battle conditions, not tricked by conflicting impressions presented by alarming reports submitted during battles. He knew how to command, always looking ahead and never retreating carelessly. At the end of June, after the sad days of Tiurenchen and Vafangou, in a report to the sovereign explaining the causes for our failure, General Kuropatkin wrote, "The bitter relations of Generals Zasulich and Shtakelberg, particularly of late, with their subordinates have made proper relations impossible among those subordinates and the troops." But Generals Mishchenko and Rennenkampf, he added, enjoyed "authority and affection." Actually the troops disliked Zasulich and detested Shtakelberg. As for Mishchenko and Rennenkampf, both of whom I knew well, Kuropatkin's characterization needs some modification. Mishchenko, about whom I will write later, liked people and they liked him. Rennenkampf, on the other hand, regarded the human element of his unit impersonally, as an implement for war and personal glory. But his military bearing and bravery impressed his subordinates and obliged them to acknowledge his authority, made them believe in him and willing to render unquestioning obedience. But there was never any intimacy.

Besides staff officials, there were always several "personalities" in my staff — military correspondents, officials of the highest ranks who had come with a definite purpose, as well as hangers-on or simply officers who had "detoured." Rennenkampf's military reputation attracted them and many sought some sort of military commission in order to have entered on their service list a notation of participation, even though bloody, in the affairs of the famous detachment.

Relations between the Chinese population and our troops were satisfactory. Of course there were excesses, as in all armies and all wars. But Russians are by nature gregarious and not arrogant. Our soldiers mingled amiably with the Chinese and by no means treated them as an inferior race. Because the population centers changed hands often, it was possible to compare the two "regimes." When they retreated, the meticulous Japanese usually left buildings in order while our soldiers, particularly the Cossacks, gave them an uninhabitable appearance. In order to compel our people to take better care of their lodgings, Rennenkampf ordered that when a village was occupied for a second time, companies and Cossack squadrons were to be assigned to the same buildings which they occupied earlier.

In every other way the Japanese "regime" was incomparably more oppressive, as indicated by the despicable way in which the Japanese treated the Chinese, literally as if they were inanimate objects, and by their requisitions of women, which were not individual cases but organized on higher orders. Even at outposts, when our troops seized Japanese patrols unexpectedly they would find among the Japanese soldiers several terrified and exhausted "requisitioned" women.

Our relations with the Chinese population were complicated in the theater of war even more than in the Trans-Amur district by our slavish dependence on Chinese interpreters. Off the beaten track, living conditions among the Chinese prompted many "volunteers" to offer their services as spies both to us and to the Japanese. When caught redhanded they were shot, but this did not deter others. We tried to stop these incidents, but it was quite impossible since no one could guarantee that Chinese interpreters were not denouncing those being questioned for spite or to settle personal accounts.

In my pocket field diary I entered a case our division doctor Manotskov told me about: "We had an ensign, not a good fighter, who had a good business and a young wife at home. He feared bullets and was homesick. Once his mates brought him to me with a wounded leg.

They explained what had happened. On his way to Shakhedza he stopped on the road and told his soldiers that he had to go into the bushes 'for a natural need.' His soldiers heard a shot. They rushed to the bushes and found the ensign wounded. Near him were two frightened Chinese. The soldiers tied their plaits together and thus brought the two men to the unit. The ensign testified that the two men had shot him. They were questioned. I wonder what they told the interpreter. In any case, after he had 'translated,' the two Chinese were decapitated. As for the ensign, his wound was a neat one. It seemed queer to me. The flesh looked burned, obviously by a very close shot. I went to see him in the hospital. He had an extremely high temperature. 'Where are the two Chinese?' he asked. 'They have been executed.' 'My God,' cried the ensign, 'it is dreadful. They are innocent! I shot myself to get a leave.'"

"And what happened to the ensign?" I asked the doctor. "Well, he got home. I would not report it. I am a doctor, not a prosecutor. Besides, no one could put those poor Chinese heads back on their shoulders."

In October the viceroy, recognizing the incongruity of his role as chief commander, for the third time asked the sovereign for permission to retire. In view of the significant reinforcement of the Manchurian army by corps from Russia, he suggested the creation of a second army, "placing each army under the authority of a general." By such means he sought to secure the honorable demotion of Kuropatkin, who might remain as one of the army commanders while removal and replacement would concern Admiral Alekseev alone as chief commander. But on October 26 the viceroy was relieved from duty and it was General Kuropatkin who became commander in chief! After that the Manchurian army was divided into three armies, headed by General Linevich (1st, eastern), General Gripenberg (2nd, western), and General Baron Kaulbars (3rd, central). General Rennenkampf's detachment became part of the 1st Army.

Fearing for the left flank, Kuropatkin's staff constantly directed our attention to the road from Tsianchan to Sintszintin, which led in a roundabout way to Mukden. Consequently we put out increasingly stronger patrols in that direction. On November 19 General Rennenkampf, feeling burdened by the calm, went personally with a small detachment (three battalions, four Cossack squads, and twelve guns) in the direction of the village of Uitszyiui. We went along a broad valley between double rows of *sopkas* from which hostile bullets might rain down at any moment. For safety, mounted patrols were sent ahead. The Cossacks would dismount and climb *sopkas* right and left to cover the column as we passed, later riding to rejoin us while another screen went on ahead.

When we halted to rest, I wrote my first report to the army staff. It was a cold morning; the air was crisp and clear. We heard an unceasing, intrusive whistle, *vzzi, vzzi,* monotonously droning. Rennenkampf turned to me and said, "Well, Anton Ivanovich, I congratulate you on your military baptism!" The sound came from Japanese bullets whizzing over our heads. The scene was quite ordinary. Nobody paid any attention to it.

On November 20 our detachment repulsed the enemy from the Shunkhailin mountain pass and, after forcing the Japanese from Uitszyiui, occupied the village. We spent the night there after having established outposts on outlying *sopkas*. Generals Rennenkampf and Ekk (the nominal head of the detachment actually managed by Rennenkampf) settled into one of the huts with their staffs. We awoke at daybreak, alarmed by heavy fire from the *sopkas* where our outposts had formerly been stationed. We later learned that during the night the Japanese, speaking Russian loudly, had approached our sentries and killed them. Then they took their positions and opened fire on the village from above. Bullets rained like peas on the roofs and walls of our huts. We immediately sent a battalion to reinforce the forward units. Then, according to Rennenkampf's custom, we assembled leisurely, as if in a peaceful setting. Under the bullets we went about our morning toilet in the hut yards. Under bullets we drank tea even more leisurely than usual. Later we left to join the reserves who stood exposed in a hollow at the crossroads. As we approached, Japanese started firing on our reserves. The reserves stirred about and orderlies brought out two or three wounded. I turned to General Rennenkampf: "Your Excellency, the reserves must be led to that *sopka*."

"Just wait. After a restless night, people are nervous. We must be calm."

"But all the same, while we remain here being calm, the reserves should be allowed to take cover." He agreed. As they had said at headquarters, it was difficult to keep one's head on one's shoulders in Rennenkampf's staff.

Here, according to my memory, is a fairly accurate but not a full summary of losses at various times. Lieutenant Colonels Mozheiko and Shulzhenko and Cavalry Captain Shakharov were killed, Colonel Rossiiskii and Lieutenant Colonel Gurko along with two adjutants were wounded, and a number of officer-orderlies were wounded and killed. General Rennenkampf was wounded twice by bullets in his neck and in his leg. But the tradition of none-too-cautious regard for our own skins was what created the warm regard of the troops not only toward the chief but also toward his staff.

On November 23 our outposts near Tsinkhechen were hard pressed by the Japanese and on the morning of November 24 an advance guard reported that a dense column of enemy in the valley was ready to attack us. Thus began the battle of Tsinkhechen.

General Rennenkampf went with his staff to an observation point on a commanding height from which he could view the entire panorama of battle. From the leader of the advance guard, a Cossack regimental commander, we received a report which was both alarming and vague. Rennenkampf sent him a field dispatch in sarcastic and sharp terms. "I am afraid," he told me, "this . . . will mess everything up!"

"Your Excellency," I asked, "permit me to take the advance guard."

"With pleasure. I wish you success."

I went to the advance guard, pondering on the way how to soften the blow for my predecessor. It was a needless anxiety. When the colonel learned that he was being relieved, he took off his cap, crossed himself, and said, "Praise the Lord! At least now I will not be held responsible." In the army, I met many men in both high and low posts who were otherwise absolutely courageous but who feared responsibility.

That was my first experience with independent command. I deployed the advance guard (one and a half battalions, four Cossack squads, and a mountain battery) to a forward position, having given the left flank of the detachment the task of covering direct access to the Tsinkhechen valley. That day the Japanese attacked me (left flank) and Lieutenant Colonel Beresnev of the Bugulminskii Regiment (center). All the attacks were repulsed, by me with fire and by the heroic Lieutenant Colonel Beresnev (whose position the Japanese succeeded in penetrating) with bayonets.

The night was cold, twenty degrees below zero Reaumur [−13 degrees F.]. Riflemen lay on the ridges of craters in tense expectation, holding their weapons in their frozen hands. I went down to the reserves. Concealed from the enemy small woodfires burned and small groups of soldiers were warming themselves. In spite of the cold others slept on straw strewn on the ground. There was not a single hut nearby. Having found a kind of spade somewhere, my orderly, Starkov, dug a pit in the frozen earth and lined it with straw as a bed for me. I tried to take a nap but sleep would not come. My body grew so cold that I preferred not to sleep. That night the Japanese again attacked and again they were repulsed.

On November 25 the Japanese, obviously reinforced, brought the battle to all my fronts, encircling my left flank still more and advancing toward the Sintszintin road. My Cossack squad, directed there, sent out small units on foot to ridge elevations where their firing led the Japanese to an error in judgment, thus lengthening the radius of the circle. The attack continued on all fronts with the Japanese approaching within 1,200 to 2,000 steps of various parts of our position.

On my right flank was an elevation from which one could accurately observe the Japanese shifting. The main attack came toward it. The fire was so heavy that we could not raise our heads. But the commander of the nearest company, Captain Bogomolov of the Chembarskii Regiment, was walking upright to verify targets.

"Captain, why are you doing that? Get down!"

"Impossible, Lieutenant Colonel, sir. Our men are nervous. They aim poorly." And he continued on his way.

The wounded began to crawl down. Japanese bullets were copper, of an old style, and all the injuries were grave. We carried off the slain. One noncommissioned officer, obviously a favorite of the captain, was struck down by a bullet in the head. Bogomolov went over and bent down to kiss the deceased on the forehead. For two or three minutes he knelt, covering his face with his hands, then rose and again went on, upright. I encountered many officers like Captain

Bogomolov in the fields of Manchuria. Because of them the enemy always had a high opinion of the valor of Russian officers, of whom there was a higher percentage killed than of soldiers.[2]

In the Japanese trenches, as a rule, everything alive went into the ground. Once however, during General Mishchenko's attack near Tasintun, I watched as a Japanese company tried to rid itself of the Cossacks surrounding it. The old captain commanding the company directed its fire while standing on the roof of a hut, from which Cossack bullets finally shot him down.

In the Tsinkhechen battle Japanese artillery did me little harm because the configuration of the terrain forced them to occupy virtually open positions. The battery directed against my front was reduced to silence after the third volley from my mountain battery. Artillery from the main position parried all attempts by Japanese batteries approaching the center and right flanks and quickly scattered all concentrations of Japanese.

The Japanese assaults and attacks against Tsinkhechen continued for five days. The last time that the Japanese attacked, on November 28, they were easily repulsed. It was only a rearguard action covering the retreat of their main force. Our horse patrols reported that their left column, which I had outflanked, evacuated the entire area between Sintszintin and Tsinkhechen and departed toward Tszianchan. I broke up my detachment by regiments then and returned to the staff.

At General Rennenkampf's request, General Linevich, the commander of the army, reinforced us with a brigade of riflemen and ordered an attack. The chief commander, General Kuropatkin, did not approve, considering the timing unpropitious. That very day, he ignored the army staff and telegraphed directly to Rennenkampf, "Continue to guard against movement of the Japanese toward Sintszintin, en route to Tsinkhechen." I emphasize General Kuropatkin's inordinate fear for the left flank of the Manchurian army because it later played such an important role in the course of the Mukden engagement.

Because we had received no strict orders to the contrary, on November 29 General Rennenkampf moved our detachment in for an assault on Tszianchan. He dislodged the enemy from two mountain passes and our cavalry reached the River Taitszihke. But on November 30 a categorical order arrived telling us to return.

We had no way of estimating the overall Japanese losses, but we counted 280 Japanese corpses. Probably no fewer were recovered by the Japanese themselves or lost in the wooded ravines of the craters or in the snowy glades.

So ended the Tsinkhechen battle, memorable for me as my first experience as a combat commander. And with waves of emotion I encountered the latest in the history of military names: "Rennenkampf Mountain," "Beresnev Sopka," "Denikin Sopka," the names of Tsinkhechen positions which we had held.

After significant reinforcement of General Rennenkampf's detachment, an order came on December 18 to form a staff corps for it. Colonel Vasilii Gurko was to head the staff while I retained my post as chief of staff of the Trans-Baikal Cossack Division. The head of the division at that time was General Liubavin, a simple, courageous, and honest Ural Cossack who left me initiative to operate. Because tiresome inquiries about a threat to our left flank continued constantly to arrive from headquarters, Rennenkampf charged us to increase our patrols in that direction. General Liubavin and I twice beat back forward units of Japanese and went to Tszianchan, and one time with an independent detachment I threw back the Japanese from the encirclement of Vantselin (Ianopu). When once we succeeded in battling our way to the forward Tszianchan positions, we requested permission to move our infantry in order to insure success. The occupation of Tszianchan, that junction of circuitous roads, should have calmed the fears of headquarters. Rennenkampf shared our views but permission was still denied.

In December we became aware of preparations for a cavalry attack on the rear of the Japanese army, in order to outflank the Japanese from the west. The raid, which should have been kept secret, was soon known to everyone. It was discussed in the stations, the public houses, and in private correspondence. Rennenkampf obviously wanted passionately to have this affair entrusted to him. He became nervous and negotiated privately with headquarters. Subsequently we learned that General Kaulbars, although occupying a higher command post in the army, had asked Kuropatkin for the job. Believing that he could be more useful in this role, he wanted to head the Western Cavalry. Actually army circles considered that those two natural cavalrymen were the only ones capable of carrying out such an important raid, the first to be undertaken during the Manchurian campaign.

Late in the year we received word that the branch railway had been completed from the rear, from Fushuna, to our detachment. The commander in chief himself wished to inaugurate the new road by visiting Matsziandan in our region on December 22. General Rennenkampf went to greet him, taking me along. An honor guard was displayed, a company with standards. We were situated on the flank. That was the first time since my academy days that I had met General Kuropatkin. When Rennenkampf presented me to the chief commander, General Kuropatkin shook my hand firmly and said, "Certainly, we are already acquainted, well acquainted." At lunch, to which a number of us had been invited, the chief commander was quite amiable, asking about my service experiences, but he did not mention the incident at the academy.

In conversation with Kuropatkin, Rennenkampf had evidently mentioned the matter of the raid again, because after we left he shared with me several new facts about it, morosely concluding, "Mishchenko will command the cavalry."

On January 1, 1905, Port Arthur fell. This event, although not unexpected, was sadly discussed in the army as well as in the country. The commandant of the fortress, General Stoessel, was not master of the situation.[3] Afterward he was sentenced by a military court to death by execution, a sentence which was commuted by the sovereign to ten years' confinement in the stockade. His chief of staff, General Kondratenko, was the spirited defender of Port Arthur and had he not been felled by an enemy bullet, the fortress would perhaps have held for several weeks more.[4] But no more than that.

In any case the Port Arthur garrison displayed unusual bravery. In the incomplete and imperfect defenses of that fort, a force of 34,000 repulsed fierce attacks by the Japanese for 233 days, holding off almost a third of the Japanese armies (four or five of Nogi's divisions, that is, 70,000 to 80,000 men not counting reinforcements). We lost 17,000 men killed or dead from illness, while about 110,000 Japanese were eliminated. At the time of the surrender the garrison numbered only 13,500 of whom many were ill, especially from scurvy and snow blindness. Port Arthur was a glorious page in the history of the Manchurian campaign.

That affair, which freed all of Nogi's army for action in the main theater, stirred the commander in chief to make haste with the raid, not awaiting, as he should have done, development of our general attack. General Mishchenko's cavalry, composed of seventy-seven squadrons and Cossack squads and twenty-two pieces of ordnance, entered the campaign on January 9 charged with inflicting capital damage on the railroad from Khaichen and Saichzhoi, seizing the station and port of Inkoi, and destroying military supplies there.

General Mishchenko, a distinguished military chief under ordinary circumstances, was not equal to this particular task, which required athletic skill, speed, and initiative. His detachment moved too slowly, being burdened by a large pack train, excessive because of superfluous supplies, allowing the Japanese time to take countermeasures. He inflicted only insignificant damage to the railway and ruined several warehouses. After suffering failure near Inkoi, he further overburdened his transport with wounded. On January 16 he returned to the original position.

General Rennenkampf was unable to conceal his contempt for the raid. He originated a phrase which spread rapidly through all the command circles, "This was not *nabeg* but *napolz!*"[5] Mishchenko surely heard about the wicked pun and it served to sharpen the animosity between these two outstanding generals placed far away from each other at the front all during the war and who, as far as I know, never met. I must say, though, that General Mishchenko's military reputation was so solidly established that the Inkoi failure did not lessen his prestige in the eyes of the commander in chief and the army.

In spite of a series of failures, the army did not lose courage but waited with impatience for a new and genuine offensive. And when it was ordered, everyone's spirits, officers' as well as soldiers', rose once more. Still, some did not rejoice. There were those who felt too deeply the bitterness and disappointment of past failures.

Our strength was almost equal to that of the Japanese (220,000 to 240,000 bayonets). General Gripenberg's 2nd Army was to deliver the main thrust along the Japanese left flank in a general attack on the railroad. The offensive promised success. There was level terrain, to which our soldiers were accustomed, and Gripenberg's significant numerical superiority over Oku's confronting army was encouraging. But further strategy led to an impasse. According to instructions, the entire front was to halt awaiting the success of the 2nd Army's first movement. The 2nd Army, meanwhile, was initially assigned a limited objective, to take the village of Sandepu. January 25 was designated as the day for attack.

Headquarters did not abandon its pathological fear for the left flank of the army. On January 18 the Japanese pressed lightly on the outposts of our detachment and General Kuropatkin went into a state of anxiety. He ordered two brigades of reinforcements previously designated for the 2nd Army offensive to be sent to us for help. Only after protracted protests from Gripenberg was the order rescinded. The commander in chief telegraphed us directly, "Watch out at Tsinkhechen." His interference extended to giving orders to General Rennenkampf as to where to place this company, where to transfer that one, and so forth. Rennenkampf grumbled, since he did not share Kuropatkin's anxiety and merely for the sake of form sent me on patrol with several Cossack squads. By January 23 I had reached the mountain pass of Vanzelin without finding any changes in the enemy arrangement.

January 25 came. We were prepared in Tsinkhechen. Impatiently we awaited orders to begin the offensive. And we waited. As January 26, 27, and 28 went by, we were perplexed. Meanwhile Gripenberg, disregarding Oku's deeper intrusion, attacked Sandepu. The attack, conducted by improper tactics, did not succeed. There were other bloody attacks in this region, but the Japanese, untroubled on other fronts, were reinforced. These attacks also failed. Gripenberg ordered a resumption of the attack on January 29 but the commander in chief, influenced by the Sandepu failure and Japanese pressure (although insignificant) on our center (3rd Army), ordered the 2nd Army to return to its former position. Thus the "general offensive" of the Russian front amounted only to an attack on Sandepu. And failure there served as cause for abandoning the entire operation. We lost 368 officers and 11,364 soldiers while the Japanese lost about 8,000 men.

On January 30 Gripenberg sent a telegram to the war minister

CHAPTER 23 THE END OF THE JAPANESE WAR

The last battle of the Mounted Detachment, which was the final battle of the Russo-Japanese War, was fought on July 1 near Sanvaiza when we took the left flank support point of the enemy by storm and destroyed a whole battalion of Japanese infantry.

In mid-July a rumor began to circulate in the army that the president of the United States, Theodore Roosevelt, had offered his services to our government for concluding peace. The quietness reigning at the front seemed to confirm the rumor. How was it received in the army? I think that I do not err in saying that for the majority of officers the prospect of returning home (for many after two years of war) was dulled by the poignancy of the oppressive, futile, and (as we all acknowledged) unconcluded campaign.

Negotiations began in Portsmouth. No representative from the Manchurian army command was sent to the peace conference. No military representative from the scene of action was included in the personnel of Witte's delegation. No one asked the chief commander's opinion about the expediency of concluding peace or the determination of treaty conditions.[1] The army was not consulted.

Rightist members of Russian society harshly condemned Witte, alleging "criminal surrender" and giving him the wicked nickname "Count Half-Sakhalin."[2] The accusation was entirely unjust, especially considering that the concession of half of Sakhalin was made by order of the sovereign, not at Witte's insistence. Witte displayed masterly finesse and firmness in negotiations and accomplished all that he could under those difficult conditions. He was not regarded sympathetically by the leftists either. The well-known socialist Burtsev, who was to assume an entirely "defensive position" during World War I, wrote to Witte in the Portsmouth days, "It is necessary to abolish autocracy. If peace will hinder this, then we must not conclude peace."[3]

Initially Witte had no sympathy from President Theodore Roosevelt, who several times corresponded directly with the sovereign and accused Witte of obstinacy. But the Japanese were actually impudent in the first stages of negotiations. They demanded from Russia the payment of an indemnity, limitation of our land and sea forces in the Far East, and even Japanese control over their composition. Repelled by these demands, the sovereign categorically rejected them with one word, "Never!"[4]

The conference was protracted and on two occasions delegates laid out their suitcases and packed. Meanwhile the American clergy and the press came more and more to favor Russia.[5] In the press voices began to resound more frequently with warnings about the potential danger to American interests of an excessively strong Japan in the Pacific. Under the pressure of changing public opinion, the president sent a telegram to the Mikado saying that "public opinion in the United States inclines sympathetically toward Russia" and that "if the Portsmouth negotiations come to nothing, Japan will no longer find in the United States that sympathy and support which she encountered earlier." Indubitably such testimony influenced the course of the negotiations. Whether it was in England's interests to continue to support Japan, events of the years 1941–1945 have shown.

Truce was concluded in Portsmouth on September 5, 1905, and the peace treaty was ratified on October 14. Russia forfeited her rights in Kwantung and South Manchuria, renounced the southern branch line of the railroad as far as Kuachendz station, and gave up to Japan the southern half of Sakhalin island.[6] To those of us not included in the conference, the central question lay in none of the treaty provisions. For us the center of gravity was the insoluble dilemma: Might the Manchurian army again go on the offensive and gain victory over the Japanese?

This question, both then and in following years, disturbed the Russian public, especially the military, and caused heated debate in the press and at assemblies, but it still remained unsolved. Human intellect possesses the characteristic of intuition but it is incapable of prescience.

I will return to purely objective data. At the time peace was concluded, the Russian army in the Sipingai positions had 446,500 soldiers (about 300,000 of them near Mukden). Troops were deployed not in thin lines as before but in depth by echelons. We had in general reserve an army consisting of more than half our personnel to protect us from accidents. It promised a more active possibility. Army flanks were well protected by the corps of Generals Rennenkampf and Mishchenko. The army had supplied and rejuvenated its personnel and significantly improved its techniques. It had howitzer batteries, machine guns (374 instead of 36), personnel for the field railroad, wireless telegraph, and so forth. Communications with Russia were maintained not by three pairs of trains as at the start of the war, but by twelve pairs.[7] Finally, the spirit of the Manchurian army was not broken. Units of reinforcements coming to us from Russia were willing and eager to fight.

The Japanese army situated opposite us had 32 percent fewer personnel. Their country was exhausted. Among the prisoners we had taken were old men and young boys. Their spirits were no longer high. During the six months following our defeat near Mukden, Japan was unable to mount an offensive, largely due to lack of confidence in its own strength.[8]

But our troops were still commanded by many of those officers who had led them near Liaoyuan, at the Sha-ho, near Sandepu and Mukden. Had the recent bloody experiences taught them anything? Would Linevich's staff have manifested greater strategic knowledge or more firmness, determination, and authority in regard to subordinate generals than Kuropatkin had done? These questions occurred to us and naturally aroused skepticism in many.

As for me, considering all the pros and cons, facing our deficiencies squarely, in answer to the question, "What would have been the result if we had gone on the offensive from the Sipingai positions?" I said then and I say now, "Victory!" Russia had not been defeated. Her army could have continued fighting. It was St. Petersburg that was tired more than the army. Alarming signs of approaching revolution — more and more frequent terrorist acts, agrarian disorders, strikes, and unrest — deprived the government of its will to decide and to dare and forced it to sign a premature peace.

By August the impression had gradually been created that the war was over. Military interests were pushed to the background and monotony set in for the army. Regiments hurriedly began to put in order administrative matters which had been neglected during the war, such as accounts and estimates. In that atmosphere an episode occurred that was characteristic of the Cossack way of life.

Our Mounted Detachment was redesignated at last as a regular corps with General Mishchenko officially confirmed as commander. General Bernov was appointed head of the Ural–Trans-Baikal Division. During General Bernov's initial review of the division, I escorted him as chief of staff. Everything went well in the Trans-Baikal Regiments. We went on to the 4th Ural Regiment. The regiment was drawn up for the examination of complaints as required by regulations, officers and Cossacks separately. The officers had no complaints. The new division chief addressed the customary question to the Cossacks, "Have you any complaints, Cossacks?"

Instead of the usual answer, "No, none!" there was profound silence. The general was astonished. He repeated the question a second and a third time. Gloomy faces. Silence. He took me aside, asking, "What is this, insurrection?"

I too was at a loss. This was an excellent fighting regiment, competent and disciplined.

"May I suggest, Your Excellency, that you question them individually?"

The general walked to the right flank and asked the first Cossack, "Have you any complaints?"

"I certainly do, Your Excellency," and the Cossack began to speak rapidly, as if from memory, pouring out an entire series of statistics. "From January 12 until February 5, the squadron was at posts. I was allowed no supplies for six days. On March 3 near Mukden, our platoon missed connections with army staff. For ten days my horse and I received nothing to eat."

And he went on and on. Another spoke, then a third, then a tenth. I tried to take notes of the complaints but soon gave up. I could have gone on writing until morning. General Bernov broke off the interrogation and took me aside. "This is the first time in my life that I have encountered such a thing. The devil himself could not shut them up. I must stop it."

Turning back to the lines he said, "I see that you have disorder here and some misunderstandings. I did not expect this from such a brilliant regiment. I will return in three days. See that everything is in order!"

I must point out that Cossacks, especially the Ural Cossacks, were entirely different from the rest of the army. The Ural Cossacks had no class subdivisions. From the same family one son might become an officer, another a simple Cossack. It was just a matter of chance. In one case a younger son commanded a Cossack squadron and the eldest son was his orderly. Family relations and the lack of class distinctions between officers and Cossacks produced the traits characteristic of the Ural Regiment.

During the two days following the inspection, there was a great deal of activity in the regiment. Adjacent to the division staff, in the meadow near the village where the regiment was quartered, one could see groups of men gathered in a circle and making exasperated gestures. A friend of mine from the Ural Mounted Cossacks explained to me what was going on there. "The Cossacks hold 'trials' of their squadron commanders. This is an ancient custom with us after each battle. The premature inspection threw everything awry. The Cossacks did not wish to complain to the inspecting general, but had they not done so, they feared that they would lose their rights and not get what their commanders owed them."

On the eve of General Bernov's next review I asked a *Uralets*, "Well, what now?"

"We have finished," he said. "Tomorrow you will hear for yourself. In most squadrons the business was quickly settled. In some, though, it was a hotter matter. The commander of N Squadron was especially berated. He threw his cap on the ground and got down on his knees. 'Be merciful. You ask too much. You want me to become so poor that my wife and sons will be left without a roof!' And the squadron replied, 'We know how much you owe us. We know how to count. You will not swindle us.' But they finally came to an agreement. The squadron said, 'All right, drink our blood, you so and so.'"

The next day when the division chief asked for the second time whether or not there were any complaints, all the Cossacks loudly and gaily answered as one man, "No, not one, Your Excellency!"

I received for my part great moral satisfaction in my personal life. By an order of the sovereign dated July 26 I was promoted to colonel "for distinction in the affair against the Japanese." Besides, General Mishchenko presented me with two high military orders.

When the war was over, the Ural–Trans-Baikal Division was subject to reorganization. I was rather attracted to Europe and did not wish to remain in Manchuria or Siberia. I took leave of my military comrades and went to headquarters. There I requested a telegraphed order from the administration of the General Staff in St. Petersburg reserving a post for me as chief of staff of a division in European Russia. Because no answer was expected soon (strikes had already begun on the telegraph line, and headquarters had to confer with St. Petersburg via Nagasaki and Shanghai), I was commandeered for the interim to the 8th Corps staff, in which I served for a long while in peacetime staff duties.

After duty with the *"Zaparozhskoi sech,"* as General Mishchenko's Mounted Detachment called itself, I passed suddenly into a completely different setting in the 8th Corps staff. General Skugarevskii commanded the corps. Cultured, knowledgeable, direct, and honest, he enjoyed, despite his fairness, a longstanding and widespread fame as a difficult chief, a restless subordinate, and an unbearable fellow. He had received his post only a short time before, after the war was over, but he was already detested in the corps. Skugarevskii knew the laws, the rules and regulations. Everything else was a matter of indifference to him. The human soul, individuality, the motivation for this or that behavior, even the military merits of his subordinates, were as nothing. He seemed to search actively for violations of regulations, important or petty, and he punished promptly, whether the offender was a division chief or a private. He punished with equal severity important violations of sentry duty or an administrative error, some "improper turn of a soldier's heel," a misplaced period in the artillery chief's inspection order, or an "unauthorized length of fur" on a *papakha.*[9] In the dissatisfaction following the Mukden failure, on the threshold of new shocks from the first revolution, such a rigorous regime was especially oppressive and foolhardy.

From the atmosphere of terror and alienation which accompanied his tours, Skugarevskii knew very well what the troops thought of him. And individuals close to him tried to talk to him.

I traveled to the corps in a railroad car which was crammed full of officers. Their conversation exclusively concerned the new corps commander. I was struck by the singular malice with which they all referred to him. In the same car sat a middle-aged sister of mercy. During the conversation her facial expression changed. She began to cry and rushed from the car to the vestibule. A confused silence settled over the officers. It turned out that she was Skugarevskii's wife.

The staff had a particularly oppressive mold, especially during the public dinners with the commander at which participation was mandatory. By established etiquette, only the man with whom the corps commander conversed could speak in normal tones. Others spoke in a whisper. At such a melancholy table nourishment did not go past the throat. Reprimands were the main course at those dinners. On one occasion a captain of the General Staff, Tolkushkin, was reduced to hysteria during dinner by Skugarevskii's outbursts. The captain sprang from the hut and through the thin walls we could hear someone calming him as he cried, "Let me go. I will kill him!"

A deadly quiet settled over the table. Everyone involuntarily glanced at Skugarevskii but not one muscle moved in his face. He continued a conversation begun earlier.

Once the corps commander addressed himself to me: "Tell me, Colonel, why do you never share your war impressions with us? You were in such an interesting detachment. Tell me, what do you think of General Mishchenko?"

"Certainly." And I began, "There are leaders and there are leaders. For one commander the troops will go anywhere. But for another they will not go a step. For example . . ." I proceeded to draw a parallel between Skugarevskii, of course without naming him, and Mishchenko. Skugarevskii listened attentively, even with apparent appreciation, and finally thanked me for an "interesting report."

Vengeance was not one of Skugarevskii's traits. I must add that three years later, when he became head of the Committee for Training of the Troops, he requested that the War Ministry name me to the committee. But life in his staff was unpleasant and so, taking advantage of the beginning of evacuation and the last severe injury to my leg, I departed for Russia at last.

PART V

CHAPTER 24 THE FIRST
REVOLUTION: IN
SIBERIA AND IN THE
THEATER OF WAR

Arriving in Harbin where direct railroad communication with European Russia had been restored, I was plunged into the very depths of an escalated revolutionary mood. Harbin was the administrative center of the Chinese railroad as well as the administrative center of the rear of the army. Masses of reserve soldiers were assembled there awaiting evacuation.

The publication of the Manifesto of October 30, which was issued under the pressure of popular agitation and bestowed a constitution on Russia, went to people's heads.[1] They behaved as though they were intoxicated. Instead of appeasement the manifesto evoked more agitation. Some misunderstood the meaning of that reform; others rushed to achieve all freedoms at once and install the "power of the people." These absurd notions were fed in significant measure by the widespread propaganda of the socialist parties, of which the Social Democrats were most visible in the Far East.[2] They did not actually control revolutionary organizations nor did they present any definite constructive program. All the proclamations and appeals from local divisions of that socialist party began with the same negative premise, "Down with . . . !" Down with the "untrustworthy autocratic government." Down with local authority, down with military authority. "All power to the people!"

Such demagogic propaganda was successful with the masses and in many places, especially along the great Siberian road, self-styled "committees" were formed, "soviets of workers' and soldiers' (rear echelon) deputies" and "strike committees" which challenged authority. The Siberian railroad administration was taken over by the "Mixed Strike Committee," which actually prevented either civilian or military administration of the railway. These self-proclaimed authorities by no means represented the people. They acquired their positions by chance, by their reputation for being "more revolutionary" or for having a name for being "politically unreliable" in the past.

In my long journey along the Siberian road I read manifestos posted on every station and town wall and heard speeches by delegations which greeted the trains. I must sincerely say that they produced an impression of political illiteracy, sometimes of actual naïveté. Aside from the watchword "Down with — !" the first revolution had no actual program, no strong leaders, nor, it seems, even sufficiently propitious soil in popular attitudes.

But official authorities lost their composure. In Vladivostok the commandant of the fortress, General Kazbek, became the prisoner of unrestrained city mobs and soldiers. In Harbin the chief of the rear, General Nadarov, took no measures against the arbitrary committees. In Chita the military governor of Trans-Baikal, General Kholshchevnikov, completely submitted to the committees, placing weapons at the disposal of organizations calling themselves "committees of popular self-defense." He confirmed decisions made by soldiers' meetings, relinquished all postal telegraph service to the revolutionaries, and so forth. Linevich's staff, cut off from Russia by a series of frequent postal telegraph strikes, was completely prostrated, and the chief commander arranged conferences in his car with the strike committee of the Chinese Eastern Railway, yielding to its demands.

The ill-chosen staff of military and civil administrators possessed neither firm character nor initiative. The fact that they relinquished their authority so lightly may partially be explained by the fact that, having been accustomed all their lives to the ancient tradition of autocracy, they regarded the manifesto which had fallen on their heads as having authorized some new form of national arrangement for which the rules had not been revealed to them. Moreover, for the first time the customary "Highest Orders," which always followed a new law, did not arrive because of the ruptured connection with the capital. From Russia came only dark rumors about insurrection in Moscow and St. Petersburg and even about the downfall of the tsar.

Revolutionary propaganda affected an insignificant portion of the officer corps, predominantly those of the rear. I know of only one such case. All the officers of the Chitinsk Regiment stationed in the city of Chita, with their commander at their head, made the absurd decision by which, among other things, they declared "sympathy for transfer of authority to the people" and stated that they considered it "dishonorable to suppress by force of arms such expressions of popular will as political parties." They promised "in case of disorder threatening bloodshed to take part in the prevention of fratricidal wars according to the demands of civil authority." Apparently they meant "revolutionary authorities" because others in Chita were quite inactive.

A new element was introduced into the revolutionary movement, insurrections by demobilized reserve soldiers. Political and social programs interested them little. They skeptically scoffed at propaganda proclamations and speeches by delegates sent to the depots by the "people's government." Their only slogan was the shout "Homeward!"

"Freedom" for them meant "no chiefs" and "impunity." They created disturbances and acted indecorously all along the rear of the army, especially those soldiers and sailors returning from Japanese prisons where they had been propagandized. They listened neither to those in authority nor to the committees. They demanded to return home at once, out of turn, without considering the condition of rolling stock and all the difficulties rampant in that huge expanse, the ten thousand kilometers of Siberian road.

Under pressure from the boisterous masses and the demands of the "railroad committee," Linevich, who had obedient troops of the regular Manchurian army at his disposal for preserving order in the rear, revoked the normal evacuation schedule by corps, the equitable system, and ordered the transport of reserves to begin. Instead of organizing supply points along the Siberian railway and dispatching reserves with armed staff escort, he let them go by themselves after they were given an allowance in Harbin for the entire trip. That money was spent on drinking at Harbin and the next few stations, then soldiers sold all they could on the way. When there was nothing left to sell, their hungry mobs grumbled and plundered depots, buffets, and small villages between.

It was amazing that under such circumstances corps of former Manchurian army soldiers maintained organization and discipline. Thousands of kilometers from their native hearths, oppressed by futile sacrifice in the abortive and unconcluded campaign, fatigued, thwarted in their expectation of returning home, in cold and impoverished lands with no information (due to the strikes) about what was happening in their homeland and at their homes, overwhelmed by the Harbin revolutionary propaganda, they nevertheless bore up magnificently. They bore up because officers familiar to the soldiers from the time of the Manchurian sufferings preserved authority and influence by fair discipline and that same good sense which did not waver among the soldiers on active service.

During the stormiest period, from November 1905 to January 1906, I went by train through the Siberian provinces, literally fighting my way from Manchuria to St. Petersburg. I rode for an endless time through a series of new "republics" — Irkutsk, Krasnoyarsk, Chitinsk, and others. I lived for several weeks among echelons of reserves, rolling like locusts homeward across the Urals. I observed closely the waves pouring out on the shore from the sea of soldiers. At times dissension over the boundaries of the "republics" and several partial strikes completely blocked our progress. In Irkutsk we (about thirty troop units and several train passengers) had to wait several days. At that time it was extraordinarily difficult to obtain provisions along the road. Before long we existed only by supplies acquired in Irkutsk.

Our train, crammed full of officers, soldiers, and called-home railroad personnel, tried to proceed "legally" by a sort of timetable, but we moved no more than 100 to 150 kilometers a day. Stranded reserves greeted us at the stations, jeering and preventing us from leaving. Once we were detained in a small half-destroyed way station with neither buffet nor water and we went a full day without food or drink. A group of reservists whose locomotive was damaged had uncoupled ours and absconded with it.

It was soon apparent that legality would get us nowhere. Four of us colonels who happened to be on the train chose a senior commander from one of the Siberian regiments as commandant of the train. We set a guard on the locomotive, a duty unit of officers and soldiers armed with revolvers collected from the officers, and appointed an elder for each car. From the generous contributions of passengers, the soldiers standing guard were paid sixty kopecks a day so we soon had more volunteers for duty than we really needed. Only from two "revolutionary cars" in which evacuated railroad men were riding did these measures meet protest, but only once and not very energetically.

The first time a unit failed to proceed by timetable, we uncoupled their locomotive. After that with two locomotives our train went full speed. Groups coming after us wanted to impede our progress. But seeing our organized and armed command unit, they decided against conflict with us. The only opposition we met was from occasional rocks and logs heaved through windows. Several times we saw officials of the way stations, terrorized by menacing telegrams demanding our detention from echelons left behind, running with their serving personnel into the forest near the tracks. We went through without permits because God preserved us.

We traveled for more than a month. Finally we rolled through the Urals. With Christmas approaching, everyone wanted to get home, but near Samara we were stopped near a semaphore. There was a special strike of engineers. The road was closed and movement was impossible. When it would be restored, no one knew. To complete our misery, our own engineer ran past the guard and escaped. Imagine the general astonishment when a delegation came from the "revolutionary car" of our train to the commandant, proposing to use two engineers among them but only on condition that we would pretend to be using them by force so they would not lose face in front of the strikers. So we staged a convoy and dragged out the two "resisting" trainmen by their collars. To the duty official at the Samara station we gave a categorical order by telephone, "In half an hour our train will come through at full speed. Do not try to stop us. The way must be open!" Fortunately we proceeded. After that the train went normally and I reached St. Petersburg on the very eve of Christmas.

That modern-style raid of which Mayne Reid would have approved illustrates how, in revolutionary days, a handful of bold people may cut their way through thousands of kilometers amid chaos, a succession of illegal wayside "republics," and ferocious hostile mobs.[3]

Meanwhile St. Petersburg had regained its composure and had begun to employ decisive measures. By initiative of the head of government, Count Witte, troops were sent to restore order along the Siberian railway.[4] General Meller-Zakomelskii's detachment went from Moscow to the east and Rennenkampf moved westward from Harbin. Later General Mishchenko went to Vladivostok, where the most turbulent mobs of reserves had already receded. He calmed the city in his peaceable way.

General Rennenkampf left Harbin on January 22, 1906, with his division and proceeded without opposition, restoring railroad administration and pacifying boisterous units of reserves. The usual method of pacification was to evict rebellious troops from the train and force them to walk about twenty-five kilometers in the Siberian cold (30 to 40 degrees Reaumur) to the next station where a vacant car would wait for them at a scheduled time.

Near Chita, which was considered to be the most formidable bulwark of the revolutionary movement, Rennenkampf halted and demanded the surrender of the city. After several days of negotiations, Chita was surrendered without a battle. Rennenkampf altered the Trans-Baikal provincial administration, stripped the population of weapons, and arrested the principal leaders of the sedition, giving them a military trial.[5] He followed a similar procedure elsewhere. Later the leftist press tore Rennenkampf to shreds, accusing his courts of violating legal process, of injustice, and of excessive severity in sentencing. Probably there were judicial errors but one must take into account the chaos then existing. His courts at least gave advance notice of the accusations, providing an opportunity for defendant and defense counsel to reply to the charges.

General Meller-Zakomelskii behaved differently. I had known him during service in the Warsaw area. He commanded the 10th Infantry Division on the staff of which I had kept camp rolls in 1899. His disposition then was harsh but in a peacetime situation, of course, there was little evidence of it. Meller-Zakomelskii's report to the sovereign about the results of his expedition contained these lines: "Rennenkampf's generals made a grave error by negotiating with the revolutionaries and allowing them to surrender. A bloodless conquest does not affect a city or produce much of an impression." Proceeding from this point of view, with a detachment of only two companies, two machine guns, and two pieces of ordnance, Meller-Zakomelskii went by train from Moscow to Chita in only three weeks, more than six thousand kilometers, establishing harsh repression everywhere.

By mid-February the revolutionary movement had subsided in the

Siberian provinces. In Harbin the "strike committee" was arrested and normal evacuation of the Manchurian army began.

The sovereign, extremely dissatisfied with General Linevich's inactivity in the face of the revolutionary movement, ordered him to come immediately to Russia without waiting for his relief, General Grodikov, to arrive. General Kuropatkin received a similar order. Although he had held firm in regard to the revolution and had behaved prudently, he was ordered to go by sea via Vladivostok to one of the Black Sea ports, there to await further orders. This was, in a word, banishment. Feeling offended, Kuropatkin answered by telegraph and stated that for health reasons he could not undertake such a lengthy journey, nearly encircling the world. He requested permission instead to complete, along with his collaborators, his "Account" of his command. Apparently St. Petersburg knew about this "Account" and dreaded some unexpected disclosures, which was the reason for such unusual measures toward Kuropatkin. He finally received orders to go by rail "with the next departing group" but not to stop in St. Petersburg or its vicinity. He was ordered to live on his estate Sheshurino (in Pskov province), avoiding all interviews or any justification or opinions in the press.

Finally the restrictions were lifted. At Sheshurino Kuropatkin finished his "Account," which comprised four solid volumes.[6] Although it was characterized by self-justification and often described events in a biased way, this work nevertheless provided copious factual material. The fourth volume, in which he summarized and examined army deficiencies and reasons for our failures, was of special interest. Although the existence of the work became widely known, it did not see the light of day. The War Ministry, guarding the reputations of several high officers whom Kuropatkin had accused, this one deservedly, that one unjustly, categorically refused to allow publication of the "Account." In time, however, excerpts from Kuropatkin's work began to appear in the foreign press and the newspaper *Golos Moskvy* published the fourth volume, claiming to have translated it from the American edition. For more than two years the struggle continued between the ministry and Kuropatkin; then the ban was lifted from his books.

At Sheshurino a friend of mine helped Kuropatkin write the fourth volume. That was Krymov, a lieutenant colonel of the General Staff.

Krymov told me that the scope of Kuropatkin's diary astonished him. Kuropatkin had noted daily and in detail the circumstances of his personal life as well as military and state activities. Krymov's attention was caught by signatures in the field diary of a number of individuals who had played historic roles in the country's destiny. "Correct. So-and-so." It seems that Kuropatkin, after recording an important conversation, at the next session would request that individual to certify the accuracy of his notes.

Kuropatkin told Krymov that once, before the war, the sovereign had said to him, "I hear, Aleksei Nikolaevich, that you keep a diary. It would be interesting to read some of it."

"Certainly, Your Majesty."

Kuropatkin deliberately chose two or three notebooks of rather innocuous content and at report time delivered them to the sovereign. Returning the notebooks later, the sovereign had said coldly, "Yes, interesting."

Great was Kuropatkin's distress when he noticed that one of the notebooks contained an extremely harsh reflection on the motive behind a proposed imperial reward to an individual participating in the Yalu concessions. Kuropatkin believed that it was then (the beginning of 1903) that the sovereign began to cool toward him.

CHAPTER 25   THE FIRST REVOLUTION: IN THE COUNTRY

Among the Russian masses there did not appear to be sufficiently propitious grounds for a political revolution. But from 1902 until late 1907 in the countryside, especially along the Volga and in the Pre-Baltic, by incendiarism and by the plundering and seizure of landowners' estates, the peasants attempted to solve the exclusively agrarian problem of the peasant smallholder, which was considerably complicated by the low level of agricultural production.[1] In the Pre-Baltic, besides, the national element played a large role, on the grounds of that sharp and long-standing enmity between the Estonian and Latvian peasantry and the German landowners and the all-too-common alienation of these two elements.[2] Under the banner of national freedom and without the participation of native masses, terror was widely employed in Poland by only one battle organization, that of the P. P. S. under Pilsudski's leadership. An attempt was made on the life of the Warsaw governor-general, Skalon, and on other individuals high in the administration. There were murders of policemen and raids on the treasury. At Bezdana station near Vilna, the future dictator of Poland personally participated in the extortion of two hundred thousand rubles from a postal car. One may recall that the future dictator of the U.S.S.R., Stalin, began his career with extortion from the Tiflis treasury, a raid that cost many lives. In Finland during that entire time there were only two terrorist acts, but in one of them Governor-General Bobrikov was murdered.[3] The nation seethed but calmed down when it received constitutional guarantees.

An insignificant number of townspeople and working proletariat in the cities wanted to improve their standard of living, but only a few were consciously influenced by the program of demands of the Socialist Revolutionary party. Except for the insurrection in Moscow, disorders in the cities were rather swiftly and easily liquidated.

The political element was even less significant in the soldiers' mutinies, which arose on the basis of revolutionary propaganda against the excessive regimentation of barracks life and the sometimes unhealthy relationship between enlisted men and officers, especially in the navy. In the "demands" of rebelling units there was a unique mixture of alien party phraseology with pure soldiers' folklore. The "four-tailed formula" stood side by side with the demand to "cut the hair short but not shave the head."[4]

In view of such popular attitudes, the revolutionaries, as I have already stated, incited the people with their simplistic mutinous slogan "Down with!" And because in the traditionally loyal army they considered mutiny to be a hopeless business, revolutionaries devoted all their strength to transforming the very spirit of that army. Obviously this meant only enlisted men because, according to an acknowledgment published in Paris at the time in the revolutionary journal

Krasnoe znamia, "We have been able to entice only the very sorriest officers, of whom two or three would become swindlers of revolution and would wish to divert it to obscene paths of military adventurism so as to appear in the role of dwarf Cromwells." The judgment pronounced in *Krasnoe znamia* was incorrect. There were officers going into the revolution with conviction, but their number was small. We were convinced of this in 1917 when all that was secret became clear, and when their underground activities offered people the road to honor and elevation. In later polemics by those two coarse revolutionaries Savinkov and Deich, comical details emerged of a quest which they undertook in St. Petersburg ("to establish connections") for the revolutionary "Union of Officers," which either never existed or was entirely inactive.

At the end of 1905 and the beginning of 1906, a series of military mutinies broke out which were bloody in some places, especially in the navy. There were Sveaborg, Kronstadt, Sevastopol, the mutiny on the armor-clad *Prince Potemkin Tavricheskii* which escaped to a Romanian port, and so forth.[5] The mutinies were sporadic and unorganized, lasting only a few days before being suppressed by loyal units. So it was at Sevastopol during the mutiny prepared by the Socialist Revolutionaries, when Lieutenant Schmidt began by attaching a red flag to the ship *Ochakov*. The seditious ships were sunk by fire from shore batteries and from loyal vessels of the fleet. The Brestskii Regiment, influenced by three maritime officers, joined the mutinous sailors, but soon "repented" and took part in suppressing the revolt. Characteristically, the three officer-revolutionaries fled, leaving to the mercy of fate their soldier-assistants, who were captured and executed.

The most serious revolt occurred in Moscow. As far as the military was concerned, only the 2nd Grenadier Rostovskii Regiment mutinied, and it was pacified in two days. The remaining troops of the garrison, although affected by propaganda, maintained an indeterminate state of mind. Relying on participation of the Moscow garrison, a "Soviet of Workers' Deputies" was formed in Moscow which proclaimed a general strike on December 20 and called upon the populace to revolt.[6] Barricades appeared in the streets. Whole rows of factory buildings were transformed into fortified support points and weapons which had been secretly cached were distributed to the workers.

Meanwhile, the governor-general of Moscow, Admiral Dubasov, doubting the loyalty of the Moscow garrison, petitioned St. Petersburg for reinforcements. The Semenovskii Guards Regiment from Petersburg and the Ladozhskii Regiment from the Warsaw area were dispatched. These units, assisted by local artillery, joined battle with the rebels. In the course of several days they moved step by step, destroying barricades, occupying one house after another, laying waste with artillery, and burning support points. By the ninth day they had suppressed the rebellion.

A small episode. Voices from the Moscow rebellion. 1925: Brussels. I was an émigré. General Pliushchevskii-Pliushchik, the former quartermaster general of my staff in southern Russia, and Astrov, a former member of my government and a prominent Moscow liberal leader, happened to visit me at the same time. Due to our crowded situation they spent the night in the same room. They began to share reminiscences. In 1905 Pliushchevskii had commanded one of the companies of the Semenovskii Regiment and he told this story: "Moving along one of the streets, my company met stubborn resistance. Bullets rained down from the upper floor of a house occupied by revolutionaries. It was impossible to proceed. I happened to notice on the lower floor the signboard of a pharmaceutical store. It was a blessing. With two soldiers I hurled myself toward the store and forced open the door. As I had expected, there was a great supply of alcohol, benzine, and ether. We threw it all in a pile on the floor, cautiously holding our breaths. We succeeded in exploding it and the house flew into the air."

Astrov sat up in bed. "May I ask where this was?"

Pliushchevskii named the street.

"But I was there and saw all this with my own eyes!" It seems that Astrov had been nearby and had observed the explosion of the house with indignation and civilian distress.

These two psychologies, two world views, were characteristic of the epoch of the first revolution. But my guests did not break off friendly relations. Two revolutions, and the advent of bolshevism with the latter of them, had caused many representatives of liberal democracy to change their view of the past. Even several barricade builders came to the belated conclusion that "revolution was unnecessary."

In the main, among the seditious masses the movement had a nonsensical character, in spite of the efforts of party agitators. Also absurd were their demands. For example, the Samurskii Regiment (Caucasus) demanded that their officers hand over their weapons and the standard. When the officers refused, the commander of the regiment, the colonel-priest, and three other officers were killed. The Sevskii Regiment (Poltava) demanded the release of criminals from provincial jails and the proclamation of a "Poltava Republic." The neighboring Eletskii Regiment (Poltava), also incited, only demanded an end to regimental economic irregularities and beat up Jews and agitators in the regiment. The Kronstadt revolt began with demands for a "Constituent Assembly" and ended with the destruction of eighty-five stores and sixty-eight smaller shops.

Nevertheless, uniform features appeared in many of the demands, brought in from outside, like those in the later renowned "Order Number One" of the "Soviet of Soldiers' and Workers' Deputies" (1917) which definitely began corruption of the army.[7] The following resolution by the above-mentioned 2nd Grenadier Rostovskii Regiment composed with participation of the Moscow committee of Socialist Revolutionaries was typical.

General Demands

Abolition of capital punishment
Two-year terms of service
Abolition of uniforms outside of the service
Abolition of military courts and disciplinary punishment
Abolition of oaths
Election of platoon leaders and sergeant majors
   by the soldiers themselves
Increased salary

Soldiers' Demands

Better treatment by officers
Improved food and clothing
Construction of libraries
Free forwarding of soldiers' mail
Provision of table gear (knife and fork), bed linens,
   pillow, blankets
Freedom of assembly
Free leave from camp
Prompt delivery of soldiers' mail

It is significant that the morning before they presented the demands to their superior, the soldiers thought it over and decided that the general demands were unnecessary and they presented only the soldiers' demands. But columnists for the Moscow night newspaper wrote that the demands in their full text had been delivered to the head of the Rostovskii Regiment.

The first peals of revolutionary thunder, as I have stated, challenged a prostrate authority. There was a lack of decisive measures and direct instructions. There was inaction in regard to the prolonged anarchy on the Siberian road. And there was rebellion throughout the country which allowed such outrages as the brief revolutionary "government" of Khrustalev in the capital itself.[8] The government did not listen in time to the demands of the sensible segment of society and had to grant, unwillingly, new Fundamental Laws.

Command personnel were perplexed, chiefly from ignorance as to how to combine troop management with the new state regime. This situation sometimes took on a tragicomical character, as for example in the Caucasus, where a commander lost his composure and, on the advice of an obvious revolutionary, Social Democrat Rashvili, issued to his organization several hundred imperial arms for the "suppression of popular disorder."

In the absence of authority, things appeared in some places which were hitherto unknown in the military environment, such as the organization of officers' secret societies, not for any sort of political aims but for self-protection. I knew about three such societies. In Vilna and in Kovno, officers, recognizing the threat of terrorist acts directed at the highest military authorities, gathered information in the city about revolutionary leaders and warned them privately about the retaliation which they might expect. In Baku the affair was more open and simpler. An open meeting of the garrison officers decreed and published as general information, "In the event that a single officer or soldier of the garrison is murdered, we will hold responsible not only the criminal but also the leaders and agitators of revolutionary organizations. Criminals may know that henceforth they will be seized and executed. Nothing will stop us from restoring order." In such cases it was terror challenging terror, lynch law answering lynch law.

As authority recovered, the first order of business was to satisfy the army by improving its material conditions. Soldiers' wages as well as rations allotments were increased. Blankets, bed linens, and such were provided. Knowing human nature, the military section established daily allotments for the troops restoring order that were generous for that time, thirty kopecks a day for soldiers. I witnessed the willingness with which squadrons of the Saratov garrison went to restore order and how jealously they watched not to miss their turns.

Forcible suppression of soldiers' mutinies continued, however. In January 1906 the Council of Ministers presented a report to the sovereign concerning the necessity for severe repression "against propaganda attempts in violation of the military code." The sovereign disagreed, preferring instead his own resolution: "Strict internal order and the trustee relationship of officers toward the soldiers' way of life will best of all protect the troops from hostile propaganda in the barracks situation." This resolution was given wide publicity but it created a not entirely accurate impression among us about the sovereign's position in the struggle then current. Later we learned that he had issued a different series of resolutions demanding "application to the rebels of the most decisive repression," which proceeded from the premise that "every hour of delay may cost rivers of blood in the future." But Witte, the head of the government, kept all such resolutions under lock and key to avert from the sovereign the odium of such inevitable but sometimes aimlessly cruel measures that would increase the agitation of public opinion in the country. Cruelty appeared, however, on both sides, especially in the Pre-Baltic. Such episodes as the burning alive in Gazenpot (Courland) by revolutionaries of a soldier of the dragoons' horse patrols could not have improved mutual relations.

According to the Bolshevik historian Pokrovskii, the number of victims during the years of the first revolution in all of Russia was calculated at 13,381 persons.[9] It is impossible to suspect the Bolsheviks of minimizing the figures as they conducted an inquiry about the "guilt" of the tsarist regime. According to the Bolshevik scale and Bolshevik expertise, however, this figure seems rather insignificant.

Under the pressure of the Manchurian failures, officers painfully felt their share of guilt in the occurrences and stolidly endured the campaign against themselves and the army that was inaugurated after the October Manifesto.[10] The press, which enjoyed absolute freedom in the first year after the manifesto, aroused passions and discord. Organs of the extreme right tendency (*Zemshchina* and others), identifying themselves closely with army circles, saw redemption of the country and the army not in reforms but in the "dissolution of the convict Duma" and in the "return of the rod." The rightist press expressed itself vaguely and simplistically as favoring a "return to native beginnings." Having accurately deduced that the army had broken the revolution, revolutionaries continued to work for the army's corruption. In collaboration with radical democracy, they ridiculed the army in meetings, in the press, from theater stages, in sessions of the *zemstvos*, and in the cities. Humor magazines emerged in the beginning like mushrooms after rain, with text and caricatures that abused military people and the notions about duty which were inculcated in the service. The dais of the first two State Dumas was used more than once to insult the army and undermine its discipline, and even some speeches of counselors in military courts aimed at the same effect.

In liberal circles, in the camps of the Russian intelligentsia, there was disorder and dull incomprehension. As an outstanding example I submit the polemics of two typical intelligentsia who exchanged views in the columns of the newspaper *Russkaia vedomost* in 1906. One was a young lieutenant colonel of the General Staff, Prince A. M. Volkonskii, representing liberal military youth, and the other was a prominent Kadet party leader, Prince P. Dolgorukii.

Dolgorukii: While the government and the people through their representatives present themselves as two hostile camps, while government persists and prefers, contrary to the clear expression of the people, to follow the counsel of some few, while conformity is lacking between the authority of the legislative and the executive branches, it is impossible to expect any pacification. It is impossible to expect that the troops, sons of these Russian people, will be unconcerned by this murderous dissension and remain blind weapons in the hands of the government. It is, therefore, impracticable and fruitless to ask the army to stay out of politics and to remain nonpartisan. It is impossible to oppose the soldier with impunity, son of the people that he is, to those same people.

Volkonskii: Both camps summon the army to their side. Unfortunately internal processes cannot continue painlessly in the heat of the passion. One camp still cries for the dissolution of the Duma. The other still binds the army to an oath. And among the insulted, slandered ranks may be heard calm voices, "Leave us alone! We are not the concern of your party. A change of laws, that is your business. We are people bound by an oath, obedient to today's law." So I say, leave us alone! If once we break our oath, then of course you will not trust us either. Then there will be chaos, internecine war, and bloodshed.

The subsequent fate of the two brothers, Princes Peter and Paul Dolgorukii, was tragic. Since they were both outstanding liberal leaders, it was impossible to accuse them of "reactionary acts."[11] Both became emigrants. Paul, homesick, returned secretly to the U.S.S.R., where he was seized and executed. Peter, eighty years old and ill, was arrested by the Bolsheviks in Prague in 1945 and taken to the U.S.S.R., where he disappeared without a trace.

But the army stood firm, thanks to the officer corps which, although after 1905 began closely to scrutinize, to analyze, and more than once to criticize various areas of military and public life, maintained throughout the character of a national protective force. This was its historic merit and in this was predestined its subsequent tragic fate.

By early 1906 the revolutionary movement had definitely subsided. Toward April the battle organization of the Socialist Revolutionaries was dissolved in Moscow and St. Petersburg, although terrorist acts still occurred in Poland.[12] And in the countryside sporadic agrarian disorders recurred until the end of 1907.

No doubt the autocratic bureaucratic regime of Russia was an anachronism. No doubt also evolutionary change would have occurred earlier had not crime gone mad, as for example when the 1881 revolutionaries, members of the "Party of the People's Freedom," assassinated Emperor Alexander II after his Great Reforms and on the eve of the election of representatives of the people (*zemstvos*) to public administration.[13] This crime delayed evolution of the regime for a quarter of a century.

Though belated, the Manifesto of October 30 was an event of great historic importance, opening a new era in Russian national life. The arrangement provided by the Russian constitution was not parliamentarianism of the West European variety, a fact significant today when parliamentary government everywhere is experiencing a crisis and its validity is rather questionable. The rights allowed to the State Duma were restricted, particularly with regard to the budget.[14] But for all that, this act pledged the beginning of legal order, of political and civil freedom, and opened the way for legal struggle for further achievement, genuine popular government.

Nevertheless the radical-liberal intelligentsia would not enter a coalition or collaborate with the ruling bureaucracy.[15] They demanded the replacement of all government personnel with persons of their own camp. The sovereign did not wish to deliver all authority into the hands of the opposition. Moreover, the laws issued by the first two Dumas made him apprehensive. A situation arose which prevented the possibility of replacing the Council of Ministers with individuals enjoying public confidence. As a result of aggravated opposition by radical-liberal democrats, although they did not desire revolution, a revolutionary state of mind was promoted in the country and the Social Democrats worked with all their might for a second revolution.

CHAPTER 26 MILITARY RENAISSANCE

In his "Account" about command personnel in the unfortunate Japanese campaign, General Kuropatkin wrote as follows: "Persons of strong character, independent individuals, were unfortunately persecuted rather than promoted. In peacetime they seemed to many commanders to be too restless. As a result such men often left the service. Conversely, men without character or convictions but accommodating, always ready to conform to the opinions of their superiors, were promoted."

The Japanese taught us something else, that it is essential to train command personnel. Until that war officers could take command of a regiment and get along with only such scientific baggage as they had brought from military or officers' school. They did not have to keep up with the progress of military science. No one ever questioned their knowledge. Any kind of examination would have been considered offensive. Generally the only criterion for the appraisal of an officer was the way his soldiers behaved on maneuvers, and even then obvious mistakes were easily forgiven.

In 1906 the first higher order was issued to "establish suitable training for high command personnel, from commanders of units (regiments) to commanders of corps inclusive, that training being intended to develop military knowledge." This innovation caused widespread irritation in the upper ranks. The old men growled, seeing it as an "affront to gray hair" and an "undermining of authority."

The project progressed little by little, although at first not without friction and incidents. Training for old commanders normally consisted of two phases of military games, planning and field maneuvers. As I repeatedly participated in these schools, I became convinced of their genuine utility. In addition to their educational value, they gave participants the opportunity to become acquainted with each other and contributed to both voluntary and compulsory elimination of ignoramuses.

An episode which occurred in 1911 indicates how galling to high military leaders was the idea of the necessity to learn new techniques. At the initiative of War Minister Sukhomlinov, military games were organized in the Winter Palace. Summoned for participation were commanders of district troops, the future army commanders. The games were to be conducted in the sovereign's presence, and as future commander in chief he took a personal role in the establishment of the initial directives.[1] Everything had been prepared for the games to be held in the palace halls. But an hour before the designated starting time, the chief commander of the St. Petersburg military district, Grand Duke Nikolai Nikolaevich, extorted an order for cancellation from the sovereign. Sukhomlinov, placed in an awkward position, tendered his resignation, but it was not accepted.

Not until 1914 in Kiev, just before the war, did the chief administrator of the General Staff succeed in conducting military games. Two of the higher ranking participants were to become chief commander and commander on the Austrian front. Basic to the instructional games, in which I took a modest role as head of one of the outposts, were the actual war plans, both ours and the Austrian, which an agent from the General Staff had obtained in Vienna not long before. Subsequently, because the matter had received publicity, the commander of the Austrian General Staff, Conrad von Hötzendorff, altered their plan in the final weeks before the war.

As a result of the introduction of the new pension statute, new certification regulations, and examinations for older commanders, there began a voluntary departure of many officers and compulsory elimination of others, a movement which army humor christened the "slaughter of the innocents." In the course of 1906–1907, fifty to eighty percent of our commanders were dismissed and replaced, from commanders of regiments to commanders of districts. The maximum-age law had been suspended in 1906 but it was reestablished in 1910, promoting rejuvenation of the officer corps. Educational requirements were also raised so that by 1912, 55.2 percent of our generals had completed one of the military academies. Although these measures could not produce new command personnel instantaneously, officer corps standards were considerably elevated by comparison with those of the Japanese War era.

This period also presaged the potential danger to the state of army deficiencies. The failures and defects of the war and the relationship of the people and the press to the officer corps shook the faith of many officers in their profession. An exodus began which lasted until approximately 1910. By 1907 army officer personnel had decreased by about 20 percent.

But not all were so affected. Along with the "desertions," the Manchurian failure served for the majority as a moral awakening, particularly among the youth. Probably never yet had military thought functioned so intensively as in the years following the Japanese War. The necessity for reorganization of the army was talked about, written about, shouted about. The urgent need for self-education received a significant revival of interest in the military press.

At that time the military department formulated and partially proceeded with a series of reforms such as rejuvenation and improvement of command personnel, elevation of the educational level of military schools, organization of cadres of reserve divisions, strengthened artillery, new manuevers, and so on. This went terribly slowly, thus arousing anxiety and discomfort within the army. For example, new regulations about military duties, far sketchier than expected, came only in 1912. The new policy regarding the field administration of troops was confirmed only at the beginning of World War I. A series of commissions for reorganizing the way of life and administration of troops did not complete their task of working out new norms until the war started.

In 1909 the war minister communicated by secret circular with the higher commanders about the formation of secret officers' societies, which had allegedly been established for the purpose of accelerating by forcible measures the (in its opinion) "slow and unsystematic course of reorganization of the army." The minister demanded that measures be taken against these organizations. I never heard of any such organizations and assume that they did not exist. But there were cases of another type.

During the fall of 1905, after conclusion of peace with Japan, Captain Khagandokov, a chief staff adjutant in Mishchenko's detachment, initiated an assembly of several officers to consider forming an "officers' union." Elections were held, the purpose being to assist army recovery. I attended two such gatherings before my departure to European Russia. The intent was good but the form in which the society was molded was something like an officers' council of deputies, which seemed alien to the military system. I declined, therefore, to take part in implementing the project. Later I read in a newspaper that in May 1906 a new session of the society under the new name of "Restoration" was being held in St. Petersburg with permission from War Minister Ridiger. The open meeting attracted a large number of officers to the auditorium, largely because of a rumor that the popular General Mishchenko was a member of the society. Captain Khagandokov, the temporary chairman of the organization, explained the very well-intentioned program of the society: self-restoration and self-improvement, the preparation of cadres corresponding to the contemporary requirements of war, a struggle against the boredom and stagnation which had "brought so much pain to the sovereign and to the Fatherland." The charter of the society was submitted to the war minister but he did not approve it. With that the matter was finished.

This episode had an unexpected sequel for me. Anyone who draws "historic material" from Soviet sources risks, as is well known, refraction from the false Soviet mirror. In 1928 a certain Mstislavskii, all of whose activities compel one to surmise that he was a provocateur, printed in a Soviet "historical journal" his reminiscences about this mythical officers' union in which he allegedly played a guiding role.[2] He wrote: "Among the members of the secret officers' revolutionary union in 1905, although he was very conspiratorial and showed nothing of himself, was the future 'hero of counterrevolution' Denikin. He was in the Far East at that time and his entry into the union when he was already in high ranks made an extraordinary impression on our Far East comrades."

The Paris émigré newspaper *Poslednaia novosti* made a thorough critique of that magazine and quoted the above excerpts from Mstislavskii's article. I sent the paper a refutation, saying, "All my life I have worked openly, not in any secret organization ever established, nor was I acquainted with a single revolutionary until 1917. If any one of them saw me, it was while I was sitting in sessions of military courts."

Fourteen years passed. I was living in a lonely little village in the south of France under the close surveillance of the Gestapo.[3] In the Russian-language German propaganda newspaper *Paris vestnik* there appeared an article by another provocateur, this time one from the right, Colonel Felichkin, who, disclosing the role of the "Jewish freemasons" in the Russian revolution, brought up completely out of context some phrases of Mstislavskii's, along with a denunciation: ". . . a fierce opponent of Russian rapprochement with Germany, paralyzing the farsighted policy of General P. N. Krasnov, Denikin in our eyes had already shifted to the Jewish freemason camp."[4] Felichkin did not succeed, by his fawning and flattery, in ingratiating himself with the Germans because he was soon dead.

From 1908 on, army interests were given attentive regard by both the third and fourth State Dumas, or more precisely by their nationalist sector. Under the Russian Fundamental Laws, all the active army and fleet were directly responsible to the Supreme Authority. The authority of the Duma extended only to the consideration of legislation requiring new appropriations. The war and navy ministries jealously guarded from the Duma's curiosity the substance of registered legislative proposals. On this basis a conflict began, as a result of which the Duma, having formed a Commission for National

Defense, attained the right to deliberate by points, to "make inquiries through specialists" (the right of interpellation) of such important matters as, for example, the multimillion-ruble appropriation for construction of a fleet and the reorganization of the army.[5]

"Making inquiries" took two paths. One was by means of the official secretaries of the military and naval departments, who gave the commission only formal information, fearing that excessive candor would be used by the left sector of the State Duma to harm the business of defense. The other was in a confidential way. At the initiative of A. I. Guchkov and General Vasilii Gurko and under the chairmanship of the latter, a small military circle formed of individuals who held responsible positions in the War Department made contact with the moderate Duma representatives of the Commission for National Defense.[6] Many participants in the small circle, such as General Gurko, Colonel Lukomskii, Danilov, and others, subsequently played significant roles in World War I. None of them had political aims although they were given the droll name of "Young Turks." In private sessions with members of the Duma, military questions were discussed widely and candidly before they were entered for deliberation in the Duma. War Ministers Ridiger and later Sukhomlinov knew about those meetings and did not hinder them. Joint work thus went on for two years until there was a schism in that small military coterie, the day some of them criticized sharply and validly a few legislative proposals that had been handed over to the Duma before being previously discussed by themselves. Sukhomlinov heard of the incident and was disquieted. Lukomskii and three other participants left the small circle. "It was impossible," Lukomskii subsequently wrote to me, "to try and make the Duma reject legislative proposals which seemed to have been endorsed by us." In regard to other more obstinate "Young Turks" such as Gurko, Sukhomlinov moved to eliminate this "co-government," as he called it in a report to the sovereign, by giving them responsible posts outside of St. Petersburg.

Involuntarily one makes comparisons. How would the autocratic Stalin have handled a situation with only a suspicion of deviation from the "party line"?

Those were the mild forms in which military opposition was expressed. Only the military press which, as we have seen, enjoyed more freedom than in other great Western nations, continued to disturb those in power.

CHAPTER 27 IN THE WARSAW AND KAZAN MILITARY DISTRICTS

When I arrived in St. Petersburg from the Far East, I received devastating personal news. The chief administrator of the General Staff did not wait for the officer-evacuees of the Manchurian army to return home. He had hastened to fill all vacant posts with junior officers, without considering their lack of war experience, as well as with those who had been invalided home with severe or light injuries (the "risen dead," as army wits called them). When I stated that headquarters had telegraphed two months earlier that a division-staff commander post had been reserved for me, the colonel supervising appointments answered that no such order had been received. On investigation, of course, he found the telegram. The confused colonel suggested that I temporarily select a lesser post as corps-staff officer. I chose the staff of the 2nd Cavalry Corps, quartered in Warsaw where I had served before the war. That "temporary" assignment lasted a whole year.

The Warsaw district still lived by the "Gurko" tradition. Field Marshal Gurko had left the district in 1894 and after him many generals had served as troop commander there, men such as Count Shuvalov, Prince Imeretinskii, Chertkov, Skalon, designated because of considerations of internal order. The command of troops in Poland was combined with administration of the frontier (a governor-generalship). This combination was theoretically correct because it averted many conflicts, but in practice both civil and military administration suffered. The Warsaw governors-general were persons of a high cultural level and, except for the aristocrats, they had nothing in common with the broad circles of Polish society. They drew information about life on the border exclusively from reports of their close assistants and the *okhranka*. As for troop administration, they acknowledged their inexperience and made no attempt to take an active lead.

Having served on the district staff for nearly a year in 1900, I was well acquainted with the situation. For ten years the Warsaw district had been ruled by a "Gurko" chief of staff, General Puzyrevskii. A brilliant professor at the War Academy, author of a prize-winning Academy of Science work, teacher of the history of military arts to the future Emperor Nicholas II, participant in the Russo-Turkish War, Puzyrevskii was a man of cutting words and thin irony, and was pitiless in evaluating people. He belonged to the category of "restless ones" and had made many enemies. He was not, therefore, drawn into the Japanese War and to the end of his life received no military district of his own. He found consolation later in a calm armchair position as a member of the State Council (the upper chamber), after which he soon died.[1]

"His Serene Highness suggests" or "the Commander of the troops has ordered" were just official stamps on our staff papers. Although sometimes such papers were important, they had not gone farther than Puzyrevskii's study. True, His Serene Highness Prince Imeretinskii had, at the beginning of his command, tried to free himself from Puzyrevskii's wardship. Imeretinskii was motivated by an incident which occurred at the farewell dinner given in St. Petersburg on his departure. When someone proposed a toast for the new commander's success, the war minister's wife, Madame Kuropatkin, an exceedingly outspoken lady, addressed herself loudly to the prince: "Well, what is there to say! You will go to Warsaw and fall into Puzyrevskii's hands like all the rest."

The prince blushed and said nothing. But this is how the new commander's initial steps were described to me by the staff. In reaction to a report from our chief of staff, the prince was cold and seemed to be dissatisfied with the prepared solution presented to him. "I wish to know the background of this question," he said.

"Yes, sir!"

The next day Puzyrevskii brought to the palace a large stack of papers from which he proceeded to read prolix excerpts to the commander for several hours, acquainting him with the "background of the question" to the point of immoderate boredom. Prince Imeretinskii endured such torture for a week before he finally submitted. Orders and decisions began to flow from General Puzyrevskii's study as before, stamped with "His Serene Highness suggests" and "the Commander of the troops has ordered . . ."

In 1902 General Puzyrevskii was named assistant troop commander of the Warsaw district. His successors in the post of chief of staff were men of lesser caliber, but they continued that odd administration in the Warsaw district, that district which was so strategically important since it was a potential front and contained the greatest number of troops! Nevertheless troops of the Warsaw district continued in a satisfactory state of preparedness, strong in military ways of life and traditions.

Having little to do in the 2nd Cavalry Corps, I published articles on military history and the military way of life in military journals and read reports about the Japanese War at gatherings of the Warsaw general staff and in the provincial garrisons. My articles in *Razvedchik*, written in a liberal spirit, about life and customs in the Warsaw district commissariat did not go unnoticed. But in general the lack of meaningful activity was a burden to me, especially when we received orders to reorganize the corps and I became involved in protracted and boring clerical work. For diversion I spent my leave abroad, touring Austria, Germany, France, Italy, and Switzerland.

A year of my temporary assignment had already passed but still the promised appointment was delayed. I reminded the chief administrator of the General Staff in not quite proper terms, I guess. After some time an answer came: "Suggest to Colonel Denikin the 8th Siberian Division staff. If he refuses, he will be stricken from the candidates' list." Never had there been a compulsory appointment on the General Staff, especially one to Siberia! Provoked and irritated, I answered in even less correct form with only the words, "I do not want it." I expected fresh troubles but instead received a civil query proposing that I join the staff of the 57th Reserve Brigade, excellently quartered in the city of Saratov on the Volga.[2]

At the end of January 1907 I went to Saratov, which was located in the Kazan military district, a district as large as central Europe. The district was remote from the attention of the highest sphere and always somewhat behind both metropolitan and frontier districts. At that time the district was in a crisis. The old life, serene and patriarchal, had ended and something new and entirely different was rushing in. Three brigades had returned from the war in which they fought brilliantly. Quite a few officers with battle experience had returned. There were new commanders and new influences and the work was in full swing. The district had awakened. At that very time there arrived in Kazan a fellow who stamped his foot angrily and shouted loudly to the entire district, "I will make you knuckle under!"

What I say about the Kazan district, where I spent the next four years of my life, by no means applies to the entire Russian army. Nothing similar occurred in other districts either before or after. It is characteristic of army life, however, that an individual personality can be significant, either positively or negatively. General Sandetskii, the new troop commander in the Kazan district, managed to set his seal of moral repression on the district for several years.

He was never in a war. In 1905 he commanded the 34th Infantry Division, which remained in Ekaterinoslav charged with suppressing rebellion there. The following year he occupied the post of commander of a grenadier corps in Moscow. At that time the entire Volga region blazed up.[3] The frontier was put under martial law and not only all the district troops but also reserve Cossack units were mobilized. The regular cavalry, called from the western frontier, was pressed into military police duty to suppress the agrarian disorders which had erupted everywhere. General Karas commanded the district in 1906. He was a mild and good person who shunned harsh measures and clearly was unable to cope with the business of suppression. Several times he telegraphed St. Petersburg asking permission to mitigate sentences of the military courts which issued capital punishment sentences he was supposed to sign. Because these telegrams were not in cipher, Chairman of the Council of Ministers Stolypin saw Karas's activities as a cowardly effort to transfer the odium of punishment to him or to the sovereign.[4] Karas was dismissed and, to the surprise of everyone, Sandetskii replaced him.

Sandetskii laid his heavy hands equally on the revolutionary Volga region and the loyal troops. His first annual report showed a parallel. General Karas had confirmed less than ten death sentences in a year. In only a few months Sandetskii confirmed more than a hundred. This is a characteristic feature: anyone can regard strict measures as a right and even as a duty; few people would boast about them.

Long before the new commander arrived in Saratov, rumors were flying about his excessive harshness and bitterness. From Kazan, Penza, and Ufa came letters about his rude orders, transfers, and reprimands applied during inspection.

We soon found that Sandetskii read all orders issued not only in brigades but also in the regiments. And he demanded detailed reports, analyses, and instructions on the pettiest questions. The whole district was put in the writing business. Paperwork replaced real, live work. A stream of paper from above gushed onto the heads of stunned officials in the district, instructing, teaching, scolding, not sparing one department of the service or of our lives, a stream of "clarification" by a commander who would not tolerate independent action and initiative. Returning from below and directed to the district staff was another stream of accounts, codes, statistics, tables, even graphs showing the increase of the number of buns in the bakery and the average number of *versts* covered by regimental scouts in the field.

In the district was a brigade commander (of the 54th), General Shileiko, a veteran of the Japanese War who had earned an excellent battle reputation.[5] When he was asked for a report about something important to no one, he wrote to the district staff, "The compilation of such a report for the regiment is impracticable. Until now, in order not to bother subordinates, the brigade staff has invented the data." He knew that such methods were practiced in other brigades as well and he asked how the matter was to be handled in the future. The district staff did not reply.

It also appeared that the commander was dissatisfied with the "weakness" of his chiefs. On orders relating to disciplinary punishment, the single notation always came back in his handwriting, "Punishment too weak. Make it more severe. I shall take this into account in your certificate notation."[6] And the pressure began. The majority of commanders maintained their dignity and sense of justice. But a few proved to be men who built their careers on the spines of their subordinates. Reprimands showered down as from a cornucopia, both with cause and without, regardless of the degree of fault, with only one view in mind, what they were saying in Kazan.

At last the day for inspection of the Saratov garrison was scheduled. The commander arrived, looked, reprimanded us violently, and departed, leaving panic in his wake. The commander had especially abused two staff officers who had been members of the military court whose concluding session had just ended.[7] Sandetskii had assembled all officers of the garrison and in their presence, torn the staff officers to shreds. He shouted, stamped his foot, and finally declared that they would never be promoted to regimental commanders because they had "displayed weakness."

This is what it was all about. In one of the regiments a revolutionary proclamation was found in the footlocker of a corporal. The judges, taking into account the fact that the paper was only being kept, not circulated, and other extenuating circumstances, credited the corporal with his ten months of preliminary confinement in prison and, stripping him of his rank, set him free. This incurred Sandetskii's wrath.

To the credit of our officers, I must say that such pressure had no result on the conscience of the court. Further verdicts in many Saratov political affairs revealed the firmness and justice of members of the military courts. Along with severe verdicts I recall, for example, the noisy and clearly exaggerated affair concerning the "Kamishinskii Republic" in which all the accused, after a brilliant defense by a well-known advocate, Zarudnii, were acquitted despite potential danger to the careers of court members. Or still another notorious affair concerning the prominent Socialist Revolutionary, Minor. Guided only by their consciences and by duty, the judges (our two lieutenant colonels among them), gave him a relatively light punishment. The decision was based on the fact that there was only circumstantial evidence. Of course in neither of these cases was there indulgence, only the expression of the court's responsibility. In the first case the judges correctly discovered the essence of the matter but in the second they erred. Minor, as it subsequently developed, was head of the foremost revolutionary battle organization of southeastern Russia.

The worst tyranny was exercised in the matter of certification, on which depended all promotion of officers. I will mention three examples of despotism which might be considered "anecdotal" if such anecdotes had not destroyed people's lives. Colonel Leontev of the Lesno Regiment was certified as excellent, deserving of promotion. He was transferred to another regiment of the brigade and took command of a battalion. The next day he had to present the battalion in review to the brigade commander. The battalion had been poorly instructed by its late commander, as was well known from a recent report. Sandetskii, having read the report but not considering the circumstances, altered Leontev's certificate and gave him a "warning about insufficient conformity." That sentence deprived him of the right to promotion for two years.

It was typical that the brigade commander, who trembled before Sandetskii, did not venture to correct the commander's error. Only on Sandetskii's arrival in Saratov did he venture, at my insistence, to protest. Sandetskii answered, "The certificate has already reached the General Staff. To change it would be awkward. I will give it my attention next year." Leontev departed that year to another district with a "free ticket."

Colonel Pliashkevich of the Bobruiskii Regiment, a distinguished battle officer, was certified as "out of line" in the regiment. In an assessment of his moral nature, the regiment commander noted, "He drinks little." Imagine our astonishment when, after some time, there arrived a harsh instruction from the commander with a "warning" to Pliashkevich because "he drinks." And the brigade commander and regiment commander were reprimanded because they had improperly evaluated the man. In vain did the regimental commander insist that he had only wanted to emphasize Pliashkevich's unusual temperance. Sandetskii replied that this did not make sense. Since he mentioned drinking at all, it must mean that Pliashkevich "drinks a lot."

So another man wasted two years of his career. Because paper served as the judge of people, it was necessary to agonize and to weigh every word in official correspondence. Adjutants from the regimental secretariat came to me constantly for advice. But nothing was safe from sad surprise.

On the excellent certificate of Captain Khvoshchinskii of the Balashovskii Regiment was written, "He devotes his leisure to self-education." Sandetskii returned the certificate with the order, "Issue a warning to this man because he does not devote his leisure to the company." I could not believe my eyes. I even went to the library to check the dictionary: "Leisure: free time from necessary duties." Khvoshchinskii fled to the Warsaw district.

Our brigade commander, General P., was a kind man, modest and completely in awe of his superiors. To be impelled to dispute the ineffable demands of the district staff or to intercede for an injured man cost him great effort. There was such a case. General Sandetskii read an order in the Khvalinskii Regiment and, erring in a family name, put one staff captain under arrest instead of another. The brigade commander summoned the injured man and tried to persuade him to "Endure it, my dear. You are still young. You will not soon receive a company anyway. Even if this problem is corrected, the evil will not go away. You know yourself that if the commander becomes angry. . . ." The staff captain endured. So it went, endlessly. Army life there was overcast by rudeness, tyranny, and capriciousness. To struggle against it was dangerous. Above Kazan there was only St. Petersburg. But in reality for the officers St. Petersburg was remote and inaccessible, and in the minds of the soldiers even more distant than the stars.

Did St. Petersburg know what went on in the Kazan district? Of course. From the court business, the complaints, the press. The sovereign knew. Sukhomlinov subsequently wrote the following: "In spite of the sovereign's kindness, in the end his patience was exhausted and His Highness instructed me to state in writing that he was dissatisfied with the regime which Sandetskii had established in his district." Later, when the war minister was preparing to visit the Volga region, the sovereign ordered, "Tell the commander for me that I appreciate his zeal but I do not approve of unnecessary rudeness to subordinates." The Volga region was still in ferment, however, and the presence of a stern commander over the troops was apparently considered a necessity.

On some occasion or other, the district commanders were gathered in Penza. Instead of Sandetskii, who was undergoing treatment in a health resort, his chief of staff, General Svetlov, presided. At the end of the conference, the commander of the 54th Reserve Brigade, General Shileiko, spoke up, saying that the head of the district was abnormal and that he considered it morally reprehensible for Svetlov and other subordinates to be silent and not to bring this to the attention of St. Petersburg. The generals, including Svetlov, were embarrassed but they did not protest.

Later Shileiko sent the war minister a detailed report about Sandetskii's activities, repeating the statement which he had made to the Penza conference and citing all the participants as having agreed with him. This report was forwarded by the war minister to be investigated — by Sandetskii!

Because the chief of staff opened all the correspondence, a palpitating Svetlov brought the packet to the commander's palace together with his own resignation. What occurred at the palace was unknown. Shileiko was retired "with uniforms and pension" but Svetlov, contrary to expectation, remained in his post.

Even in such an unhealthy environment and despite Sandetskii's excesses, we proceeded with battle training and felt the enthusiasm which enveloped the entire military sphere. General P., lacking battle experience, handled the immense task of reviews and management and left the problems of preparing the troops for battle to me. I appreciated the latitude given me. I organized systematic tactical practice with garrison officers, assisted by participants from the past war. We set up reports and conferences on various branches of military affairs. By invitation of the regimental commanders, I helped them to compose tactical assignments and carry out field training. I applied new trends in military science to brigade maneuvers as well as the results of my own battle experience, trying to bring the training closer to actual conditions of modern warfare. This satisfying work benefited both me and the regiments.

Sandetskii was kind to P. and rewarded him with the rank of lieutenant general and a decoration. But once during a maneuver the commander unexpectedly visited our staff. From conversations with P., he became convinced that the latter was not responsible and was even unaware of the orders given the brigade. He was exceedingly disappointed and deeply angered. After that his benevolence toward P. ended.

During those years I wrote a great deal in my spare time, publishing articles in military journals, mostly *Razvedchik*, under the general heading of "Army Notes." The fate of that journal, the first private military journal in Russia, reflected the evolution of military thought and that of the guardians over it. In 1885 retired Captain Berezovskii, the proprietor of a military book business, originated the idea of publishing a military journal. General Dragomirov, commander of the General Staff Academy, warmly supported him. In spite of Dragomirov's patronage and that of other prominent military professors, the undertaking met categorical opposition in the war ministry. The very thought of disseminating a private military organ in the army was declared dangerous heresy. In 1886, without specific permission and without the right to "assign title and number," Berezovskii published a journal.[8] Two years later the ministry decided to approve the title *Razvedchik*. But it was only after six years of publication, when Emperor Alexander III happened to see a copy and ordered it delivered to him regularly, that the journal received the legal right to exist.

In spite of monarchical attention and cooperation from the very conception of *Razvedchik* by such prominent individuals as Generals Dragomirov, Leer, Gazenkampf, and others, the journal scarcely eked out an existence. Only with difficulty could it convey to military circles that freedom of expression and criticism were not necessarily antagonistic to military discipline. By 1896, however, the journal was solidly on its feet, having acquired a wide circulation and reputation. Other private military journals emerging subsequently encountered less success and were not long lived.

Razvedchik was a progressive organ, enjoying like other military publications from the end of the last century and especially after 1905 the freedom to represent not only the dark side of military existence but also delicate areas of administrative order, command, government decisions, and military reforms. In any case there was incomparably more freedom than in France, Austria, or Germany. In France no officer could publish anything without prior review by a department of the War Ministry. The German military press, speaking vaguely about its restrictions, said this about its Russian counterpart: "It is amazing that Russian military writers are able to express themselves with such freedom. And their commanders are attentive to their statements. They take them into consideration." And further, from an article by General Zeppelin: "The obvious attention shown to military literature in Russia by the highest authorities gives the army a great advantage, especially in the matter of raising the intellectual level of the Russian officers corps."

Even in the most diverse questions of military affairs, service, and way of life I personally never experienced censorship or even authoritative anger from St. Petersburg, although my writings several times touched upon the authority of high individuals and institutions.

There was a little restraint from local authorities in the Warsaw district but never from those in Kiev. But in Kazan, where life consisted of sharp and sensitive issues, as I tried to lead the struggle against the regime established in the district, I was subjected to systematic persecution by the commander. The official reason for his persecution was not my journalistic work but some nonessential or nonexistent mistakes in performance of duty. Sandetskii was exceedingly sensitive to what was written about life in the district. He was apprehensive about publicity, knowing that discontent with him had already accumulated in St. Petersburg.

Once during a conference General Sandetskii burst out with a thundering indictment against his officers. "Our officers are trash! They know nothing, they do nothing. I will punish them without mercy, even if it means that I am left with only one corporal." Colonel Reinbot, commander of the Inskarskii Regiment quartered in Penza, returned from the meeting and saw fit to repeat the commander's words to his assembled officers. They told me later that those assembled sat there after his speech in dismal, depressed silence. The cowed officers painfully endured the undeserved insult. Only one lieutenant colonel uneasily asked Reinbot, "Colonel, sir, is it possible that this really happened? Is it possible that the commander really said that?"

"Yes, I have repeated his words verbatim."

The next day an officer of the regiment, Staff Captain Verner, forwarded to the war minister a complaint in his own name about the commander's insults.[9] A general from the War Ministry soon arrived in Penza, conducted an investigation, and left. The district staff in their turn fell upon the regiment with an inquest. Excitement over the incident grew, and rumors flew through the entire district.

I was heartily interested in the matter and steeled myself to respond in print in the next "Army Notes." Suddenly I received from Kazan a heavy packet marked "Confidential, to be delivered to Colonel Denikin personally." In it was all the material about the Penza affair, along with instructions from Sandetskii to leave for Penza and make a confidential investigation about the lieutenant colonel who had dared ask Reinbot: "Is it possible that the commander really said that," a question that, in Sandetskii's opinion, had undermined his authority in the regiment and caused distrust for his pronouncements. It was an awkward contrivance. Obviously the lieutenant colonel's "fault" was a mere invention. The device was, however, not without sagacity. I was disarmed, because I had no right to comment in the press on the Penza affair after it had been entrusted to me as a confidential mission.

I did what I had to do. I reported that the staff officer had behaved correctly and gave him the best of references, which he fully deserved. As a result the lieutenant colonel and the captain were transferred by the War Ministry to another unit and General Sandetskii received ("delivered to General Sandetskii personally") a blue packet containing a reproof from the sovereign.

Not long before I left the district, one of my "Army Notes" created an especially serious complication. In it I described regimental life in general and the bitter lot of one army captain in particular. I wrote that he had little hope for promotion, in spite of successful reviews, after he read in an inspection report, "There is order and cleanliness in his squad but a cricket was singing in the kitchen."[10] For such an "oversight" a reprimand followed. And because of the reprimand, the captain himself began to sing like a cricket and was taken to a hospital for the mentally ill. This was a caricature, of course, but it truthfully depicted life in the district and abounded in actual detail.

General Sandetskii was away at the time and his chief of staff, General Svetlov, after conferring with his aides and the public prosecutor of the military district courts, decided to bring me to legal accounting. Svetlov reported this immediately upon Sandetskii's return but to his astonishment received the reply, "I have read the story and found nothing offensive in it." The affair of the cricket was fancied to be under control. Soon after, however, I received three disciplinary reprimands in quick succession, reproofs suggested by the commander for some alleged neglect of my office.

Arriving in Saratov some time later, General Sandetskii called me aside after inspection and said, "You display no shame in scattering my words abroad. You are the one who writes 'Army Notes.' I know!"

"Yes, sir, Your Excellency, it is I."

"Well, I have one method of maintaining control, others have another. I have nothing against criticism. But the General Staff is extremely dissatisfied with you and suggests that you have undermined my authority. You would be well advised to leave me alone . . ." I did not answer.

In the final months of my stay in the Kazan district, a series of distressing incidents occurred. First a Colonel Veis was transferred from Kazan to one of the Saratov garrison regiments. He proved to be an informer for General Sandetskii and played his role almost openly. He was feared and despised but no one dared to show his feelings outwardly. That fall, however, there was a brigade certification conference in which Colonel Veis was unanimously acknowledged unworthy of promotion to regimental command.[11] The brigade commander reluctantly confirmed the certificate but then lost his nerve. Veis, publicly waving the portfolio in which the denunciation lay, said, "I will show them! They will remember me!"

At the end of the year there was a district conference in Kazan. When the brigade commander returned, he was on the verge of despair. "Well, the commander blew up at me! Believe it or not, he pounded on the table with his fist and shouted as if I were a small boy. From a piece of paper in Veis's handwriting he enumerated my 'sins,' some forty items such as this: 'Commander of brigade, on arriving in camp, stored his piano in the arsenal of Khvalinskii Regiment.' And, 'When regimental commanders were unable to execute Sandetskii's orders, the brigade commander said to the staff commander, 'We request Anton Ivanovich.[12] He will know how to write us out of this.' In a word, I am now ruined." I was so depressed by all this that I could find no word of consolation.

Several days later an order came from the commander. How dared the certification committee refuse to promote Veis, a man whom he considered deserving and had recently promoted to colonel "for distinction"! The commander demanded that the conference reconvene and reconsider the matter. We had never before experienced such coercion.

By telegraph I summoned to this conference regimental commanders from Astrakhan and Tsaritsyn. Seven of us met. The various views were rather confused but nevertheless we decided unanimously to maintain our previous decision. I composed the resulting resolution and, with the approval of the participants, began to enter it in Veis's certification list. General P. looked quite ill. Without waiting for the session to adjourn, he went home, leaving orders to send all correspondence to him for signature. An hour later the general's orderly ran in to report that the brigade commander had just suffered a stroke.

The situation was further complicated since an absolutely fantastic individual, General Fevralev, was expected to replace the brigade commander. Fevralev had been serving out his time in order to get his pension as a regimental commander and was a heavy drinker. The cruel Sandetskii knew this and to our astonishment did not react. Fevralev was attracted to me and somehow even seemed a little afraid of me. This gave me an opportunity at times to moderate his excesses. At the brigade reception for Fevralev I raised the doubt that his command would end favorably. But he reassured me. "You will never see me in the staff office. Do not bother with reports. Just send papers for my signature and that will be all." Such a regime was maintained for many weeks.

The day after the memorable conference I sent Veis's certificate to Kazan. I received a stern reprimand for presenting papers that had "no significance without the signature of the brigade commander." The district staff even expressed doubt that the contents were actually known to and approved by General P. In answer I described the meeting and sent in my draft of the resolution with General P.'s notes and corrections on it.

In Kazan they were obviously startled. After the two Penza scandals a new one might upset the commander's unstable situation. An aide to the district staff commander soon arrived in Saratov, obviously on some official mission and actually to determine how the new situation affected the life of the garrison. Discovering the circumstances of P.'s illness and my friendly relation to Fevralev, he called on me. "Do you know how this happened? What was the cause of General P.'s attack?"

"Of course I know, Your Excellency. It was the result of the moral shock the brigade commander experienced at the troop commander's conference. He suffered a stroke."

"How can you say such a thing?"

"Because it is the absolute truth."

After that episode Kazan went silent, leaving us all to our own destinies. The entire situation became more complicated. We had begun to form our reserve brigade into a division, with the exclusion of some units and inclusion of others, with intricately developed boundaries involving conflicts of interests and demands for instantaneous decisions.

Meanwhile General P. regained his health and began to take walks.

But his memory did not return. He talked nonsense all the time. Whenever the general announced his intention to visit the troops, I would dissuade him and take measures to prevent it. Once the clerk on duty ran to me. As usual he had accompanied General P. on his walk, but this time the general had climbed into a carriage and gone toward the barracks. I rushed to the barracks and witnessed the following scene in the Balashovskii Regiment.

The young soldiers of one company had been assembled by their superior officer and were standing at attention. General P. fixed a glassy stare on one young soldier and became silent. The soldier was frightened out of his wits. He blushed and sweat poured from his forehead. I spoke to the general. "Your Excellency, please do not trouble yourself. Just order the company commander to ask questions and you can listen."

He nodded. The tension eased. The regimental commander took me aside and said, "Thank you for rescuing me. I really did not know what to do. Judge for yourself how horrible it was. He told one soldier that our current heir to the throne is Peter the Great." Somehow it ended and I took the general home.

The situation had become impossible. I telegraphed to the district staff that the brigade commander wished to come to Kazan for an examination so that he might "be sent to the Caucasus to take the waters." In my heart I hoped that they would take more drastic action. P. departed. He made a serious impression on the commission since he was unable to remember even his patronymic. Nevertheless they assigned him to the nearest course of treatment and did not go beyond that!

Returning from Kazan, apparently under the impression that his trip had had a favorable outcome, General P. ordered that he was to take effective command of his brigade again. I telegraphed to Kazan but Sandetskii maintained stubborn silence. Obviously he was embarrassed by the Saratov scandal and feared publicity so much that he did not want to employ coercive measures in regard to P.

As before, I issued the orders and instructions that both the district staff and the regiment knew as my own, though they were reinforced by P.'s signature as they had previously been by Fevralev's. Again P. tried to visit the regiments and a greater effort was required to restrain him. At last his departure date arrived and he went to take the waters. For about a month after that we prolonged the fiction of Fevralev's command until a new commander arrived to take the division, which had been reorganized from our brigade.

I will conclude by mentioning briefly the fate of some of the individuals whom I have described. Generals P. and Fevralev were retired and soon died. General Sandetskii remained in his post for five years, until 1912, after which he was assigned to the War Council.[13] But during World War I they named him commander of the Moscow military district.[14] The same things began to happen as in Kazan. War Minister Sukhomlinov wrote to the headquarters of the supreme command: "Sandetskii has stirred all of Moscow against himself. I went to Moscow at His Highness's order to try to persuade him to display less sternness. . . ." Obviously it did not help. They cleared Sandetskii out of Moscow by giving him back the Kazan district. In the March days of the 1917 revolution General Sandetskii was arrested by the Kazan garrison. The Provisional Government initiated his trial on the basis of repeated accusations of "over-authority." The Bolsheviks subsequently executed him.

Reviewing my memories of the Kazan nightmare, I cannot understand why Sandetskii's tyranny was tolerated for so long. Undoubtedly such episodes as this, as well as accession to ministerial posts of individuals universally disapproved, had a causal relationship to the overthrow of the supreme authority in the second revolution.

CHAPTER 28   IN THE ARKHANGELOGORODSK REGIMENT

By a supreme order dated June 12, 1910, I was named to command the 17th Infantry Arkhangelogorodsk Regiment quartered in the city of Zhitomir in the Kiev military district. This regiment, created by Peter the Great, was among the oldest in the Russian army, having not long before celebrated the two hundredth year of its existence. It had helped to build St. Petersburg, participated in the wars of Peter the Great and his successors, served under Suvorov for the entire glorious Saint Gothard campaign, and earned battle decorations in the Russo-Turkish War of 1877–1878.[1] It was inactive only during the Japanese campaign, although even then it was present at the very end in the Sipingai positions.

In order to revive memories of the regiment's military history, I petitioned for transfer to the regiment of old regimental standards, which were stored in St. Petersburg warehouses. Thirteen were located. Those standards were witnesses to the military glory of the regiment over two centuries. Some had escaped injury but all the others were battle-torn or entirely decayed. I created a regimental museum to preserve them and was able to assemble quite a few relics of the regiment. Among the ancient memorabilia was an excellent handwritten missal that served for camp masses in the time of Peter (the early eighteenth century).

When the standards arrived, we greeted them with pomp. The entire regiment turned out in the presence of the commander in chief and the troop commander of the Kiev military district, General Ivanov. The establishment of this symbolic connection with the past generated enthusiasm among the officers. There was less reaction among the uncultured soldiers but familiarity with the regiment's past history and the triumphant welcome of the relics produced a good impression there also.

The Arkhangelogorodsk Regiment was a strong unit. According to the mobilization plan, it could develop into two regiments and a reserve battalion. There were one hundred officers, doctors, and officials in the regiment, and about three thousand soldiers.

The officers were interested in military affairs. They worked hard and conducted themselves properly. Following General Zavatskii's system, I never applied disciplinary punishment to the officers during the four years I commanded the regiment.[2] I summoned offenders for a suitable reprimand to my study or, in more sensitive cases, to the chairman of the officers' court of honor, Colonel Dzheneev, a person of the highest moral and military nature. That was sufficient. Only twice did a matter go to a court of honor. In one case the officer involved was removed from the regiment; in the other the court was content to issue a reprimand. There was not one serious scandal during my entire command.

Reprimands were not my only form of participation in the lives of my officers. They brought many difficult and "confidential" problems to me for solution, even to the determination of alimony. Such an "arbitration court" was more convenient than an official one because, in the first place, it did not leave the walls of my study, and secondly it required no expenditure.

Our officers, like those everywhere in Russia, were loyal to the regime and took no active part in politics. Two or three officers were close to the local "Black Hundred" newspaper of the Union of the Russian People school but they exerted no influence in the regiment.[3] There were no officers with leftist tendencies.

After the Japanese War and the first revolution, in spite of its proven loyalty, the officer corps was nonetheless placed under the surveillance of the police. Periodically regimental commanders were sent top secret blacklists of "unreliable" officers for whom the road to promotion was closed. The tragedy of these lists lay in the near hopelessness of refuting any of the accusations. Private investigations did not help. I personally conducted a prolonged battle with the Kiev district staff because two distinguished officers were blacklisted, a company commander and the head of a machine-gun command. The injustice was obvious and would have undermined both their military careers and their self-confidence, as well as burdening my conscience. But it was almost impossible to clarify this matter. Only with great difficulty was I able to defend those officers. Two years later they both fell bravely in battle in World War I.

Blacklists were composed by three departments, the department of police, the gendarmes, and a special military police created by Sukhomlinov during his tenure as war minister. In each military district staff was instituted the post of chief of counterintelligence, headed by a gendarme officer disguised in staff uniform. His official sphere of interest was uncovering foreign espionage. But in most cases his chief role was something else entirely. Colonel Dukhonin, then chief of the reconnaissance squads of the district, complained bitterly to me about the oppressive atmosphere introduced by this element which, although officially subordinate to the quartermaster general, actually kept under suspicion and surveillance not only all the staff but also its chiefs.[4]

The counterintelligence staff was independent and was headed by Gendarme Colonel Miasoedov, who was directly responsible to Sukhomlinov and enjoyed his complete trust. Large sums of ministry funds were placed at Miasoedov's disposal. This innovation ended tragically.

In 1912, during deliberation on the War Ministry budget in the State Duma commission, Guchkov challenged War Minister Sukhomlinov, demanding an explanation of the large allocation for Miasoedov's work which was concealed under the heading (knowingly abused by the minister) of "expenses known to His Imperial Majesty."[5] Guchkov informed the commission that Miasoedov, while serving in the gendarme corps, had been expelled from the service for a series of criminal matters, among them the purchase of weapons in Germany for secret resale in Russia. In spite of this, Sukhomlinov had not only appointed him to office but had placed him in charge of such a responsible institution.

A stormy scene broke out in the commission. Sukhomlinov walked out of the session. Rumors about the incident spread to the press. Miasoedov challenged Guchkov to a duel which ended bloodlessly. The incident caused displeasure at court but Sukhomlinov managed to convince the sovereign that it was all personal intrigue against him by his enemies, Guchkov and the assistant minister of war [A. A. Polivanov]. As a result the latter was removed from office. But after a time Miasoedov was also dismissed from service.

At the beginning of World War I, thanks to a flattering recommendation from Sukhomlinov, Miasoedov resurfaced with an appointment to the western front and charged with reconnaissance work. But in 1915 he was convicted of espionage for Germany, tried by a military court, and executed. Because of certain trial irregularities and the hasty execution, a legend arose that the executed man had been innocent. The enemies of the supreme commander (Grand Duke Nikolai Nikolaevich) set in motion rumors that the whole affair had been created and carried out artificially in order to justify the significant failures then occurring on our front. During the second revolution and afterward, polemical articles on the subject often appeared in the press and the Miasoedov affair became to many people one of the most mysterious of criminal cases, one of those that remain secret and unsolved in history.

Personally I do not doubt Miasoedov's guilt because of circumstances known to me which shed light on this dark affair. General Krymov was my informant and he was close to Guchkov, having worked with him. At the start of the war a Japanese military agent came to Guchkov and, after obtaining his word that their conversation would remain confidential, informed him that Miasoedov, who had just been named to a responsible post, had worked for Japan in espionage service against Russia. The military agent added that he considered it his duty to warn Guchkov but, since traditionally names of secret collaborators are never revealed, he requested that his visit and information be kept secret. Guchkov began an energetic campaign against Miasoedov which ended in his exposure but, bound by his word, did not reveal the source of his information.

A letter from Sukhomlinov dated April 2, 1915, to the chief of staff of the supreme command, General Yanushkevich, confirmed this information: "I have just received your letter and realized that the deserved punishment had taken place (execution of A. D. Miasoedov). That he was a scoundrel may be judged from the letter which he wrote to me (blackmail) when I dismissed him. But it is odd that Guchkov and Polivanov did not wish to give evidence for the trial which might have cleared up this mess."[6]

The officer personnel of my regiment were predominantly Russian, of course, but there were several Poles and totally Russianized Germans as well as an Armenian and one Georgian. Throughout the Russian army nationalistic divisions among officers and among soldiers were completely erased and did not at all affect the amiable course of regimental life. Absent in military life in particular was the concept of a "Ukrainian" as something separate from the idea of a "Russian."

In 1908 when the press accused the army of increasing the number of "foreign races" in the command composition, the semiofficial organ of the War Ministry, *Russkii invalid*, carried this rebuff: "Russians are not those who bear Russian surnames but those who love Russia and consider it their Fatherland."[7]

Government policy actually promoted such an attitude among

Ivan Efimovich Denikin (1807–1885), the father of Anton Denikin

Denikin at the age of forty.
Below: Denikin, wearing a
black *papakha*, in Manchuria
during the
Russo-Japanese War

Colonel Denikin, photographed in 1913, when he was commander of the 17th Infantry Arkhangelogorodsk Regiment stationed at Zhitomir in the Ukraine

General Denikin and Grand Duke Nikolai Mikhailovich, 1915

Denikin, commander of the 4th Rifle "Iron" Brigade, and Colonel S. L. Markov, his chief of staff, at the Austro-German front in December 1914. Below: Denikin with his staff in September 1916

War Minister A. F. Kerensky
with Denikin, commander of the
western front, in June 1917

General L. G. Kornilov
(from a painting)

General A. M. Kaledin

General Denikin at his desk in 1917

officers with regard to all foreign nationalities except the Poles. In defiance of the law, secret circulars placed rank restrictions against them which were unjust and offensive. And I must say that, even in the comradely military way of life, officers felt the burden of such constraints, condemning them and when possible avoiding them.

Access to officer ranks was absolutely closed to Jews.[8] But there were officers and generals who had accepted Christianity before entering the service and who afterward applied to military schools. In both of the classes adjacent to mine in the General Staff Academy, I personally knew seven officers of Jewish descent of whom six were promoted to the rank of general before World War I. They spent their military careers normally, unhindered by any restraint in either their official or their social lives.

The nationality question did not exist in camp. If soldiers of non-Russian descent experienced difficulties in service, it was mainly due to their ignorance of the Russian language. Actually Latvians, Tatars, Georgians, and Jews who did not speak Russian were a terrible burden to the commander of the company and the company itself, and circumstances created animosity toward them. The majority of such soldiers were Jews. In my regiment and in others with which I was acquainted, complete tolerance was practiced toward Jewish soldiers, but it is impossible to deny that in some units there was a tendency toward oppression of Jews. This by no means resulted from the military system but was brought into the barracks from the outside, from the national way of life. The majority of Jews were townspeople, living poorly in the main; therefore, they sent sickly recruits, boys who were less well-developed physically than the peasant youth. This immediately placed them in a rather inferior position in the barracks. The inadequate education received in the *heders* and their frequent ignorance of the Russian language still further complicated their situation. All of this created, on the one hand, an extreme hardship in training these boys to military order, and on the other significantly increased their burden in the service. I must add that some common traits of the Jewish character, such as hysteria and love of speculation, also played a significant role.

On this basis, taking into consideration the low cultural level of the Jewish masses, a strange phenomenon occurred. As one of my duties as regimental commander, many times in the course of four years I had to examine potential military conscripts, together with representatives of Volynsk province. Before my eyes passed hundreds of deformed human bodies, mostly Jewish. They were naïve and ignorant people who crudely shammed disability in order to escape military obligations. It was miserable and annoying of them but people all through the Jewish Settlement crippled themselves.[9] Legal records in various cities presented a morbid picture of self-mutilation and revealed the existence of a widespread institution, that of underground "doctors" who practiced such operations as cutting off toes, piercing eardrums, causing acute inflammation of the eyelids or ruptures, pulling out all the teeth, and even dislocating hip bones. Such was the lot of the poor and wretched, while the Jewish intelligentsia and plutocracy went through military service in normal privileged circumstances, under conditions of volunteers.

The barracks regime could not have caused such dread. People not only disfigured but also maimed themselves, destroying their health for life. If the authorities were guilty of restricting Jews excessively, no less blame lay on intelligent and wealthy members of the Jewish upper class who, though ardently and passionately struggling for equal rights, did not once take measures (which were possible) to raise the cultural and economic level of the local unfortunates of their own race. In any case, in the Russian army the Jewish soldiers, sharp-witted and conscientious, created a normal situation for themselves in peacetime. And in war distinctions tend to become obliterated, with only individual valor and quick wittedness receiving recognition.

General Perekrestov commanded our 5th Division. He was not strict nor a formalist, and he treated us with benevolence. Neither he nor the corps commander (General Shcherbachev) nor the commander of the troops of the district (General N. I. Ivanov) in issuing general orders interfered with the authority of regimental commanders, and we were allowed to conduct our business peacefully.

In parade and ceremonial marching my regiment lagged behind the others. I placed no special emphasis on this. More important to me was the fact that the regiment fired well and maneuvered better than the others. My experience in the Japanese War with the latest tactical innovations enabled me to go beyond the training program in moving my men by forced march (with light packs). Thus on maneuvers my regiment could fall upon their surprised "enemies" as snow falls upon the head. Without bridges or pontoons, we forded rivers considered impassable by other regiments using only the materials that came to hand, such as planks, rope, sheaves of straw, and the services of my best swimmers. It was amazing to see the enthusiasm with which all ranks of the regiment participated in the extra program of practice and how much natural ingenuity, resourcefulness, and goodwill they displayed. Even the musicians swam, holding on to their floating Turkish drums. The machine-gun command ferried their machine guns and cartridges using unscrewed wheels placed on a tarpaulin as an improvised pontoon. Individuals held sheaves under their armpits as buoys. It was both instructive and amusing.

When I relinquished the regiment just before World War I, I felt that it was well prepared for battle. The Arkhangelogorodsk Regiment, as I have already mentioned, was split according to mobilization plans into two regiments. I did not encounter the first regiment in battle during the war, but in the spring of 1915 the second regiment (the one which inherited the name) came temporarily into the composition of a larger group which I commanded and occupied an exceedingly critical position on my front. I will have more to say about this episode.

In 1911 the regiment participated in imperial maneuvers near Kiev. This was the second time for me, the first having occurred when I was a company commander and took part in imperial maneuvers in the Warsaw district in 1903. On September 1 the maneuvers ended. The sovereign visited the troops, who remained in the positions where they had been surprised by the all clear. I was touched to see the almost mystical enthusiasm which was elicited everywhere by the appearance of the tsar. He was met with loud, continued cries of "Hurrah," and in the feverish brilliance of eyes and trembling of hands as they presented arms could be seen the inexplicable effect on officers, generals, and soldiers, the "men in greatcoats." Amazingly, a few years later some of those same men visited inconceivable cruelty upon everyone connected with the tsarist family, even allowing their brutal murder.[10]

On the morning of September 2 we moved to an assembly point for the tsarist review. My regiment, as senior in the district, led the ceremonial march before the sovereign. From it was chosen the honor guard consisting of an officer, a corporal, and a soldier to be presented personally to the tsar. This was a singular event in the life of the regiment, causing much excitement as we selected, equipped, and trained the honor guard.

As soon as we arrived at the assembly point, we were stunned by news that spread like lightning. The previous evening, at a festive performance in the Kiev theater in the sovereign's presence, the revolutionary Bogrov with a revolver shot had gravely wounded P. A. Stolypin, the head of the government.[11] There were riots in the city. By night three Cossack regiments from the maneuvering troops had been hastily sent to Kiev to prevent a Jewish pogrom anticipated because Bogrov was Jewish.

The mood of the officers, most of whom expressed sympathy with both the personality and policies of Stolypin, fell heavily. But the soldiers, not understanding such matters, were rather indifferent toward the event. The question which engrossed them was this: "Will the review occur or not?" It occurred. For several hours troops passed before the sovereign. The magnificence of the parade captivated everyone. As always, the troops were enveloped by high enthusiasm and the tsar's presence caused exalted excitement.

That was six years after the first revolution and six years before the second one. The attitude of the army then was still entirely loyal and favorable to the monarchy. It might have remained so but for a subsequent series of unfortunate circumstances and fatal errors which turned the popular psychology upside down and injured the prestige of both authority and dynasty. I will speak of this in further detail.

On the day before, we had received invitations addressed to commanders including regimental commanders to attend "an imperial dinner" at the Kiev palace on September 2. Knowing that Stolypin was dying in a Kiev hospital, we suggested that the dinner be cancelled. But contrary to expectation, the entire program for the visit of the tsarist family to Kiev — receptions, reviews, dinners — remained unchanged. Dining tables were set up in several halls. Dinner passed in a sober, even depressed atmosphere. There was no music. Everyone spoke quietly. At our table and probably at all others the conversation was exclusively concerned with Bogrov's crime. Low voices expressed the apprehension that the conspirators had perhaps aimed higher.

In the hall where the sovereign was seated, his guests — the heir to the Romanian throne and high generals — went through the usual ritual. The district troop commander, General Ivanov, spoke several words of welcome in the name of the army. The sovereign replied with a few words, then proposed a toast to the Romanian heir which was drunk silently, all rising.

Dinner ended. We were directed into the garden where black coffee was served at small tables. The tsar visited the tables conversing with the guests. He came to me. This was the third time I had conversed with him.[12] The sovereign was obviously a timid person and, out of his usual milieu, at a loss for a topic of conversation. He spoke with me about the last day of maneuvers, about the fortifications which had raised my regiment to the position which he had noticed. It was apparent that he wanted to compliment both the regiment and its commander.

When he moved on, a small group of officers formed around him. I joined them. All of us were waiting for something. We all wanted something to remember. But I only heard trite, insignificant phrases. The stifling routine of etiquette, the affected courtiers surrounding him, and his personal shyness prevented the tsar from approaching the military heart, from learning how devoted it was. And he spoke no words which would stir the soul. To that group which by tradition, by atavism, and by devotion to his person was especially responsive, he was unable to speak. That was my last meeting with the sovereign. I never saw him again.

Stolypin's fate was tragic. A profound patriot, a strong, intelligent, and authoritative person, he liquidated the first revolution and reestablished order in the country with little bloodshed and without shock to the foundations of the state. Although he bound his destiny to the concept of a State Duma, he was forced to dissolve the first two assemblies, which were leading the country directly to revolution. Although he was a supporter of the state regime, he nevertheless violated the Fundamental Laws by enacting a new electoral law, that of June 3, 1907, which placed a property qualification on representation, essentially to rescue the very concept of a parliament which was then threatened with abolition.[13]

He passed agrarian reforms allowing the peasant to leave the commune and strengthening him on his own plot of land.[14] Those reforms, had they been carried to conclusion, would have ended the isolation of the peasant class and solved one of the sharpest and most delicate social questions of Old Russia.[15] In opposition to Stolypin were radical circles which demanded immediate expropriation of the landlords' land for the use of the peasant, as well as Slavophile and noble circles which demanded the preservation of the commune.[16]

Stolypin sincerely sought public support for his government, but he met with incomprehension and rejection. From radical democrats came demands to transfer all authority to them, from the moderate right declarations that the government was impotent and connected with "dark forces behind the scenes."

By the leftists Stolypin was considered reactionary, by the right (court circles, the right sector of the State Council, the unified nobility) as a dangerous revolutionary. Quite simply, there was something suspicious about the fact that Stolypin was killed by a member of a revolutionary battle organization who was working simultaneously for the *okhranka*. In those days not only among Kievans but all over Russia went the rumor that Stolypin "was killed by the *okhranka*."[17] There is still no proof of this, or at least I have never encountered it in print. But it is necessary to recognize that the *okhranka* displayed criminal negligence bordering on connivance in the affair.

Although Stolypin attempted in every possible way to support the already wavering throne, he had incurred the sovereign's displeasure by the end of his career. If he had not been killed, he would soon have been dismissed.

Stolypin died on the night of September 5. I was in Zhitomir the next day and attended the requiem at which Volynsk Archbishop Antonii officiated. A remarkable person, highly educated, and a member of the extreme right wing of Russian society, as a member of the Holy Synod he took an active part in St. Petersburg politics. Subsequently, in emigration, Antonii was a dignified metropolitan heading a section of the émigré Orthodox Church, the so-called "Karlovatskii jurisdiction," which proved the most resistant to American Orthodox subordination to the Soviet patriarch.[18] But he still showed a reactionary political tendency.

Archbishop Antonii said a few words before the requiem. He coolly reproached the deceased for following a "policy too far left" and said that Stolypin "had not deserved the sovereign's confidence." He stated that he was consoled only by the fact that, after being fatally wounded, Stolypin, "realizing his error," had turned to the tsarist loge and blessed it with the sign of the cross. The archbishop ended his speech with the phrase, "We pray that the Lord has forgiven his sins." Having previously had a high opinion of the archbishop's intellect, I was shocked that he found it necessary to speak in this way of the great statesman who attempted to save the Russian ship of state from sinking, flooded as it was by waves raging from both left and right.

The years 1912 and 1913 brought restless conditions. In a victorious struggle the Balkan Slavs broke the final fetters binding them to the Turks and Austria-Hungary openly prepared to curtail the results of their victory.[19] In the summer of 1912 Austria moved six corps to the borders of Serbia and mobilized three corps on the Galician border next to Russia.

Tension grew and at one point my regiment received secret instructions, in accordance with the early stages of the mobilization program, to send a squadron to guard an important point on the southwestern railroad going toward Lvov. They remained there in full battle readiness for several weeks.

From 1908 on, after the annexation of Bosnia and Herzegovina, Austria-Hungary had prepared with full speed for war against Serbia and her natural protector Russia. Our neighbor's German and Magyar military parties by word, pen, and deed worked toward creating in the country a hostile attitude toward Russia and especially to incite the Poles and Ukrainians. Appeals called on them to fight "in the forthcoming conflict" on the side of Austria-Hungary. Circulars inundated our border provinces, especially Volynsk and Podolsk, although without apparent success. In short, our neighboring "friendly" country rattled the saber and we, repeating our error of the period before the Japanese War, were silent.

Again as in the 1870s waves of sympathy for the Balkan Slavs spread through Russia, far transcending the bounds of Slavophile circles and widely arousing the Russian people. Fearing that bitter public indignation against Austria would increase diplomatic difficulties, the government employed a series of restraining measures, prohibiting lectures, assemblies, and demonstrations connected with Balkan events and influencing the press by reprimands and punishment. Sometimes these measures took a revolting turn. In St. Petersburg mounted gendarmes dispersed sympathetic demonstrations directed toward the Serbian and Bulgarian embassies. In our remote province the police forbade playing the anthem of the Balkan Slavs and tore down their national flags from the platform of a charity concert to benefit the Red Cross in Slavic countries.

Not long before the war, from peace-loving motives of course, a highest order came strictly prohibiting military officials from conducting discussions on contemporary political themes (the Balkan question, the Austro-Hungarian conflict, Pan-Germanism, and so on). On the very eve of the inevitable Fatherland War our authorities assiduously avoided exciting the people to a healthy patriotism. They did not explain the aims, causes, and problems of possible conflict, or acquaint troops with the Slavic question or our eternal conflict with Pan-Germanism.

Strictly speaking, like many others I did not obey the order but prepared the attitude of the Arkhangelogorodsk Regiment suitably. And in the military press I wrote a passionate article, "Do Not Extinguish That Spirit!" against the order.[20]

I wrote: "In secret laboratories with shutters tightly closed against the eyes of the Russian people, Russian diplomacy is brewing a political mash which the army will have to sip. The army has cause to distrust those authorities who in the past centuries have systematically placed obstacles in the path of strategy and later deprecated the results of our victories."

I pointed in turn to the administrative measures taken by government censors "to reduce the enthusiastic spirit of the country and to extinguish that precious response which springs up by impulse and suggests victory." I concluded, "Chauvinism is not necessary. We do not need to rattle the saber. But a firm and clear public understanding of the mood of Russian state policy and a victorious spirit in the people and army is necessary. Do not extinguish that spirit!"

On March 23, 1914, I was promoted to general for instruction under the commander of the Kiev district troops. Because I had genuinely grown to like my regiment, I said goodbye to them with real sorrow and left for Kiev. On June 21 I was promoted "for distinguished service" to major general and confirmed in my new duties.

PART VI

CHAPTER 29　ON THE THRESHOLD OF WORLD WAR I

As a result of the fall of Austria-Hungary and the Russian and German revolutions, people have had access to facts and diplomatic documents which in other circumstances would have remained hidden for many years, perhaps forever. It is already possible to say, therefore, that indisputable guilt for World War I lay with the Central European powers.

Nevertheless this question has been interpreted otherwise. How can this be? Dishonesty, preconceptions caused by patriotic sentiment, inadequate knowledge. The United States, more objective because it entered only at the end of the war and was not bound in a direct sense by the Versailles Treaty, might still have answered that question correctly. But an extraordinary difference of opinion about the origins of the war runs extensively through American historical literature. One of the local [American] journals composed a questionnaire and interviewed 215 professors. The resulting opinions, of all shades within two categories, produced these amazing figures: 107 of the individuals questioned declared that they blamed the Central powers and 108 the Entente.

In my essay "The Role of Russia in the Origins of the First World War" (Paris, 1937), I analyzed that question in detail. I will not dwell on proof of such commonly known events as the stormy ascent of German industrial imperialism, which had a direct connection with the special spirit of the German breed, who claimed for themselves the "historical mission of renovating decrepit Europe" by means based on their concept of being the "super race."[1] With steady perseverance they systematically prepared the minds of the masses in their literature, in schools, and even in church. The Germans long ago expressed unrestrainedly their opinion of Slavs as "ethnic material" or, more simply, *"Düngervölker,"* that is, dung for the cultivation of the German culture. Their contempt extended to the "decadent" French with the belief that the French should submit to "full-blooded" Germans. "We will organize a great forcible eviction of the lowest peoples." This was the old leitmotif of Pan-Germanism.

The candid boldness and impunity with which the German press outlined the path of expansion was astonishing. Probably the most specific writings on the subject came from the famous Bernhardi, ideologue of the military party.[2] In his *Kriegsbrauch* he demanded from England a "division of world authority" and non-intervention in questions of German territorial expansion. "War with France is necessary, war to the death," he added, "war which will destroy forever its role as a great power and lead in the end to its downfall. But our chief efforts must be directed toward conflict with the Slavs, our historic enemy."

What, essentially, did Hitler subsequently say or do that was new? He attempted to fulfill the plan of his predecessors, only with greater flexibility. Lulling and deceiving in turn first the west and then the east, blackmailing them and others, he only concealed his obvious intent of expansion under an ideological motif.

Austria-Hungary's *Drang* was somewhat more moderate. "Austrian hegemony in the Balkans" was the basic slogan of Austrian policy, more clearly developed after 1906 when Aehrenthal became minister of foreign affairs and General Conrad von Hötzendorff chief of the General Staff. In the year of Russia's greatest military unpreparedness (1905), the semiofficial Austrian organ *Danger's Armeezeitung*, quoting a "highly authoritative source," ventured to write: "If it proves impossible to achieve Austrian hegemony in the Balkans by peaceful means, then we must look for a solution not in the Balkans but in another theater of war."

Austria-Hungary, suffering from such internal infirmities as the fragmented composition of its population, German-Hungarian rivalry, and Slavic rebellion, lacked sufficient resources to fulfill her objectives. But mighty Germany stood behind her, supporting her aggressive undertakings. Germany was an ally but was also the leader. When in June 1913 Austria decided to ignite world conflagration by attacking Serbia and so informed the Berlin cabinet, Berlin considered action at that particular time inappropriate and responded harshly.[3]

"An attempt to deprive Serbia of her achievement," said the German minister of foreign affairs to Austrian envoy Count Secheni, "would mean European war. Austria-Hungary, with its exciting but unfounded nightmare of a great Serbia, must not toy with Germany's fate." And Austria hesitated, temporarily.

Across Austria-Hungary's path lay Russia, the traditional protector of the Balkan Slavs, clearly perceiving the threat of militant Pan-Germanism to the narrow mouth of the Bosphorus because of Balkan proximity to the Aegean Sea and the Sea of Marmora.[4] Across that path also stood the idea of a South Slav national revival and the critical political and economic interests of England and France. It was necessary to consider these things. But despite these tensions and conditions, there were sufficient potential causes for world conflict, and Germany and Austria only awaited the appropriate time. And occasion. If there had been no Sarajevo shot, they would have found another motive without difficulty.

From extensive materials concerning the genesis of the war, I will examine several facts in order to reconstruct in the reader's memory the most significant personages of that world drama, the authentic originators of the war. On June 28, 1914, the Sarajevo shot rang out. It was a response to long years of the Austro-Magyar regime, a consequence of the national enthusiasm of the South Slavs, and a result of revolutionary-emancipatory activities which involved almost all Slavic youth, especially those in occupied Bosnia and Herzegovina. The heir to the Austro-Hungarian throne, Grand Duke Ferdinand, was assassinated while visiting Sarajevo by the Bosnian Princip, an Austrian subject.[5] The Austrians, for all their efforts, were unable to implicate the Serbian government in the affair but several Serbian citizens were involved in the plot.

On the day after the assassination Austro-Hungarian Chancellor Berchtold conveyed to Hungarian Premier Count Tisza his intention to "use the Sarajevo crime to settle accounts with Serbia." But Germany's concurrence and assistance were necessary. To that end Emperor Franz Joseph sent a memorandum to German Emperor Wilhelm in which he defined the aims of his forthcoming declaration in the following words: "Serbia, which appears today to be the prime mover of the Pan-Slavic movement, must be annihilated as a political factor in the Balkans."

On July 5 Wilhelm gave his reply to the Austro-Hungarian envoy, Count Secheni. "If the matter should come to war, Austro-Hungary against Russia, you may be assured that Germany, with her customary loyalty to her alliances, will stand at your side. If Austria acknowledges the necessity for military action, it would be a pity to let such a favorable opportunity escape." That meant that the time was appropriate. At this tense moment Wilhelm, in order to cover his tracks, decided to depart for a "rest" in the skerries.

On July 19 the Austro-Hungarian government definitely decided the question of war with Serbia. The customary resolution was made public, of course. Before all the world Austria declared her territorial disinterest. Not made public, however, was the possibility of dividing Serbia among Austria and her neighbors, nor was the possibility excluded of "delivering Serbia into a dependent relationship to the Monarchy (Austro-Hungarian) by overthrow of the dynasty and other measures." Even German Chancellor Bethmann-Hollweg, informed by a dispatch about this decree, made a handwritten statement in the margin, "Unbearable hypocrisy!"

In essence the basic conditions for the ultimatum to Serbia were conveyed on July 11 and sent to Berlin for approval.[6] But before presenting them to Serbia, Austria delayed until the departure from St. Petersburg of French President Poincaré, who was visiting Emperor Nicholas II.[7] Berlin was dissatisfied with the delay and Wilhelm wrote in a report, "How wretched!" That same day the Austro-Hungarian ambassador, Count Secheni, telegraphed his chancellor, Berchtold, "The Minister of Foreign Affairs deeply regrets this delay and fears that sympathetic regard and interest in this move may abate within Germany."

Nevertheless it was only on July 23 that Austria presented Serbia with a defiant and offensive ultimatum whose shocking contents produced a stupefying impression everywhere except in Berlin. The ultimatum, which allowed forty-eight hours for compliance, demanded among other things the immediate exclusion from office of all Serbian officials and officers accused by the Austro-Hungarian government of "circulating propaganda against Austria." Point Five demanded the establishment within Serbia of "an Austro-Hungarian agency for suppression of the revolutionary movement against the Monarchy (Austro-Hungarian)." Point Six was the "admission of Austrian officials to conduct inquests in Serbian territory."

Serbia accepted with minor reservations eight points of the Austrian demands, rejecting only Point Six outright. The Serbian response impressed everyone with its extreme moderation and compliance. Even Wilhelm noted on a report to the ministry, "A great moral victory for Vienna. But it precludes all cause for war." This above all Berlin was seeking, a proper cause. The question of war had already been decided.

Having received the Serbian reply, the Austro-Hungarian mission left Belgrade without even consulting their ministry. Diplomatic relations were thus interrupted. In the next seven days all forces went into action, all behind-the-scene diplomatic influences, with both concealed and open motives.

By direct intercourse Russia attempted several times to persuade Austria to resume negotiations on the basis of Serbia's reply, but we met categorical refusal.[8] All further attempts of our ministry were unsuccessful because, as we know now, the Austrian ambassador to St. Petersburg, Count Szapary, had secret instructions from Berchtold to "continue conversations without making any commitments, dwelling only on common ground." England, supported by France and Italy, suggested to Berlin and Vienna that the problem be submitted to a conference of the four great powers. They refused. Count Secheni telegraphed from Berlin to Vienna, "They advise us to proceed with haste, to place before the world a fait accompli."

Serbian Prince-Regent Alexander appealed to the Russian emperor for assistance, placing the fate of Serbia in his hands. The sovereign replied on August 9, "While any small hope of avoiding bloodshed remains, all my efforts will be directed toward this goal. If . . . we do not attain it, Your Highness may be assured that Russia will not in any case remain indifferent to the fate of Serbia." But already there was no hope.

July 27: The English minister, Grey, repeated his proposal, asking Berlin to influence Austria. Bethmann-Hollweg telegraphed the Viennese government: "By rejecting all peaceful proposals, we will appear in world eyes to be originators of war. This would make our internal situation impossible. We must appear to our own people as unwilling to go to war." This official telegram was accompanied by another to Count Secheni: "The German government assures you in the most categorical manner that it does not at all agree with the proposal (meaning Grey's), that it emphatically opposes it, and is sending this correspondence to you only for appearances." Who said, "Unbearable hypocrisy!"? Under such circumstances Austria-Hungary, having rejected both the Russian and English proposals, declared war on Serbia on July 28.

The substance of the interrelated treaties binding the powers involved in the conflict may be summarized as follows:

1. Germany, approving Austria-Hungary's aggression against Serbia, agreed to move against Russia if the latter interceded for Serbia.

2. France would come in on Russia's side if the latter, intervening on behalf of Serbia, should experience aggression from Germany.

3. England's position was less definite. For several days Sazonov and Poincaré tried to obtain from England an official declaration of solidarity with them. Those words were not said which, if pronounced clearly and at the proper time, might have halted the Austro-Hungarian madness.

On July 29 London proposed another alternative to Berlin. Grey conceded the occupation by Austria-Hungary, "in the nature of a pledge," of some Serbian territory including the capital city of Belgrade, and the suspension of further attack pending clarification by mediating powers. For the first time the English voice contained the hint of a threat that if Germany and France were to become involved in conflict it would be impossible for England to remain indifferent.

Berlin clearly felt anxious that day. During the night the German chancellor bombarded Vienna with six telegrams, one nullifying the other, containing insincere advice to continue discussions with the powers. The advice was obviously insincere because the same basic motif recurred: "If Vienna rejects all proposals, it will be impossible to place the odium of war upon Russia." To push Russia to take the first step, to place the blame on Russia, that was the primary objective.

At the same time parallel conversations were leading to other decisions. On July 30, by order of von Moltke, chief of the German General Staff, the Austrian military agent in Berlin, Binert, telegraphed to General Conrad: "Every moment lost increases the danger of our

position and gives advantage to Russia. Reject the conciliatory proposition of Great Britain. European war is the last chance for the salvation of Austria-Hungary. Germany absolutely guarantees to support
you." On the night of July 31 von Moltke himself telegraphed: "Be on
guard against Russian mobilization. In order to save Austria-
Hungary, mobilize swiftly against Russia. Germany is mobilizing."

That evening a government meeting took place in Vienna and the
resulting protocol stated: "His Majesty announced that cessation of
military action against Serbia is impossible. . . . His Majesty approved the proposal to evade acceptance of the English offer diligently while answering in such a way as to demonstrate our conciliatory
attitude." That same evening Emperor Franz Joseph signed a decree
authorizing mobilization of the remaining army units, concentrating
them on the Russo-Galician border. Thus Vienna and the national
leaders of the Central powers competed with each other in hypocrisy,
trampling elementary human morals, shoving their monarchies into
the abyss.

Russia was not prepared for war, did not desire war, and exerted
every effort to prevent war. The condition of the Russian army and
navy after the Japanese War, the exhaustion of material reserves, and
the known defects in organization, training, and administration were
truly threatening. Military authorities acknowledged that until 1910
the army remained defenseless in the fullest sense of the word. Only
in the last years before the war (1910–1914) did reconstruction and
reorganization of the Russian armed forces improve them
significantly.[9] In technical and material aspects, however, they remained entirely inadequate.

Legislation authorizing the construction of a fleet was passed only
in 1912. The so-called Great Program, which aimed at significant
strengthening of the army, was confirmed only in March 1914. Nothing substantial was realized from either program. Corps departing
for war had from 108 to 124 pieces of ordnance as compared with the
German 160 and were almost devoid of heavy artillery and supplies of
rifles. Our supplies of cartridges consisted of 1,000, according to the
old norms, against 3,000 of the Germans.

Such defects in the supplies of material for the Russian army were
not justified by the financial condition of industry. Military credits
provided by both the Ministry of Finance and the last two State

Dumas were adequate. What went wrong? Our factories were slow in filling supply orders because of the obligation to use domestic presses and machines and the fact that the introduction of foreign machinery was limited. Our inertia, our bureaucratic red tape, and inter-departmental frictions were also to blame. Finally, the administration of War Minister Sukhomlinov was deeply at fault. Sukhomlinov was an extremely shallow person, entirely ignorant of military matters. For example, before the war the question was not even raised about the means of replacing military supplies after peacetime stores were exhausted. There was no discussion of mobilizing war industries![10] A bewildering question involuntarily arises. How could those in author-ity have tolerated such a man as Sukhomlinov for six years, a man whose actions and inactions led unswervingly and methodically to the ruin of our state?

Because of our obvious unpreparedness and our enemies' advan-tage in swift mobilization, our plans to meet aggression on the western front assumed a defensive character. Sukhomlinov's prewar strategy dismissed the use of Poland as an advance forward theater, disman-tled the fortifications there, and withdrew several divisions deep into the country. Those measures had caused excitement at the time in both Russia and France.[11] The last directives of 1913 were somewhat more decisive but still carried the stamp of passiveness, both in dis-tribution of forces and license for the commander to deploy the army to an area far inside the country, along a line from Kovno to Brest to Proskurov. In the face of the international situation, neither the Aus-trian army nor Austrian policy was regarded as autonomous. Our war plans on the western front anticipated only one combination, a conflict with a combined Austro-German force.

The actual Russian situation combined with the prevailing mood in the country shows incontestably that Russia did not desire and was in no position to desire war. An entirely different picture could be seen in Germany. According to our evaluation as well as that of the Ger-man General Staff, Germany was thoroughly prepared for war in 1909. In 1911 and 1912 the Reichstag passed laws for a special war levy to enlarge contingents and increase the number of formations of special units. In 1913 a new levy was set enlarging the peacetime size of the German army to 200,000 men, a 32 percent increase. The Austro-Hungarian army was also increased significantly and according to the opinion of its actual chief, General Conrad, it was "ready" as early as 1908 and 1909. Of course, we appraised it as drastically less than the German, and its multinational composition with significant contingents of Slavs represented obvious instability. Nonetheless, in order to achieve swift and decisive destruction of this army our plan provided for the deployment of sixteen corps against the anticipated Austrian thirteen.

The center of gravity for the forthcoming conflict lay, of course, in Berlin's plans. Long before the war their literature, the correspondence of their military authorities, and the secret reports and plans of the German General Staff had laid out clear and firm plans not only for definite attack as a strategic doctrine but for aggression, which corresponded to Germany's historical and political purpose.[12]

The German war plan, finally worked out by General von Moltke (the younger), foresaw the infliction of an initial blow against France by a main German force of thirty-five and a half corps and the active defense of Eastern Prussia by four corps.[13] Simultaneously the Austro-Hungarian army was to strike at Russia.

At the end of May 1914, one month before the Sarajevo shot, in a conference at Karlsbad Generals Moltke and Conrad agreed that "each delay will decrease our chances for success." To Conrad's question about how the future looked to him, Moltke answered, "We hope to be finished with France in six weeks after opening military action or, in any case, to be able by that time to transfer the greater part of our forces to the East."

CHAPTER 30   RUSSIAN MOBILIZATION

Immediately after the rupture between Austria and Serbia and in view of Austrian mobilization, which was obviously directed not only against Serbia but also against Russia, an imperial council at Tsarskoe

Selo decided on July 25 to announce not actual mobilization but a "premobilization period," providing for the "return of troops from camps to permanent quarters" and a roll call plan of calling up reserves. In order not to be caught unaware, it was further decided that in case of necessity ("necessity" to be defined by the minister of foreign affairs), partial mobilization of the four military districts of Kiev, Kazan, Moscow, and Odessa would be effected. The Warsaw district, which adjoined Austria and Germany, was not to be mobilized in order to avoid giving the latter cause for alarm and retaliation. But a grave misunderstanding ensued.

This decision could only have resulted from Sukhomlinov's incredible lack of information.[1] It was presented to the council without the knowledge of his experienced staff. As I have already indicated, in view of the treaty relations between Austria and Germany, the Russian plan of mobilization for war foresaw only one possibility, conflict with a united Austro-German force. No plan of partial mobilization (against Austria only) existed. Partial mobilization, therefore, was a pure improvisation in the last days before the war and threatened us with disaster. As evidence I submit the following facts:

1. Our mobilization plan involved full military districts, not corps.

2. We had no strict territorial system of completing mobilization and consequently the corps mobilized were not predesignated to receive reinforcements from unmobilized districts.

3. According to the plan, several corps of the Moscow and Kazan districts had to be concentrated in the Warsaw district, which was not consistent with the rationale for "partial" mobilization.

4. Modification of railroad plans, in case it proved necessary (and it seemed more than probable) to transform partial mobilization into a general one, would have caused incredible confusion if not full paralysis of our transport. Meanwhile, in view of the immense distances in Russia (and the absence of automobile transport), our army required from twenty to thirty days for large concentration while the Austrians were on a fifteen-day schedule and the Germans ten.

5. Above all, if the Warsaw district were not to be mobilized simultaneously, then the southern part contiguous with Austria would be unprotected, especially that area between the Bug and the Vistula, where the Austro-Hungarian command directed their main blow with a force of twenty-eight and a half divisions.

Anticipating such awesome eventualities, the Russian General Staff felt it their duty to advocate general mobilization to the supreme authority, considering that even a delayed announcement would be less dangerous than an improvised partial mobilization.

Our former enemies have hypocritically placed the question of mobilization in causal connection with our declaration of war upon Germany. But we did not know, as we know now, that on July 30, on the eve of general Russian mobilization, war was already for them a foregone conclusion. For the most part foreign histories bearing on this question accept the German treatment of it.[2] Regrettably, several prominent Russian leaders (Nabokov, Miliukov, Gan, and others), laboring under an unpardonable delusion, also described Russian mobilization as the "adventurism and militarism of the generals" who "deceived the sovereign."

What actually occurred in St. Petersburg during those tragic days? On July 28 information was received that Austria had declared war upon Serbia. Then Berchtold rejected direct negotiations with St. Petersburg. Minister of Foreign Affairs Sazonov ordered the General Staff to proceed with mobilization. At the insistence of the General Staff leaders, General Yanushkevich prepared two bills to be signed as decrees by the supreme commander, one for general and one for partial mobilization. Together with the declaration memorandum, they were dispatched to Tsarskoe Selo. On the morning of July 29 the decree for general mobilization, signed by the sovereign, was returned.

That same day the German ambassador, Count Pourtales, handed Sazonov an ultimatum: "The continuation of military preparations by Russia will compel us to mobilize, and then it will scarcely be possible to avoid European war." "Military preparations" in this ultimatum meant partial as well as general mobilization, although Russia had not even begun to mobilize. Between eight and nine o'clock in the evening, as the central telegraph was preparing to transmit the imperial decree to all the corners of Russia, a change came. "The sovereign orders partial rather than general mobilization. . . ." And mobilization began on the night of July 30. What had happened?

Emperor Nicholas II had decided on one more attempt to avoid conflict. He suggested by telegraph to Emperor Wilhelm that differences be submitted for deliberation by the Hague conference.

Wilhelm did not mention The Hague in his answering telegram. Pointing to the "grave consequences" of Russian mobilization, he concluded: "Now the entire weight of this decision rests on your shoulders. You bear the responsibility for war or peace." Reviewing the facts mentioned above, one is involuntarily led to the now ritualistic phrase, "Unbearable hypocrisy!"

On July 30 Foreign Minister Sazonov made a last desperate attempt to prevent conflict. He sent Ambassador Pourtales the following statement: "Recognizing that the Austro-Serbian question has become a European question, if Austria demonstrates readiness to withdraw ultimatum points which encroach on the sovereign rights of Serbia, Russia will pledge to halt her own military preparations." By this formula both Sazonov and Pourtales, by their own statements, understood that Russia would require from Austria neither rapid cessation of her military activities in Serbia nor demobilization on the Russian border in exchange for Russia's complete rejection of mobilization.

This proposal, which exceeded all normal bounds of conciliation, was made, according to Sazonov, on his own initiative and without authorization from the sovereign. He declared to Pourtales that no Russian government could do more "without exposing the dynasty to serious dangers." After several hours an answer came from Berlin. It was a categorical refusal. The die was cast.

The Russian General Staff was well aware that within the next few days all parties would announce general mobilization, and chaos deepened. On July 30, the first day of partial mobilization, there was still the possibility of a painless transition to general mobilization, because that first day was spent entirely on administrative affairs. Transportation still had not begun.

Reflecting the mood of the General Staff, after a conference of Sukhomlinov, Yanushkevich, and Sazonov, the latter informed the sovereign of the necessity to announce general mobilization immediately. In his memoirs Sazonov described those historic moments in detail.[3] After the minister's report and a brief reply by the emperor, grave silence ensued.

"This means condemning hundreds of thousands of Russian people to death! How can one not hesitate before such a decision?" Then, speaking with difficulty, the sovereign added, "You are right. We can expect nothing else but the enemy's attack. Give the chief of the General Staff my order for general mobilization."

All the vacillation, changes, delays, orders, and counterorders from St. Petersburg were the product of an illusory hope up to the last moment of preventing war. But they created bewilderment, unrest, and confusion in the country, especially in Kiev, which was the organizational center for the Austrian front.

General V. Dragomirov, chief of staff for the Kiev military district, was on leave in the Caucasus, as was his second in command. I replaced the latter and on my still inexperienced shoulders rested mobilization and organization of three staffs and all institutions of the 3rd and 8th Armies for the southwest front.

The new mobilization Timetable No. 20 was supposed to have been completed by the end of 1914. Coordinated with it were plans to deploy the Russian armed forces in the event of war with the Triple Alliance. Meanwhile the army operated by an old timetable (No. 19). Mobilization plans did not correspond, therefore, to the order of deployment. For example, no plans existed for forming a staff and administering the new 8th Army. High personnel for the army were designated by telegram from St. Petersburg on July 31, the first day of mobilization. But I had to recruit other personnel as I could, which was difficult in the chaotic first days of mobilization. Rear institutions were not formed for the 8th Army until the fifteenth day of mobilization.

No fewer difficulties were caused by the new Regulations Regarding the Field Administration of Troops, confirmed only on July 29, two days before mobilization actually began. As we set about it, we had no new data about rights and responsibilities, posts, allowances of staff, and officers. I received a telegram from St. Petersburg on July 30 that the new regulations were generally no different from the "Proposed Regulations" which had been sent to the staff earlier.

Since the Kiev staff had only one copy of the Proposed Regulations, there was a veritable pilgrimage to the staff from every side. People swarmed into my study at all hours for information and to copy such and such an item of the Proposed Regulations. Hundreds of bewildering questions arose which required clarification from the General Staff. The overloaded telegraph and the more overworked General

Staff were unable to give instant answers, so I had to take responsibility for decisions on many important questions. We managed, but with difficulty. New lists of individual personnel were prepared. Three days later a field courier from St. Petersburg brought several copies of the freshly printed regulations and they proved to be quite different from the Proposed Regulations. All our work of the preceding days was wasted. Everyone feverishly undertook the recomposition of their lists. Generally speaking, my colleagues and I retained an impression of sheer nightmare from the first week of mobilization.

If all this confusion testifies to the excessive carelessness of the St. Petersburg central administration, at the same time it also proves that we did not expect war even though thirty-three days had passed since Sarajevo. Still and all, mobilization proceeded throughout huge Russia rather satisfactorily, and the concentration of troops was accomplished within the deadline.

General N. I. Ivanov became chief commander of the southwest front. He owed his career to a series of accidents, among them the suppression of the Kronstadt rebellion. A modest and peace-loving person, he lacked strategic knowledge. He was more interested in the economic life of the district. But M. V. Alekseev was assigned to him as chief of staff. Alekseev was an authority on strategy and one of the principal formulators of our war plan for the Austrian front. After the Galicia victory General Ivanov enjoyed great popularity in Russian public opinion and among our allies. The general press and subsequent works on military science created the impression that many corps were motivated to victory under the command of General Ivanov. Actually his role was exceedingly minor. The real leader of the army was General Alekseev.

General Brusilov was appointed to command the 8th Army, with General Lomnovskii as his chief of staff. General Brusilov lacked experience in leadership techniques of large scale forces and was at first under the influence of his chief of staff. But later he was emancipated and assumed personal initiative and independence of decision.

I was named quartermaster general of the 8th Army. With relief I relinquished responsibility for the Kiev staff to General Dragomirov's second in command when he returned from leave, and I was free to become absorbed in study of deployment and problems in store for the 8th Army.

On August first Germany declared war on Russia and on the third on France. When Germany invaded Belgian territory on the fourth, the English government informed Berlin that it would "take all measures in our power to protect the neutrality of Belgium which we have guaranteed."[4] Austria delayed. The Russian tsar, still hoping to extinguish the conflagration, decided not to open military activities until the declaration of war upon Russia. This came at last on August 6. Subsequently our cavalry, in spite of the planned four-hour mobilization preparedness, could not throw its front squadrons at the border until the sixth day.

The great war began, that supreme exertion of national spiritual and physical strength, that greatest sacrifice in the name of the Fatherland. The great war began, with economic devastation, moral disintegration, and a loss of life running into the millions. The great war, which led humanity to the brink of the abyss.

In contrast with the mood of the country at the beginning of the Russo-Japanese campaign, Russians entered World War I in a patriotic spirit. True, the radical-liberal circles did not support "outright war" immediately and without hesitation. Typical of their attitude was the position of the Kadet party organ *Rech*.[5] In July that newspaper had protested against Russian and French armament as a "grievous sacrifice on the altar of international militant nationalism." As late as July 25 it demanded "localization of the Serbian question and abstention from anything that would involve us in it." But after the Austrian ultimatum, *Rech* acknowledged Austria's "traditional policy of political annihilation of Serbia" and called the Serbian reply "a maximum concession." Stormy debates in their editorial conferences reflected the contradictions of liberal thought gone astray. On the day war was declared *Rech* was suppressed by authority of the supreme high command, but on August 4 it reemerged, defining its new position in a lead article with the following words: "In this awesome hour of trial, internal conflict should be forgotten in order to fortify more strongly the unity of the Tsar and the people" and "the remarkable words of the Highest Manifesto indeed express the fundamental problem of the present time."

The question of participation in the war created a schism in the socialist camp. "Priziv," the Paris group of Socialist Revolutionaries (Avksentev, Rudnev, and others) demanded "participation of revolutionary democracy in the self-defense of the people," explaining that "the path to victory will lead to freedom." However, such St. Petersburg revolutionaries as A. F. Kerensky and others opposed this "defensive" policy.

Similar contradictions caused paradoxical scenes. For example, the Socialist Revolutionary Burtsev, influenced at the beginning of the war by patriotic motives, decided to stop his revolutionary activities and return to his birthplace, where he intended, as a public service, to conduct a campaign in support of the war. Instead, the authorities planted him in Peter and Paul Fortress and brought him to trial. Two of Burtsev's party comrades, the lawyers Kerensky and Sokolov, were asked to defend him. Kerensky visited Burtsev in prison and told him, "You have placed us in an embarrassing position. We cannot defend you. We consider it necessary to protest this war with all our might, but you show support for the government by defending it." The Kadet Maklakov finally defended Socialist Revolutionary Burtsev at the trial.

Schisms also occurred among the Social Democrats. A large group of Social Democratic economists such as Yordanskii, Maslov, Tugan-Baranovskii, and others declared that war against Germany was justified. Their views were even shared by the patriarch of anarchists, Kropotkin. Only the Social Democratic Bolsheviks remained utter defeatists from the beginning of the war until the end, entering into remunerative collaboration with the Central powers and directing propaganda from abroad according to Lenin's theme, "The lesser evil is defeat of the Tsarist monarchy."[6]

But this was a single blot against the general background of patriotic fervor in Russia. When the storm broke in August 1914, the State Duma in a historic session responded to the tsar's appeal to "arise unanimously and self-sacrificingly to the defense of our Russian land."[7] Nationalist groups such as Poles, Lithuanians, Tatars, Latvians, and others formally expressed their "firm conviction that in the hour of trial, all the peoples of Russia are united in their feeling for the Fatherland, firmly trusting in the justice of this matter, at the call of their sovereign prepared to arise in defense of our Fatherland, its honor, and its fortunes." This was actually more than a formal declaration. It testified to faith in the historic process of the building of the

Russian nation, in spite of errors in government policy and manifestations of nationalist chauvinism frequently introduced from outside.

In any case, as circumstances were to prove during the course of
more than three terrible war years, in spite of our varying degrees of
success and in spite of the immensity of our multiracial empire, there
was not a single episode of unrest on nationalist grounds, a fact of
great positive significance.

CHAPTER 31 1914: AT THE FRONT

World War I began. The comparative power of the armed forces
on each side was as follows. After the completion of mobilization, the
combined strength of the Entente compared with that of the Central
powers was as ten to six. But it is necessary to consider the weakness of
the Belgian army as well as the lack of organization and the complete
absence of modern armaments and munitions in the Serbian army,
which was valiant but had the nature of a militia. On the other hand,
the Austro-Germans had superiority in quantity of artillery, especially
heavy artillery. The Germans had 160 pieces of heavy artillery per
corps, the Austrians 132, the French 120, and we had 108. In techniques and organization the German army made even more difference
in the balance of power.

Russia's position was particularly difficult. Immense distances and
an insufficient network of railroads complicated the concentration,
supply, and transfer of troops, while the backward industrial situation
made it impossible to cope with increased wartime requirements. It is
possible to say that if on the Western European front the opposing
sides vied with each other in courage and technique, then in the East,
especially during the first two years, we opposed the murderous techniques of the Germans with courage and blood.

The Germans, still operating according to the plans of their high
military authority, the late General Schlieffen, aimed at making short

work of France and directing the main blow through Luxembourg and Belgium. For that purpose seven times more strength was amassed on the right wing than on the left. The fixed axis for the pivot and strike was the region of Metz.

Von Moltke, the new chief of the General Staff, lacked the talent of his famous father.[1] He changed the Schlieffen Plan, weakening the "striking fist" to five corps. He assigned three corps for the protection of Alsace and Lotharingen and later sent two corps to Eastern Prussia when the Russians penetrated there. Thus he sacrificed strategy to the preservation of prestige.

The French, completely unprepared for a blow through Belgium, had deployed almost all their armies along their eastern borders. On August 16 the Germans took Liége and easily threw the Belgian army back to the sea, to Antwerp. Partial attacks by the French in Alsace and the Ardennes were unsuccessful. Four English divisions suffered serious defeat and General Kluck, chief commander of the German shock troops, was approaching Paris.

By the end of August all fronts of the French army had retreated to the Marne. The new (6th) army of General Maunoury, supported by the English, actively defended Paris, which was experiencing mortal alarm. The French government evacuated to Bordeaux and sent the Russians an odd and impracticable appeal to transfer four Russian corps to France through Arkhangel. In addition, President Poincaré, General Joffre, and French Ambassador Paléologue requested that we accelerate our attack on the German borders.

According to the Russo-French Convention, if the Germans assaulted France the Russian northwest front was obliged to begin attack by the fourteenth day of mobilization and the southwest front by the nineteenth day. This promise, thoughtlessly given by representatives of the Russian General Staff, placed our troops, especially those of the northwest front, in an extremely grave situation. Mobilization would be in its twenty-eighth day before we could assemble thirty infantry and nine and a half cavalry divisions. At the beginning of the attack on August 17, we had only twenty-one infantry and eight cavalry divisions. Moreover, our troops had not yet received an adequate supply of transports or even of bakeries. Some units, such as the 2nd Army, lacked so much as division carts. At the end of the opera-

At the end of January Brusilov's 8th Army went on the offensive, with Gumennoe as its main objective. But our somewhat lengthy preparations had not been sufficiently concealed from the Austrians and, bringing all available forces to the threatened front, they met us with a counteroffensive especially strong from the direction of Mezoliaborch-Turka, where Linzingen's army was situated. Our left wing, a weak screen in Bukovina, was attacked by thirteen and a half Austrian divisions and thrown back to the Dniester and the Pruth. Lechitskii's 9th Army was transferred there from the left bank of the Vistula. During February, March, and April bloody battles raged in the Carpathian foothills with variable success. In the end we repulsed the Austro-Germans and they failed to achieve their objective, the relief of Peremyshl. We again seized control of the main Carpathian passes but our efforts to force the Carpathians were unsuccessful.

On March 22 Peremyshl surrendered. Into our hands fell 9 generals, 2,500 officers, and 120,000 soldiers, as well as 900 guns and an immense quantity of equipment and supplies of all kinds. General Shcherbachev's 11th Army, which had been besieging Peremyshl, was thus freed and Ivanov assigned him to the Carpathians also.

Meanwhile Germans on the East Prussian front began to advance. In February a battle broke out near Avgustov in which both sides suffered heavy losses. In March we took the offensive, aiming to throw back the Germans to the Varta-Narev line. Not all the March battles were equally successful. Twice near Prasnishem we hit the enemy hard, but the operation ended in a draw. Finally the Germans retreated to the frontier and assumed defensive positions all along the East Prussian front. About that time (March 26) General Ruzskii suffered illness and General Alekseev became commander of the northwest front. General Vladimir Dragomirov was assigned as General Ivanov's chief of staff.

General Ivanov was at last able to persuade the supreme commander, Grand Duke Nikolai Nikolaevich, and on March 19 the directive went out. The northwest front was to assume the defensive while the southwest was to drive through the Carpathians toward Budapest. The sovereign approved the decision, saying, "That is exactly what I would do." The new directive, while ostensibly opening great opportunities for our front, in essence only confirmed existing conditions.

From December on, the armies of the southwest front employed superhuman effort in an attempt to force the Carpathians. In freezing cold, in snowstorms, up steep ice-covered mountain slopes, our forces were literally devastated, creating gaps and melting our ranks. Mobilization plans did not provide for the specific composition of cadres, only numbers, so that the lists of supply corporals, that essential framework of the army, were completely unrealistic. When the war began, therefore, squads marched off to war with five or six officers and up to 50 percent of the corporals serving as privates. The majority of this valuable element perished in the first battles. As cadres melted away, reinforcements arrived untrained and, what was worse, unarmed.

By late 1914 there was already a keen shortage of supplies and cartridges, but the careless and ignorant war minister, Sukhomlinov, succeeded in convincing the sovereign, the Duma, and the public that all was well. Toward the spring of 1915 a terrible crisis became evident in equipment and especially in military stores. The strain of artillery fire in that war reached unprecedented and unexpected dimensions, upsetting all the theoretical calculations made by both our and western European military science. But while industry in the western countries, by extraordinary effort, coped with the critical task of creating huge arsenals and stocks, we were unable to do so.

Only toward the spring of 1916 did we manage, by colossal effort and foreign orders, to acquire heavy artillery and replenish our stock of cartridges and supplies. Of course it was still not on a scale with that of our allies but it was sufficient for prolonging the war with some hope of victory.[1]

The difficulty we encountered in our foreign supply sources was well described in Lloyd George's memoirs.

In the summer of 1915, when Russian armies were shaken and afflicted by the artillery superiority of Germany, military leaders of both countries (England and France) still did not conceive of sharing the undertaking with Russia, did not understand that the success of this enterprise depended on uniting all resources so that each of the participants was placed in the most favorable conditions to attain common goals. To each proposal concerning equipment of Russia, French and British generals answered in 1914, 1915, and 1916 that they could spare nothing which would not prejudice their own needs.

We left Russia to her own fate and by that very act hastened the Balkan tragedy, which played such a role in prolongation of the war.[2]

At that time we had only 155 heavy guns on the entire southwest front while the French, having concentrated huge reserves of equipment in the fall for the battle in Champagne (1915), had twelve times as many on a narrow 25-kilometer front and could afford the fantastic luxury of releasing three million shells.

I recall that in the 8th Army that summer we had only two hundred shells remaining for each gun and had not been promised supply replacement from the artillery department before early fall. Batteries consisting of eight guns each were reduced to six guns and empty ordnance depots were dispatched to the rear as unnecessary.

That spring of 1915 will remain in my memory forever. Grievously bloody battles. Neither cartridges nor shells. The battle near Peremyshl in mid-May meant eleven days of cruel fighting for the Iron Brigade. Eleven days of the dreadful boom of German heavy artillery, literally razing whole rows of trenches along with their defenders. And the silence of my batteries.

We were unable to answer. There was nothing with which to answer. Even rifle shells were rationed. Nearly exhausted regiments repulsed one attack after another with bayonets or, in extreme cases, by firing point blank. I watched as the ranks of my brave riflemen diminished, and I experienced despair as I realized my absurd helplessness. Two regiments were almost annihilated by one burst of enemy fire. When after three days' silence our six-gun batteries received fifty shells, it was reported by telephone to all the regiments. And all companies, all the riflemen, breathed more easily. Under such circumstances no strategic plan toward either Berlin or Budapest would or could be carried out.

During the Carpathian battles, the Iron Brigade fulfilled as usual the role of "fire brigade." Of a series of battle episodes I wish to describe two. In early February the brigade was rushed to the aid and relief of General Kaledin's detachment near Lutoviskii, toward Uzhgorod. That was one of our worst battles. There had been a heavy storm and snow lay in drifts. Kaledin had already sent in his last reserves, an unmounted cavalry brigade. I will never forget that dismal battlefield. Along the road my riflemen took, motionless figures marked the path, protruding from the snow with rifles clutched in their hands. The dead froze in those fields, standing where they were stopped by hostile bullets during sorties. And among them, sinking in snow, mingling with the dead and using corpses for shields, the living went to meet death. The brigade was melting away.

In the line with the Iron Rifles under merciless fire was the one-armed hero Colonel Noskov, who personally led his regiment to attack up the sheer icy cliffs to a height of 804 meters. Death spared him then. But in 1917 two companies calling themselves "revolutionaries" appeared in the regimental staff and killed him. There were wholesale murders then entirely without reason and without punishment, because military officials had been stripped of authority and the Provisional Government was impotent.

During those February battles General Kaledin arrived unexpectedly. He climbed a cliff and sat down with me in a spot that was under merciless bombardment. Kaledin calmly conversed with the officers and riflemen, asking about our activities and losses. That unaffected commander encouraged us all and inspired confidence and respect. Kaledin's operations were crowned with success. The Iron Brigade seized a series of commanding heights including the village of Lutoviskii, the central enemy position. We also took more than two thousand prisoners and threw back the Austrians to the San. For that battle I received the Order of George, third class.

In the background of the Lutoviskii operation there was one amusing battle episode. Mountaineers from the Northern Caucasus who were not subject to military conscription, Chechens, Ingushi, Circassians, and Dagestani, formed on a voluntary basis the Caucasus Native Division, better known by the nickname "*Dikaia*" (Savages). The bravery of their horsemen as well as their wild customs were well known and their flexible understanding of the term "war booty" was heavily experienced by the inhabitants of regions occupied by regiments of the division. Temporarily one brigade of Savages was attached to me and guarded my flank.

At the time the division was commanded by the sovereign's brother, Grand Duke Mikhail Aleksandrovich.[3] His chief of staff, Colonel Iozefovich, was under secret instructions to guard the grand duke's life and to keep him away from areas of actual fire as much as possible. Mikhail Aleksandrovich, modest by nature but by no means a coward, clearly felt oppressed by such guardianship. Once when Iozefovich was sleeping, as was his custom after lunch, the grand duke ordered a mount saddled and with his adjutants came to visit us in the forward positions. When his absence was discovered, the division staff put out the alarm. The awakened Iozefovich rushed after the grand duke and, overtaking him, tried to cajole him into returning to staff. Mikhail Aleksandrovich, obviously embarrassed, ignored him and remained for some time with us.

In early March the Iron Brigade was sent to Mount Odrin with orders to bridge a gap and found itself in a trap. Our position was half-encircled by the enemy's commanding heights from which came individual fire. The situation was untenable and losses ran heavy. Each day lengthened the list of killed and wounded officers and riflemen. The commander of the 16th Regiment, Colonel Baron Bode, was among those killed. I did not see the advantage of maintaining those positions where destruction threatened us, but our departure would have meant abandoning the neighboring 14th Infantry Division, whose chief declared to the staff, "My blood runs cold to think that should we retreat, we would have to fight again for possession of these heights which have cost us rivers of blood." So I remained. The situation was so critical that it required total proximity to the troops. I transferred my field staff into position in the village of Tvorilno.

To illustrate our situation: once at dinner a bullet broke the window and landed on someone's plate. Another stuck in the back of a chair. When anyone went from one hut to another, he took a machine gun with him. The Austrians several times tried to cut us off from the San but were thrown back with great loss. This action was accomplished by the fearless lieutenant colonel of the 13th Regiment, Timanovskii, nicknamed "Iron Stepanich" by the soldiers.

The brigade was dying away. To the rear there was one pathetic bridge with no pontoons over the San, and spring was upon us. Would the turbulent San swell or not? If it swelled, would it carry away the little bridge and leave no exit?

At such a crucial moment, the commander of the 13th Regiment, Colonel Gamburtsev, was gravely wounded by a rifle bullet as he climbed the steps of our staff hut. All staff officers of the regiment were already killed or wounded and there was no one to replace him.

The situation was desperate and I gloomily paced the hut floor. My chief of staff, Colonel Markov, came to me and said, "Your Excellency, give me the 13th Regiment."

"My dear fellow, please don't feel that you must. You see what is going on."

"That is why I am proposing myself, Your Excellency."

So began the battle career of the future famous General Markov, a significant name which will more than once appear in these pages. The comradeship uniting us on the bloody battlefield bound our fates together until his very death. Young, brave, extremely talented, with a marvelous enthusiasm and love for military affairs, Markov preferred front-line duty to staff service. From that time on, he led the glorious regiment from one victory to another. Later he shared with me the sad administration of the 1917 revolutionary army and acquired legendary fame in the civil war. One of the basic regiments of the Volunteer army bore his name.

Having struggled half a day along a road impassable with thick mud, then climbed a mountain path, the chief of our troops, General Count Keller, came to Tvorilno. He familiarized himself with the impossible conditions under which the brigade was perishing and left with the firm intention of removing us from the trap. Several days later we were ordered to withdraw beyond the San.

In early April I received notice from army staff that promotion awaited me. I was to be head of the N-skaia Division. I seriously petitioned them not to "promote" me, persuading them that I could accomplish more with the Iron Brigade than with any division. The matter finally ended there. At the end of April came a welcome alternative. The rifle brigade was named a division and I automatically became chief of the Iron Division.

About the same time the sovereign decided to visit Galicia. Headquarters had intelligence about preparations near Krakov for a blow by Mackensen's German army which was expected to fall upon us very heavily. The tsar's visit, therefore, seemed untimely. Although visits of the tsar to the armies were quite natural, this particular visit to Lvov, the capital of Galicia, that Austrian province being reunited to Russia, seemed premature and overdemonstrative, threatening to lessen the sovereign's prestige. But it appeared that headquarters did not dare point out these facts to the tsar. So he came.

The sovereign visited Lvov on April 22. The next day he arrived in Sambor, where the staff of the 8th Army was located. The Iron Division had the privilege of greeting the sovereign with an honor guard, and the 1st Company of the 16th Rifle Regiment was summoned from the Carpathians for this purpose. In his memoirs General Brusilov said, "I suggested to the sovereign that the 16th Rifle Regiment as well as the whole rifle division nicknamed Iron be honored, having performed with special valor. The 1st Company had fought particularly brilliantly in those days, having annihilated two enemy companies."

The sovereign, as I have already noted, was timid and did not know how to speak with the troops. Perhaps this explains his lack of popularity among the masses also. On the recommendation of Grand Duke Nikolai Nikolaevich, he decorated the entire company with George's Crosses. The company returned with decorations, therefore, but with little to tell their comrades. There were no memorable words.

Since forcing the Carpathians was clearly beyond our strength and supply crises were occurring regularly in battle, on April 11 the high command of the front ordered the 3rd and 8th Armies to assume defensive positions. Toward the beginning of May, the Iron Division occupied a front southeast of Peremyshl opposite Austro-Germans commanded by General Linzingen. The division did not withdraw. We repelled enemy attacks and even counterattacked successfully, but they pressed us heavily.

In view of the importance of this area General Brusilov gradually sent reinforcements and in May eight regiments were placed temporarily under my command. On the extreme left flank of my position stood the second best regiment, formed from cadres of the Arkhangelogorodsk Regiment which I had commanded before the war. I could not resist the temptation to visit my old regiment, so with difficulty I made my way to their position. All approaches to them were already under such heavy fire that kitchens and supplies could be brought in only at night. I spent two or three hours with my old officers, reminiscing and becoming acquainted with their battle situation. I did not suspect that this would be our last meeting.

The division chiefs had not been briefed on the extremely critical nature of our general situation at the front. Among the troops of my detachment, for example, our front conditions were considered firmly under control.

Mackensen's 2nd Army, composed of ten German divisions with seven hundred guns, struck at our 3rd Army with its five and a half divisions and one hundred sixty guns. Our front was soon broken near Gorlitsa. Only then did General Ivanov, who had previously concentrated all available troops in the Carpathians, send corps to reinforce the 3rd Army. But it was too late.

A situation developed which required swift retreat by the army. This was the opinion of the chief of staff of the southwest front and commander of the army, General Radko-Dmitriev.[4] General Ivanov and headquarters ordered, "Do not give up an inch of ground."

An unequal battle ensued. The 3rd Army was beaten and driven back. The 24th Corps fell into an especially grievous situation. Kornilov's division (the 48th) was entirely surrounded and despite heroic resistance almost annihilated, its remnants being captured. General Kornilov and his staff, barely escaping from the hands of the enemy, hid in the forest for several days trying to make their way through to us. But they were discovered and captured. For more than a year Kornilov sat in an Austrian prison until in July 1916 he managed to escape with rare boldness and dexterity, dressed in the uniform of an Austrian soldier. After hardships and many adventures he made his way across the Romanian border to Russia. For this he received the Order of George, third class, and was named commander of the 25th Corps.

But the 3rd Army retreat bared the flank of the 8th Army and on May 10 the southwest front was ordered to fall back to the San and the Dniester.

During that first year of war I came to advance as well as to retreat in response to conditions at the front. But retreating appeared to me as some kind of temporary maneuver. Now the situation and even the tone in which orders were given from above testified to the catastrophe facing us. For the first time I felt something resembling despair. That despair increased as I learned that the unit situated just east of me had orders not to withdraw and that as a result our front had been bent, nearly in a direct angle, toward units of my detachment, particularly toward the position of the former Arkhangelogorodsk Regiment. In other words, the regiment was enveloped and was under fire from both sides by the advancing Germans.[5]

The army staff withdrew in such haste that they severed telephone connections and there was no way to contest their orders. I realized that the regiment was doomed. Under cover of night I led my troops out, experiencing dread for the fate of the regiment. By the next morning it was destroyed. Most of my former brothers-in-arms had perished. The Great Retreat of the Russian army began.

CHAPTER 34   1915: CONTINUATION OF THE WAR

The armies of the southwest front held for a time on the line from Peremyshl to Mikolaev and farther along the Dniester. They held out against ever-stronger attacks by the Austro-Germans, even enjoying some successes in which they defeated and threw back the Austrians who made an attempt via the Dniester to drive to the rear to Lvov. On May 24, however, General Mackensen renewed the attack and by June 3 he had taken Peremyshl and controlled the central San.

Those battles south of Peremyshl were the bloodiest of all for us. The Iron Division suffered especially. The 13th and 14th Regiments were literally blown away by incredibly heavy German artillery fire. The first and only time I saw my brave Colonel Markov in a state approaching despair was when he brought the remnants of his squad out of battle. He was covered with blood which had gushed all over him when the 14th Regiment commander, walking beside him, had his head torn off by a bomb splinter. The sight of the colonel's headless torso standing for several seconds in a living pose was impossible to forget.

Retreating step by step, our army left the San and on June 22 we lost Lvov as well. The Russian counterattack and the necessity to pull the rear tighter forced Mackensen to halt the attack a while in the first half of July. It was resumed, however, and toward August we withdrew from the Bug.

A large German force, even before bursting through our front at Gorlitsa, attacked General Alekseev's northwest front and pushed our troops back in Courland, capturing Libav. In these difficult circumstances we gave battle on that front, from which I will cite two episodes.

Prosnyich, with the 1st Russian Army, sustained in the course of six days the strongest shock from the 12th German Army, one and a half times superior in numbers, and was overwhelmed by a strength represented by 1,264 guns as compared with our 317.

At the end of May, south of Warsaw on our 2nd Army front, the Germans unleashed their first gas attack. We repulsed their attacks despite the unexpectedness of this unlawful method of war and our lack of anti-gas equipment (as a result of which we had nine thousand men poisoned).

In early July, in conjunction with the retreat from the southwest front, headquarters abandoned the untenable situation in Poland, and General Alekseev received orders to lead the troops behind the Vistula. Thus began the great three-month retreat which was marked by heavy battles and punctuated with severe losses for us. The worst circumstances occurred near Vilna (in late August and early September) when, with a simultaneous frontal attack and breakthrough in our rear by six horse divisions near Sventsian, the Germans made an extraordinary effort to encircle and destroy our 10th Army. But the persistence of the Russian troops and the skill of General Alekseev neutralized the breakthrough, and our army was extricated from the encirclement.

Toward the end of September the retreating Russian front stabilized along the Riga-Dvinsk-Chernovits line. More significant was the direction of the German movement toward the capitals (Moscow and Petrograd). Headquarters therefore gave seven armies to Alekseev, leaving three armies, south of Polesya, to Ivanov.

The great retreat cost us dearly. Our losses ran to more than a million men. Huge territories, part of the Pre-Baltic, Poland, Lithuania, part of Belorussia, and almost all of Galicia, were gone. The cadres were thinned. The armies' spirits were low. Yet in spite of this our retreat by no means had the character of panic. We dealt the

Germans heavy losses, and due to our unceasing counterattacks the Austrians lost hundreds of thousands in prisoners alone. Our front, lacking ammunition and under strong pressure from the enemy, retreated slowly, step by step, avoiding encirclement and captivity for whole corps or armies, as happened later under the Soviet regime in 1941 during the first period of World War II. In the fall of 1915 the Austro-German attack began to falter.

Part of Russia's forces were concentrated in the Caucasus theater. In late October 1914 Turkey had entered the war on the side of the Central powers. Our forces, though they were rather weak at the time, stopped three Turkish corps, attacking the frontier from Erzerum to Kars. We spent the winter there. But in December the Turkish chief commander, Enver Pasha, risked an attack on Kars with a force of 90,000 during a cruel ice storm, moving along mountain roads drifted with snow.[1] In a battle near Saryikamyish the Turks were completely routed. Half of them froze to death and the others were killed or taken prisoner. Throughout 1915 relative calm reigned on the Caucasus front.

In 1915, the most difficult year of the war, the center of gravity for the entire world war shifted to Russia. At the beginning of the year the Anglo-French launched a series of special attacks in Champagne and near Arras, attacks lacking strategic significance. On May 9 Foch and the French attacked the Germans in Artois in a battle which lasted one and a half months. At great loss they altered the front, taking forty kilometers of territory.

In late June an inter-allied conference held at Chantilly decided that in view of conditions on the Russian front the Anglo-French would take the offensive again in Champagne and Artois. Preparations began on July 12, but for reasons which I will not attempt to analyze here the attack was delayed until September 25, when our great retreat was finished. The French ordered an attack in Champagne, being in a position of superiority. They applied an immense quantity of artillery. Seven days of artillery preparation were rewarded by seizure of the front lines of German fortifications. They took 25,000 prisoners plus 150 guns. But in the second lines the attack bogged down. Heavy losses then made General Joffre stop the attack. While attributing due heroism to our allies, I must note their general reluctance to engage the broad task and their obsessive desire to exhaust the enemy. Those flaws influenced circumstances on our front and partly explain our lack of success.

For the Entente 1915 was generally a year of failure. The Gallipoli operation conducted by the Anglo-French at Churchill's initiative from March 20 until December 20, notwithstanding the immense superiority of the English fleet, ended in catastrophe: the loss of 146,000 men (as opposed to Turkish-German losses of 186,000) and evacuation of the western near-coastal regions of Gallipoli with the abandonment of all matériel units. At the end of 1915 the English suffered a serious defeat from the Turks in Mesopotamia near Baghdad.

In October Bulgaria joined Germany, contrary to the traditional alignment of its people, because of its Germanophile dynasty (Coburg) and the government. On October 15 several French and English divisions landed at Salonika to which were later added four Russian brigades, all commanded by French General Sarrail. This army, stretching from the Aegean to the Adriatic, had one German and two Bulgarian armies opposing it. It tried several times to penetrate the enemy front without success, then assumed defensive positions.

Perhaps compensating the Allies, Italy moved against Austria on May 23, 1915. Italy did not declare war on Germany until August 27, 1916, but German troops had fought even earlier on the Italian front. Italy diverted part of Austria's strength but I consider that the ability of the Italian troops was rather insignificant, adding little to the Allied military potential. As evidence I would point out that although Italy had twelve corps and several divisions of a militia nature and raised one million men in the first mobilization call, it concentrated its main strength at Izontsa and attacked four times without success. Certainly the Austro-German command did not suspend general attacks on Russian frontiers. While keeping an eye on the Italian front, they reinforced it with two and a half divisions from the Russian front, five divisions from the Serbian front, and one German division of heavy artillery. But they organized only temporary defenses on the Italian front.

The ineptitude of the Italians, the immobility of the Salonika front, and the great Russian retreat hastened Serbia's fate. For more than a year the small Serbian army had fought tenaciously, lacking essential equipment but possessing a strong spirit, repulsing three attacks by Austria-Hungary. In October 1915 an enemy force three times stronger fell upon Serbia (twenty-nine Austro-German-Bulgarian divisions against eleven Serbian) and the Serbian army, after two months of desperate resistance, was crushed. With Prince Alexander at the head, its remnants (55,000 men), carrying their injured king on a litter, abandoned guns and baggage and with incredible difficulty made their way over mountain paths through Albania to the Adriatic Sea, where they were transported by the Allies to the island of Corfu.[2] Rested and replenished, these troops reentered the war in 1916 under General Sarrail in the Macedonian theater.

On arriving at the Riga-Pinsk-Chernovits line, the German high command ordered their exhausted troops into battle positions. The Austrian chief commander, General Conrad, went on asking for further attack, with the purpose of recovering the entire portion of Galicia still remaining under Russian authority and seizing the important railway junction of Rovno which opened, through Baranovichi, direct connections between the Austrian and German fronts. These disagreements led to the transfer of all German divisions from the Austrian front to the north German front. However, General Conrad led an attack on Lutsk-Rovno.[3]

At the end of August I received an order from General Brusilov to go immediately to the hamlet of Klevan, situated twenty *versts* from us between Lutsk and Rovno, where the 8th Army staff was located. Leading the division in a forced march to Klevan, I found by night complete chaos there. In the region of Lutsk the Austrians pressed so hard on our military guard and mounted cavalry that no front actually remained. The road to Rovno was open.

I deployed the division along both sides of the highway and after a lengthy search finally established telephone contact with the army staff. I learned that the situation was critical and the staff proposed to evacuate Rovno. Near Klevan they were hurriedly forming a new corps (the 39th) from militia guards who, in Brusilov's words, "fell first in battle and did not represent any real military strength." I became subordinate to the head of that corps, General Stelnitskii. Brusilov added that he hoped the front would "gain satisfactory stability, thus reinforced by the Iron Division, to halt the enemy on the Stubel River."

The situation of the division was unusually precarious. Austria brought fresh troops to the battle and positioned them to the left, opposite our army's right flank. Because of this my front was overextended, finally reaching fifteen kilometers. The enemy significantly outnumbered us, almost three to one, and to defend ourselves under such circumstances was impossible. I decided, therefore, to attack. From August 21 on I attacked three times. These three attacks from the Iron Division attracted about three Austrian divisions to its front and stopped an encircling movement by the enemy. But in heavy battle on September 8–11 the Austrians succeeded in pushing us back beyond the Goryin River.

Meanwhile General Brusilov ordered General Zaionchkovskii's 30th Corps toward the Goryin to find an outlet from the increasingly difficult situation. They were to attack with the right wing of the army (the 3rd Corps) and establish themselves on the River Styr. After prolonged controversy with General Ivanov (the chief commander was reluctant to move on such strong forces), Brusilov prevailed and the attack began.

The Iron Division formed the center of the front. Brilliant attacks by columns of General Stankevich and Colonel Markov put the enemy to rout on September 16 and 17 after part of their troops had been destroyed and part taken prisoner. On September 18, on their own initiative, our division followed the rapidly retreating Austrians by forced march to Lutsk.

On September 19 I attacked frontally the already-strong Lutsk fortifications. The battle continued unceasingly all day and all night. Before us were two and a half divisions of Austrians solidly ensconced in well-prepared entrenchments. Our riflemen tore into their positions, taking machine guns and prisoners and seizing the first two rows of trenches. But further movement proved beyond our strength. We had suffered severe losses and the troops were in disarray. General Stelnitskii did not offer me his militia units since he understood the hopelessness of it.

To assist my no longer successful frontal attacks General Brusilov ordered General Zaionchkovskii to attack Lutsk from the north. I must insert a remark here which is not entirely of a military nature, so as to explain the further course of events.

By a peculiarity of his nature Zaionchkovskii contributed a comical element to the otherwise harsh and epic war atmosphere. He relayed Brusilov's order to the corps in his own verbose style. He began by saying that since the Iron Division was unable to take Lutsk, this honorable but difficult responsibility rested upon them. He reminded them that the feast of the Birth of Our Lady would occur on September 21 and he invited the troops to "honor God's mother" with victory. In conclusion he declaimed, "The bottle has been uncorked. Whether we drink wine or poison will be seen on the morrow." I learned about this only after the operation. Such histrionics were not at all typical of our military leaders.

Zaionchkovskii did not "drink wine" on the "morrow." First of all, his attack did not move forward. He demanded that the army staff hand over to him one of my regiments (which they did, leaving me with only three). Besides that, on the night of September 23 I received an order from staff that since General Zaionchkovskii was so strongly hindered by enemy artillery fire, I was, at his request, to continue firing from all my batteries throughout the night "to divert the hostile fire."

To fire throughout the night when we were rationing each projectile! But I executed the order. Probably only someone who has been in battle under such circumstances can understand my feelings. The Austrians did not answer our fire. Only three shots came from them, including the one grenade which fell into the chimney of the staff hut. Luckily it did not explode. But that absurd firing had revealed to the enemy the position of our concealed battery and by morning the situation of my division became tragic. I summoned my three regimental commanders by telephone and, outlining the arrangement to them, said, "Our position is rotten. We have no alternative but to attack." All three commanders agreed and I ordered the division to attack Lutsk at daybreak.

Brusilov later wrote about that action, "Denikin, without considering the hardship, flung himself at Lutsk with one swinging movement and took it. During the battle he went personally by automobile into the city and sent me a telegram from there saying that the 4th Rifle Division had taken Lutsk." Immediately after my telegram Zaionchkovskii informed staff that he had taken Lutsk. To his telegram Brusilov made the jocular addition, "and took General Denikin prisoner there." For taking Lutsk that first time (incidentally, I had to take it again in 1916) I was promoted to lieutenant general. Zaionchkovskii demanded a George's Cross but he did not receive it. It was evident that I had made a bitter enemy.

In the entire Lutsk operation the Iron Division captured 158 officers and 9,773 soldiers, a number equal to our own personnel. But being thoroughly fatigued, we were relieved after two days and according to custom transferred to command army reserves. Our neighboring 8th and 30th Corps, upsetting the Austrians, drove to the Styr. General Conrad, weakened by the destruction of his left wing, turned to the German command for assistance. To the north of Lutsk we soon uncovered a German corps moving to challenge our right flank.

What happened afterward was utterly absurd. I cannot yet explain the circumstances from primary sources because they are in Bolshevik hands. But if one may believe General Brusilov, he received the following order from the commander in chief: "Abandon Lutsk and lead the troops back to their original positions" (to Klevan). Corps General Zaionchkovskii, with the Iron Division assigned to him, was ordered to "hide in the forest east of Kolki and when the Germans reach the road from Kolki to Klevan, strike them unexpectedly in the flank. The remainder of the front will then go on the attack." This strategy, like a children's game of hide and seek, illustrates the defective military qualifications of such men as General Ivanov and his new chief of staff General Savich.[4] The Styr-Lutsk line, which represented such an expenditure of effort, was abandoned without pressure from the enemy. The entire Lutsk operation, which had cost us so much blood and so many losses, went for nothing. The Iron Division had lost 40 percent of its personnel.

The corps did not succeed, of course, in "hiding in the forest." As a result both adversaries, Russian and German, were deployed opposite each other in the dense swampy forest. We constructed fortifications from felled trees wound with barbed wire, and both sides went on the defensive.

Using the pretext of the woody site, the staff took away my artillery and gave it to another division. When I appealed to General Zaionchkovskii, he coldly showed me his proposed directive that three of my regiments be transferred to his division and a fourth taken to corps reserves. The Iron Division thus no longer existed and I was out of command. I did not object at the time but only smiled to myself, knowing that such an order could not be executed. Actually, when he received the directive from Zaionchkovskii Brusilov quickly ordered him to "return the division to its superior and assign them some independent operation."

The corps commander deployed us along the wooded River Karmin and our mishaps began. Zaionchkovskii ordered the division to attack the Germans confronting us. I tried to attack once, then once again, suffering losses each time. As we were repulsed, I was convinced that without artillery it was impossible to achieve success in the swamp against already fortified Germans. During the course of several days the corps commander repeatedly sent sharp and categorical orders for us to attack, threatening to remove me from command for insubordination. I could not lead men to certain destruction, and since I considered the operation clearly doomed I did not answer the orders. Zaionchkovskii complained to the army staff which finally demanded direct telegraphic connection with me. General Brusilov telegraphed, "What is going on there? Please explain."

I replied that I had participated personally in the last attack by the 14th Regiment and I outlined the entire situation, explaining why it was clear to me and to my commanders that the division was headed for slaughter. An hour later Zaionchkovskii received an order from Brusilov to release the Iron Division and replace it by his own units that same night. The Iron Division was to be sent once more to the command army reserves. That was the first and only time I encountered such a cruel and offensive attitude toward the division and myself. Everywhere else our "fire brigade" had appeared, we had met expressions of relief and gratitude.

With that episode the Iron Division's "vagabond life," farmed out as it had been to various corps, ended. The new 40th Corps was formed within the effective force of the 8th Army, and my division entered it along with the distinguished 2nd Rifle Division, headed by the worthy General Belozor. General Brusilov expressed the following opinion about the corps: "Considering the effective force of its troops, this corps was among the finest in the entire Russian army."

Immediately upon formation, the 40th Corps departed to enter the war. Between the southwest and west fronts there was an interval of sixty kilometers patrolled only by unmounted cavalry. True, that was a woody, swampy line but it was not impassable. Meanwhile the Germans advanced increasingly toward the north and occupied Chartoriiskii, threatening to encircle our army's right flank and break through its junction with our western front. General Brusilov decided to repeat a short blow with the right wing (the 30th, 40th, and Horse Corps) to rectify the front, taking it again to the River Styr.

Thus began the Chartoriiskii operation, one of the most glorious chapters in the Iron Division's history. "The 4th Rifle Division," wrote Brusilov, "was charged with the heaviest responsibility, that of defeating the German division and taking Chartoriiskii."

On the night of October 16 our division turned against Chartoriiskii and Novoselok and the next night we forded the Styr. In two days we overran, defeated, and took captive the Austro-Germans on an eighteen-kilometer front. The left column (General Stankevich, Colonel Markov, and Captain Udovichenko), which I directed to the southwest and west, upset the enemy and went irresistibly forward. At the same time Colonel Biriukov's right column (16th Rifle Regiment) rushed into Chartoriiskii in one swoop. Without firing they attacked the city from the rear and took it with one burst, almost destroying the 1st Grenadier Crown-Prince Regiment located there, capturing their guns, machine guns, and baggage. Incidentally, because his regimental commander was ailing, Captain Udovichenko actually led the regiment into battle. For the Chartoriiskii operation I recommended him for a George's Cross, third degree, which he received.

The 2nd Rifle Division, having crossed the Styr on a bridge erected by the 16th Regiment, also successfully pursued the enemy to the right of us. But on reaching Lisovo, they were unable to push the attack farther because of the failures of neighboring cavalry corps.

Toward morning on October 20 the Iron Division finished its breakthrough, eighteen kilometers wide along the front and more than twenty kilometers in depth, describing the letter "π". We encountered stubborn resistance to the right and left but nothing from the front. Our artillery threatened the city of Kolki in the deep rear of our enemy, where all the staffs of their left groups were located. Austro-German confusion was so great that for two days at the front Colonel Markov received enemy baggage, transport, and mail, which of course he accepted. We happened to overhear a telephone conversation of the general commanding the region of Kolki in which he informed his superior of the hopelessness of his circumstances. Later on, studying the Austrian official history of the battle, I found in every line confirmation of their destruction then. A jolt from the direction of General Zaionchkovskii's 30th Corps, situated to the left of us, would have broken through the entire left flank of the Austrian army.

As early as October 5 I had repeatedly communicated with the corps staff and the army staff, requesting that they move the right flank of the 30th Corps forward, if only to secure my division's position. The army staff applied pressure to Zaionchkovskii, but he refused. "Denikin says," he told the operations head of the army staff, "that he has already occupied Yablonka but I doubt it because the resistance offered my front by the enemy has by no means lessened." Although only mounted units opposed the right flank of the 30th Corps after I captured Kulikovich, Zaionchkovskii did not budge during the operation.

Seeing the successful advance of the 2nd and 4th Rifle Divisions, I persistently reported the necessity to rush fresh forces into the breach we had made. The quartermaster general branch of the staff warmly supported me but Brusilov, usually so energetic, hesitated for some reason. And the moment slipped away. When the 105th Division was finally sent to me, it was already too late. Besides, this division, being militia, retreated so hastily at the first blow from the enemy that they only complicated our situation.

The enemy had also hurriedly drawn together reinforcements from all sides. In the official Austrian description of the battle I noted at least fifteen regiments in the action against my front, not counting all the command rolls. Gradually the Austro-German ring compressed around our forward zone division. Colonel Markov, who occupied the advance position near Yablonka, reported by telephone to me, "What unique circumstances. I am now supervising a battle on all four sides. It is so impossible as to be amusing."

Now, looking back on those far-off events with some "historical perspective," I still experience emotions of deep pride for the inextinguishable military spirit, heroism, and confident patriotism of my comrades in arms of the Iron Division. Not only Markov but the entire division fought on the four-sided front for two days and nights

(October 20–21). But there was no panic nor the least depression of spirit or hesitation in the ranks of my glorious riflemen.

Toward the morning of October 22 by orders from the corps commander, the division went on to Komarov. Our breaking through the enemy lines brought no advantage. The augmented enemy continued for two weeks to launch vain attacks on our Chartoriiskii front. Each time they were firmly thrown back by Russian troops. On November 9 the Iron Division for the last time counterattacked along its entire front, defeating the Austro-Germans and dealing them great losses. In the whole Chartoriiskii operation we took 8,500 uninjured prisoners.

In mid-November a full calm settled over our front which lasted until the spring of 1916, our first breathing space since the war began. Moreover the tactical chore assigned to the 8th Army had been fulfilled. We were solidly asserted on the Styr.

Now headquarters and the supreme command staff directed their attention to the loss of earlier unexpected strategic possibilities. The next step was to find the culprits. Here again Brusilov gave several characteristic sketches in his memoirs. He explained the history of our breakthrough in this way: "Two neighbors, commanders of the 30th and 40th Corps, were unable to agree and complained about each other constantly. The commander of the 40th Corps, General Voronin, was found guilty of indecision (!) and was dismissed. But time was lost. The Germans succeeded in sending significant support to their almost defeated units." Thus General Voronin, whose troops invaded deep into hostile territory and created the above-mentioned strategic possibility, was removed from command, while General Zaionchkovskii, who neither obeyed orders nor moved during the breakthrough, went unpunished.

On September 5 the sovereign had transferred Grand Duke Nikolai Nikolaevich to the Caucasus as commander in chief and personally assumed supreme command of the Russian armed forces. His decision was preceded by a series of fruitless political maneuvers, including warnings written individually by eight ministers attempting to dissuade the tsar from this dangerous step.[5] Their motive was to point out the difficulty of combining state administration with military command. The opposition ministers — to prevent the sovereign's decision and especially considering the absence of any fundamental government program in the general political views of the chairman of the Council of Ministers, Goremykin — reported that they would "lose faith and would be unable to serve him (the tsar) and the Fatherland advantageously."[6] The other official motive was the risk to the tsar in taking full responsibility for the army in this troublesome period of military failure.

The real motive, which troubled many but was never officially expressed, was fear that the new supreme commander's lack of military knowledge and experience would complicate the army's already difficult position. Also there was apprehension that Rasputin's influence would be reflected in the tsar's actions.[7]

The tsar's assumption of command, a significant act, was preceded by the following circumstances. Empress Alexandra Fedorovna suspected Grand Duke Nikolai Nikolaevich of the desire to harm Nicholas II and even to usurp his authority. Her suspicion was quite without basis because the grand duke was not only absolutely loyal to the sovereign but referred to the legitimate monarchy with an air of mysticism. Since then the tsarina's letters have become public property, those letters in which she many times with the persistence and passion characteristic of sick people warned her husband about dangers to him from Nikolai Nikolaevich. She wrote, for example, on September 30, 1914: "Rasputin fears that the *galki* want him (Nikolai Nikolaevich) to place them on the throne of Poland or Galicia. This is their aim. But I told Anna to assure him (Rasputin) that even from a feeling of gratitude you would never risk this. Grigorii loves you jealously and cannot bear that N. plays any role."[8]

June 12, 1915: "Nikolasha is far from clever, obstinate, and led by others."

June 16, 1915: "I have absolutely no trust in N. . . . . He has opposed the person sent by God; therefore his actions cannot be pleasing to God and his opinion cannot be correct."

June 17: "It is not proper for Nikolasha to meddle in other people's business. . . . It is the fault of N. and Witte that the Duma exists."

June 25, 1915: "Things are not going as they should. That is why N. stays in close contact with you, in order to compel you to accept all his ideas and bad advice."

September 21, 1916: "No one has the right to usurp your prerogative. This distresses me very much." (The matter referred to Nikolai Nikolaevich.)

On November 5, 1916, the tsarina communicated that "Nik., Orlov, and Yanushkevich wish to drive you away (this is not gossip — Orlov already has all the papers ready) and to send me to a convent."

Alexandra Fedorovna was supported and inspired in her convictions by Rasputin. Actually, to their misfortune, it was the family of Nikolai Nikolaevich which first introduced Rasputin into the tsarist circle as the "saintly *starets*" and prophet.[9] Later, when his true nature was revealed, Nikolai Nikolaevich and his kin maintained a hostile attitude toward the "*starets*." Rasputin knew this and he repaid them with malevolent hatred. Nevertheless he attempted several times to control actions at headquarters. When his worshippers hinted at this possibility, they invariably received the answer from the grand duke, "If he comes here, I will order him hanged."[10]

That Rasputin played a prominent role in the sovereign's decision to assume supreme command is certain. This is confirmed in the empress's letters.

August 3, 1916: "Do not fear to pronounce the name Grigorii in speaking with him (General Alekseev). Thanks to Him, you have remained sound since a year ago when you took command when everyone was against you. Tell him this and he will then understand His (Rasputin's) wisdom."

December 9, 1916: "Our friend says that trouble is coming and that if He (the emperor) had not replaced N. N., then He (the emperor) would have been driven from the throne by now."

There is no basis for believing that the importunate notions of Alexandra Fedorovna concerning the grand duke estranged him from the sovereign. At least neither in the tsar's relations with Nikolai Nikolaevich nor in his actions or judgments did this ever appear to be the case. And if the influence of the empress and Rasputin in this direction was that powerful, then in all probability it may be explained by the sovereign's religious understanding of his predestined role and his "God-given" authority. After the appearance of the sovereign's imperial edict taking over supreme command, Alexandra Fedorovna wrote to him, "This marks the triumph of your tsardom. He said so and I believe it implicitly." Certainly she believed it. But it is also certain that the sovereign, a quiet, well-balanced person, did not go as far as she into mysticism. He was completely sincere, for example, when he said to the ministers who opposed his intention, "At such a critical moment the supreme commander of the army must take actual charge."

The change of supreme command did not create a great stir in the army. Command personnel were apprehensive about the outcome of the war but the supreme commander's designation of General Alekseev as chief of staff calmed everyone. As for the soldiers, they were not acquainted with hierarchical details anyway. In their eyes the sovereign had always been head of the army. One disturbing notion deep in the consciousness of the people was widely reflected, however, in letters examined by the military censors. Everyone considered the tsar to be "unfortunate" and an "unlucky fellow." They mentioned as evidence such things as Khodynka, the Japanese War, and the first revolution, as well as the incurable affliction of his only son the tsarevich.[11]

General Mikhail Vasilievich Alekseev actually commanded all the Russian armed forces. Military operations were planned and conducted according to his acknowledged wise strategy, but the "order" came from the "supreme commander." It could have worked successfully but the sovereign lacked sufficient authority, firmness, and strength. For similar reasons, General Alekseev was unable to command "in the name of the tsar." As a result, in the second period of the war even more than in the first, dissension arose and commanders at the front increasingly tended to follow their own local designs. Headquarters only tried to maintain harmony by means of conditions and compromises which approached the absurd at times, as for example in the spring of 1916 when two high commanders shrugged off an important operation plan with complete impunity. I will relate that incident in the next chapter.

CHAPTER 35   1916: AT THE FRONT

Having received more or less sufficient supplies of arms, cartridges, and projectiles, the Russian army by 1916 had attracted the principal attention of the enemy, with forces one and a half times larger than those deployed on the western front. Russia became the chief theater of the world war.

The Russian command, though left to its fate during the great retreat of 1915, never refused aid to its allies, even when it was clearly prejudicial to our own interests. I emphasize this fact to show that we were true to our word, to an obligation which no one in the Russian army questioned at the time. There is lacking nowadays that basic element of respect and chivalry which is the foundation of civilization.

The year 1915 was marked by signal lack of success in the Anglo-French conflict with the Turks in the Straits, in the Balkans, and in Asia Minor. To divert Turkish efforts, the Caucasus army launched a broad offensive in the harsh mountain winter and Asiatic passes (126 Russian battalions against 132 Turkish) and on February 16, General Yudenich defeated the Turks and took the key stronghold of Erzerum. As a result of this triumph not only Turkish divisions from all fronts but also large units of general reserves were sent against the Russian army. Consequently the goals of the Turkish operation in Egypt against the Suez Canal went awry, while the situation of the English in Mesopotamia improved. The Caucasus army, continuing the attack to the end of the summer, seized Trapezund and Erzinjan and penetrated deeply across the frontiers of Turkey.

The Allies were to launch an attack by spring, but the Germans anticipated them and began an engagement on February 21 designed to breach the front at Verdun. General Joffre insistently requested that we divert German reserves and therefore our headquarters staged an offensive with troops from the northern and western fronts in March, in the spring, the most unfavorable season for us, the season when the rivers overflow and make the roads so bad.

That operation — hastily organized and poorly executed, fought in passes concealed by melting snow — literally bogged down in the mire and ended in complete failure. It was a pathetic prelude to the imminent June offensive and the failure was sadly reflected in troop morale and even more in the outlook of the high command.

At that time a change occurred in our command. The chief of staff at the front, General Vladimir Dragomirov, was blamed entirely without basis for failures on the southwest front and he was dismissed, receiving the 8th Corps. Chief commander Ivanov unjustly and pointedly accused General Brusilov, but headquarters finally supported Brusilov. As part of the insulting and unjust persecution of General Brusilov's staff, his chief of staff, General Lomnovskii, quit and went to the front, receiving the 15th Division. Ultimately however, Ivanov's unsuccessful leadership, which continued to the beginning of 1916, particularly in the operations of the 7th and 9th Armies, caused him to be relieved. On April 5 General Brusilov was appointed commander of the southwest front.

Directives for the imminent June offensive were established in a military council at headquarters on April 14. Later, as chief of staff for the supreme command, I became acquainted with the protocols of that historic session, which were interesting for their strategic and especially their psychological aspects.

The following persons were present: the sovereign, chief commanders Kuropatkin, Ebert, Brusilov (with their chiefs of staff), Ivanov, and Shuvalov, Grand Duke Sergei Mikhailovich, and Alekseev. General Alekseev announced the plan of attack. The main blow would be directed toward Vilna, and on to Berlin. It would be dealt on the western front by General Ebert, to whom were directed large reserve units of heavy artillery and all the corps from the reserves of the supreme command, a strength of arms unprecedented on the Russian fronts. For the first time we outnumbered the confronting Germans by more than one and a half times.

General Kuropatkin's northern front, reinforced by part of the general reserves and heavy artillery, would also participate in the Vilna attack. Roughly 70 percent of the Russian forces were directed to northern Polesya (on the northern and western fronts), while the south (the southwest front) retained 30 percent. The southwest front, incidentally, was to remain passive and come into play only if the main attack were successful.

Generals Ebert and Kuropatkin cited the strength of the enemy positions and especially their fully prepared heavy artillery, and thought the intended attack was hopeless. In heated words General Brusilov asserted that his troops maintained full military spirit, that the attack was possible, and that, with the present relative strength of forces, he did not doubt the possibilities for success. But, he pleaded, he could not imagine his front remaining inactive during the general offensive and requested that his troops should not be the ones to remain in reserve.

When General Alekseev objected to the pessimistic reactions of Ebert and Kuropatkin, they ameliorated their conclusions somewhat. They would attack, they said, but they could not guarantee success. And General Alekseev agreed to active participation in the attack by Brusilov's southwest front but emphasized that he could provide reinforcements of neither troops nor artillery so that Brusilov would have to be content with his own forces.

The main blow was to go, therefore, toward Vilna and a secondary one (the southwest front) toward Lutsk. The sovereign did not express his opinion but merely confirmed Alekseev's proposal. It is interesting that General Ivanov went to the sovereign after the meeting with tears in his eyes, begging him not to permit Brusilov's attack because the troops were exhausted and the action would end in catastrophe. The tsar refused to alter the plans.

Thus the decision was reached to launch a general offensive. The chief commanders on both active fronts had clearly lost spirit and lacked confidence in the success of the undertaking. Lacking the proper boldness, they could infect their leaders and troops with pessimism. I cannot understand why the two men were not dismissed and replaced by other capable leaders who favored attack.

Brusilov assembled all his marshals: Kaledin (8th Army), Sakharov (11th), Shcherbachev (7th), Krymov (9th). Shcherbachev alone expressed misgivings and aversion to the attack. All the rest supported the chief commander. The offensive was scheduled for the first of June. But on May 24 a telegram came from General Alekseev: "The Italians have suffered a crushing defeat and urgently request our assistance. Is it possible to attack now?"[1]

REFERENCE NOTES

REFERENCE NOTES

CHAPTER 1

1. According to the Julian calendar, used in Russia before 1918, Denikin's birth date was December 4, 1872, as stated. Dates elsewhere throughout conform to the Western (Gregorian) calendar unless otherwise indicated. Vlotslavsk, where Denikin spent most of his childhood years, was a district capital of 23,065 persons, predominantly Polish, at the time of the only complete tsarist census in 1897. It was situated on the Vistula River not far from the border which separated Prussian from Russian Poland. Only its river location and proximity to Warsaw prevented the stagnation typical of most Russian Polish garrison towns such as Bela where Denikin was stationed in the years preceding the Russo-Japanese War.

2. During the reign of Nicholas I (1825–1855), quotas of recruits were assigned by region and then subdivided to authorities of estates, villages, and urban communities. Recruits were drawn from those subject to the poll tax (peasants, artisans, and burghers) for a twenty-five year term. Landlords of private estates selected peasants for service and some used the army as a penal institution, choosing those peasants who were least useful to them. Nicholas N. Golovine, *The Russian Army in the World War*, p. 1; Nikolaus Basseches, *The Unknown Army*, p. 53.

3. Prince Peter Kropotkin, whose older brothers served in the army of Nicholas I, reported that beatings by officers and floggings with birch rods were commonplace. Courts-martial frequently sentenced prisoners to be dragged three to seven times between a thousand soldiers placed in opposing rows and armed with sticks. Sergeants supervised the punishment to see that blows were struck with full force. If the prisoner died in the process, "execution of the sentence was completed on the corpse." Kropotkin, *Memoirs of a Revolutionist*, p. 54.

4. Ensign, the lowest officer rank in the old Russian army, was equivalent to a second lieutenant in the United States army.

5. The people of Russian Poland hoped for a degree of autonomy when Alexander II (1855–1881) took the throne. Instead, the new emperor publicly pledged himself to continue the rigid regime established by his father in Poland. Demonstrations followed, harshly suppressed by Russian troops. The Polish statesman Alexander Wielopolski persuaded the emperor to make concessions to Polish nationalism, consistent with autocratic principles, but the Poles wanted restoration of the constitution of 1815. By conscripting the most disaffected elements in the Polish towns in an attempt to curb growing insurrection, the Russian government only emphasized the role of the military as the immediate enemy of the Polish people. Isolated skirmishes became outright rebellion. Additional troops were moved into the Polish provinces and suppressed the insurrection after eighteen months of partisan warfare. The last vestiges of Polish autonomy were abolished and the area was fully incorporated into the administrative structure of the Russian empire. Joseph Pilsudski, *The Memories of a Polish Revolutionary and Soldier*, pp. 155–156, n.1; Michael T. Florinsky, *Russia: A History and an Interpretation*, 2:910–916.

6. The Crimean War (1854–1856), a struggle of complex origins between Russia on

the one hand and the Ottoman Empire, France, and England on the other, is usually interpreted as part of the traditional Russian drive for the Straits. Hungarians, under the leadership of Louis Kossuth, rebelled against Austria in 1848; at the request of Emperor Franz Joseph, Nicholas I sent troops to help put down the rebellion in 1849. The elder Denikin was awarded the Cross of St. Ann for his participation in the Crimean War.

7. It is doubtful that there would have been any real danger. Although some European countries protested the ruthlessness with which Russia suppressed the Polish insurrection, Prussia pledged support to Alexander II and closed its borders to Polish refugees.

8. Alexander II declared war on Turkey in 1877, ostensibly to protest Turkish misrule in the Balkans. The war ended in March 1878 after less than a year of fighting.

CHAPTER 2

1. The *grosh*, now obsolete, was worth half a kopeck.

CHAPTER 3

1. The Russification of Poland, begun in the 1860s, was intensified by the law of 1885, which imposed Russian as the language of instruction, even in elementary schools, for all subjects. Denikin received his elementary and intermediate education in Russian Poland, an education which, except for the predominance of the national "minority," was the same as that offered in Russia proper. He attended elementary school in Vlotslavsk from 1879 to 1882 and entered realschule there in 1882. By the law of March 15, 1872, realschulen offered a six-year course which might be (and usually was) extended to seven years. Since the seventh grade had been abolished in Vlotslavsk, Denikin went to Lovich to attend this "supplementary" or "upper division" grade. Children of the lower classes usually received only an elementary education. Realschulen were designed for boys of the upper middle class who could afford to remain in school until the age of fifteen or seventeen and provided a technical education to prepare them for employment rather than advanced studies. Their more successful graduates were admitted to higher technical schools but not to the university. Boys of the upper class went from elementary schools to gymnasia (also seven years) which provided a general education, including classical studies, and prepared their graduates for university entrance. The Russian educational system included municipal, rural, and religious elementary and intermediate schools, all administered by government officials. Subordinate to inspectors at the provincial and district level were inspectors attached to individual schools who were responsible for the whereabouts and behavior of every student. Florinsky, *Russia*, 2:1036–1037; William H. E. Johnson, *Russia's Educational Heritage*, p. 159.

2. [A. D.:] A 1905 ukase allowed the teaching of the Polish language and religion to be conducted in the Polish language. In that unseasonable time it was deemed wise to make use of "native languages." [This is one of a number of footnotes by Denikin which appear in the Russian edition. Hereafter they are distinguished from those of the translator by the initials A. D. enclosed in brackets.]

3. In the Treaty of Riga signed March 18, 1921, the Soviets conceded much of the Ukraine and Belorussia to Poland. Among other provisions, both signatories guaranteed the religious and cultural rights of their national minorities.

4. *Heders*, elementary schools for Jewish boys aged four to thirteen, prepared students for the *yeshiva*, which served adolescent boys and young men. Like other private schools they could be opened only by permission from the Ministry of Education, the language of instruction was prescribed (Russian), and certain subjects had to be taught. Graduates of Jewish schools were not guaranteed the right to take examinations for

higher educational institutions appropriate to their social class; moreover, the examinations given them were more intensive than those administered to Russian public school graduates. Jewish children whose parents legally resided in a district had the right to attend elementary schools but were not admitted until all other children had been accommodated. Ministry of Education reports of 1905–1910 indicate that Jewish children admitted to various municipal elementary schools amounted to only 1.2 to 7.7 percent of the total enrollment in towns where the Jewish population exceeded 50 percent. Salo W. Baron, *The Russian Jew under Tsars and Soviets*, pp. 141–143; Dimitrii M. Odinetz and P. J. Novgorotsov, *Russian Schools and Universities in the World War*, pp. 25–26, 30.

5. See note 2 above.

CHAPTER 5

1. [A. D.:] The arithmetic average of all chord circles is $\pi \tfrac{7}{2}$.

2. [A. D.:] Marks from my certificate of completion for grades six and seven were as follows:

Sixth Grade
Religious instruction 5
Russian language 4
German language . . : 3
French language 3
Geography 4
History 4
Handwriting 4
Drawing 4
Arithmetic .4
Geometry .5
Algebra 5
Trigonometry 4
Descriptive geometry 5
Natural history 3
Physics 4
Chemistry .3
Mechanics .5

Seventh Grade
Religious instruction 5
Arithmetic 5
Geometry 5
Trigonometry 5
Algebra 5
Application of algebra
  to geometry 5
Descriptive geometry 5
Physics 4
Chemistry 3
Mechanics 5
Natural history 4
Mechanical drawing 3
Pattern-making 4
Land surveying 3
Architecture 3
Technology 4
Accounting 4
Gymnastics 5

3. The works of Tolstoy were officially denounced when he began openly to criticize the government and the Orthodox Church in the 1880s.

CHAPTER 6

1. [A. D.:] One was Epifanov. There will be more about him.

2. Friedrich Gottlieb Klopstok (1724–1803), a German and a contemporary of Goethe, produced his main impact as an epic poet (*Der Messias*) but his lyric poetry is more characteristic.

3. The Carthaginian general Hannibal (ca. 247–183 B.C.) swore as a boy of nine to carry on the enmity and opposition of his father, Hamilcar Barca, toward Rome.

4. [A. D.:] The Pole has an inclination to elevate people in rank. A minor writer is therefore a councillor, a teacher is always a professor, a gymnasiast is a student, a student an academician, and an individual with absolutely no definable occupation is a "Mr. Maecenas," a patron of the arts.

CHAPTER 7

1. According to Denikin's daughter, Marina Grey-Chiappe, a friend of her grand-father, Captain Rakitskii, wrote the following epitaph: "In the simplicity of his soul, he feared God, loved people, and remembered no evil." This was inscribed on the tomb-stone.

CHAPTER 8

1. Cornet was a special officer rank in the imperial Russian artillery, corresponding to second lieutenant in the infantry.

2. This measure was typical of reforms instituted by Count T. D. Delianov, minister of education from 1882 to 1897. Johnson, *Russia's Educational Heritage*, pp. 153, 296.

3. As an only son, Denikin could have been exempted from military service under the terms of the conscription law of 1874. Golovine, *The Russian Army*, p. 18.

CHAPTER 9

1. The changes actually became effective in 1912 under Lev Aristidovich Kasso, minister of education from 1910 to 1914, and Vladimir Aleksandrovich Sukhomlinov, minister of war from 1909 to 1915; there was insufficient time for them to produce concrete results before World War I began.

The word "junker," directly borrowed from the German, retained the Prussian con-notation of aristocracy until the mid-1860s. After the Great Reforms, junkers were enlisted men admitted as students to the lower class of military schools which prepared them for possible promotion to officer. When Denikin began his military ca-reer in 1890, there were three types of officer training schools. The most prestigious were those which trained young cadets who had previously attended military prep schools. The lowest in prestige were the junker schools. Denikin's school in Kiev was a hybrid of the intermediate type first created in 1888: a junker school (for volunteer enlisted men) with the same curriculum as that employed for cadets.

2. The term "third section" as a byword for official and arbitrary punishment sur-vived from the Third Section of His Majesty's Private Chancellery, which was formed in 1826 to supervise police affairs. In 1880 its function was transferred to the police department of the Ministry of the Interior. Vladimir Iosifovich Gurko, *Features and Figures of the Past: Government and Opinion in the Reign of Nicholas II*, p. 610, n. 13; Sidney Monas, *The Third Section: Police and Society in Russia under Nicholas I*.

3. This topic is treated more fully in Chapter 26.

4. [A. D.:] According to a twelve-mark system.

5. In 1869 dismay at the inadequacy of the Great Reforms triggered disturbances which resulted in mass expulsions from universities. More idle students joined the disaffected intelligentsia when the government recalled Russian students from foreign universities in 1873. In response to Alexander Herzen's *Kolokol* article, "Go to the People," hundreds of young people invaded the countryside in the "crazy summer of '74" to educate the peasantry. Peasants, suspecting double agents, handed them over to the police. Many disillusioned young intelligentsia became terrorists, following the anarchist philosophy of Mikhail Bakunin. Others abandoned politics altogether. Nezhd-anov, the hero of Ivan Turgenev's *Nov'* (Virgin Soil), committed suicide when he realized that he could never "simplify" himself sufficiently to understand "the people" to whom he had planned to devote his life. W. E. Mosse, *Alexander II and the Moderniza-tion of Russia*, p. 134; Ivan Turgenev, *Virgin Soil*.

6. N. N. Lepeshinskii's famous brother was Pantelemon Nikolaevich Lepeshinskii (1868–1944), active from his student years in revolutionary work. After the Bolshevik revolution he served in the Commissariat of Public Education. See Florinsky, *McGraw-Hill Encyclopedia*, p. 309; *Bolshaia sovetskaia entsiklopediia*, 24:588.

7. [A. D.:] From an article by Professor G. Fedotov, "The Revolution is Coming." ["Revoliutsiia idet," *Sovremennye zapiski*, no. 39 (Paris, 1929), pp. 306–359.]

CHAPTER 10

1. The Guards, traditionally the personal bodyguards of the monarch or army commander, were privileged troops in terms of post, duties, and spendid uniforms.

2. Sytin was named commander of the Bolshevik southern front in October 1918. By mid-January 1919 the Reds had pushed back the Cossacks and Volunteers on a wide front. Peter Kenez, *Civil War in South Russia, 1918: The First Year of the Volunteer Army*, pp. 173–174.

3. In 1900 an international expedition under British Admiral Seymour seized the ancient Taku forts to restore access to Tientsin, about thirty-five miles along the Pei-ho from the sea. Simultaneously part of the force went to the rescue of the Tientsin concessions besieged by Boxers. Augmented, they proceeded toward Peking to relieve besieged legations there. General N. P. Linevich commanded the Russian contingent of what grew to be an eight-nation expedition nominally commanded by German Field Marshal von Waldersee. John K. Fairbank, Edwin O. Reischauer, and Albert M. Craig, *East Asia: The Modern Transformation*, pp. 399–402.

The George's Cross awarded Stankevich in that campaign was one of the many military and civilian medals and decorations in tsarist Russia. The Order of St. George, conferred only for military deeds, entitled the recipient to wear the small white cross on a ribbon of black and yellow. Names of knights of the order and dates honored were inscribed in gold on the marble columns of St. George Hall in the Kremlin Palace, Moscow. This honor conferred rights of hereditary nobility plus a specific pension and privileges such as free tuition for sons in any of the military schools. Francis V. Greene, *Sketches of Army Life in Russia*, pp. 231–233; Henri Troyat, *Daily Life in Russia under the Last Tsar*, p. 120.

CHAPTER 11

1. Here the author used *Za veru, tsaria, i otechestvo* instead of the usual formula of so-called official nationality, *Pravoslavie, samoderzhavie, narodnost'* (Orthodoxy, Autocracy, Nationality).

2. Both leftists and liberals regarded the army as the repressive tool of a reactionary autocracy. This was a natural development since Cossacks and even regular army units were used to augment the internal police in dispersing demonstrators.

3. [A. D.:] According to the military code, any collective action was considered a crime.

4. [A. D.:] According to law, the question of permitting duels in large units where courts of honor existed was resolved there. In small camps the commander decided.

5. A long, open cart with many seats, usually two benches back to back.

6. Polish cooperation with the White forces against the Bolsheviks was never more than token, since Polish leaders believed that White leaders would expect to preserve the old Russian Empire. By the Treaty of Riga of 1921, to which the next paragraph alludes, Poland came to terms with the Bolsheviks, having withdrawn from the Russian civil war a year earlier.

7. [A. D.:] There will be more about this later.

CHAPTER 12

1. In 1890 Germany had failed to renew the Russo-German Reinsurance Treaty and in 1894 Russia completed a military alliance with France against the Triple Alliance (Germany, Austria, and Italy). In spite of the new alignment, the tradition of friendship with Germany still had many adherents in St. Petersburg. Florinsky, *Russia*, 2:1260.

2. [A. D.:] The highest military decoration.

3. Border skirmishes with Caucasus mountaineers erupted into a full-fledged campaign in 1859 to subdue them. In 1865 Turkestan was attached to Western Siberia as a Russian province. Kokand was annexed to the empire in 1876 under the name of Fergana and the khanates of Khiva and Bukhara were made vassal states. Russian expansion was justified by the rationale that constant raids of the lawless tribes made advance to establish a stable boundary unavoidable. Bernard Pares, *A History of Russia*, p. 392.

4. [A. D.:] Alexandra Fedorovna [1872–1918] and the widowed empress [Maria Fedorovna, 1847–1928].

5. Count Leo N. Tolstoy (1828–1910) was an outspoken critic of the Russian government including its "ministry of religion," the Holy Synod. As early as 1886 Alexander III characterized Tolstoy as a "nihilist" and an "atheist" whose "loathsome works" should be suppressed. In the 1890s Tolstoy championed the officially persecuted Dukhobors, a dissident religious sect whose members, like Tolstoy, advocated a fundamentalist Christianity, communal ownership of property, vegetarianism, and abstention from tobacco, alcohol, sex, and violence. When their continued refusal to serve in the army made their situation impossible, Tolstoy financed their emigration to Canada through collections and the proceeds from his novel *Resurrection*. In 1901 the Holy Synod, meeting in plenary session, excommunicated Tolstoy and forbade the celebration of a requiem mass should he die unrepentant. Thereafter his views were published in the foreign press but only hand-circulated in Russia. The Russian government considered Tolstoy a political enemy mainly because of his statements regarding private property and the peasant. His death in November 1910 went unnoticed both at the court and in the official church. *Tolstoy*, the biography by Henri Troyat, contains an excellent section on Tolstoy's political and religious views (Part 7, "The Apostle of Non-Violence," pp. 561–626). See also Aleksandr Aleksandrovich Kizevetter, *Na rubezh dvukh stoletii (vospominaniia 1881–1914)*, p. 512; *Krasnyi arkhiv*, 1 (1922), 417.

6. The liberal journal *Osvobozhdenie* (Liberation) first appeared in Stuttgart in June 1902 and was edited until 1905 by Peter Berngardovich Struve (1870–1944) in cooperation with Pavel N. Miliukov. Struve, a theorist of Legal Marxism, had drafted the Social Democratic manifesto of 1898 but finally drifted to the right wing of the socialist movement. *Osvobozhdenie* was smuggled into Russia and its editorials advocated overthrow of the monarchy and establishment of a constitutional regime, a program endorsed by the *zemstvo* constitutionalist Union of Liberation. From 1907 to 1917 Struve was a professor at the St. Petersburg Polytechnic Institute and in emigration after the October revolution he was close to monarchist circles. Aleksandr Valentinovich Amfiteatrov (1862–1938), a journalist, was exiled in 1902 for an article entitled "The Obmanovs" (from *obman*, "deceit") satirizing the tsar and his entourage. In 1905 he went abroad and published the revolutionary journal *Krasnaia znamia* (Red Banner), like *Osvobozhdenie* smuggled into Russia. Amfiteatrov never, however, favored a Bolshevik revolution. After November 1917 he went into emigration and wrote anti-Communist articles. Florinsky, *Russia*, 2:1168; Florinsky, *McGraw-Hill Encyclopedia*, pp. 19, 65–66.

7. The battle of Wagram, July 5–6, 1809, was the decisive battle of the War of the Fifth Coalition in which Napoleon put the Austrian army to rout. Russia was technically allied with France at the time.

CHAPTER 13

1. General Sukhotin later emerged as the military governor of the Siberian military district with whom Generals P. K. Rennenkampf and Baron A. N. Meller-Zakomelskii clashed as they led punitive expeditions into Siberia in 1906 under orders which transcended preexisting military and civilian authority there. *Krasnyi arkhiv*, 1 (1922), 329.

2. The term "Fundamental Laws" is anachronistic when applied to the law codes before 1906. The laws existing prior to the Duma period had been codified by Mikhail Speranskii in 1831–1832 and promulgated by order of Nicholas I on January 1, 1835. Although based on the earlier *Polnoe sobranie zakonov* (Complete Collection of Laws), the fifteen-volume *Svod zakonov Rossiiskoi imperii* (Code of Law of the Russian Empire) included only operative laws, grouped by subject. There were only partial revisions thereafter, even in 1906 when the Fundamental Laws, including provisions for the State Duma and the reformed State Council, were incorporated into the *Svod zakonov.* Sergei G. Pushkarev, *Dictionary of Russian Historical Terms from the Eleventh Century to 1917*, p. 155.

3. [A. D.:] I had received a mark of eleven in the normal way.

CHAPTER 14

1. [A. D.:] The colonel of administrative services, having supervised the recruitment and registration of reservists.

CHAPTER 15

1. *Zhid* was a derogatory term for Jews.

2. There is some evidence that Russian soldiers were encouraged to provide their own clothing. According to an 1899 document preserved by descendants of Sapper Stanislav Frantsev Zykovskii, transferring him from active to reserve status, Sapper Zykovskii, if recalled to active duty, was to "bring his own boots and white leggings no shorter than nine *vershoks* [15.75 inches] . . ." He was to be reimbursed five rubles for the boots by the quartermaster as well as for as many as two shirts at fifty kopecks each and two pairs of trousers at thirty-five kopecks each. If the summons arrived between September 1 and February 1 he was also to bring a short fur cloak for which he would receive four rubles, mittens (twenty-six kopecks), ear muffs (eleven kopecks), and at least two pairs of cloth leggings, woolen stockings, or foot socks (seventy-two kopecks each). These rates were to be effective until January 1, 1904.

3. New military regulations of 1874, as well as liberalizing punishment of soldiers, made all social classes liable to military service. An excellent exposition of all aspects of the Great Reforms may be found in Mosse, *Alexander II and the Modernization of Russia.* Chapter 3 covers the background and ramifications of emancipation of serfs, while Chapter 4 details judicial, *zemstvo*, educational, military, and economic reforms.

4. The sole national census conducted in tsarist Russia (1897) indicated that only 29.3 percent of males in the entire population were literate at that time. The law of May 3, 1908, and subsequent legislation provided for tripling the number of schools by 1922. Compulsory free school attendance for all children aged eight to eleven years was to be gradually enforced. Due to lack of funds, the plan was considerably in arrears of the original projection when World War I interrupted it. Florinsky, *Russia*, 2:1235–1237; Johnson, *Russia's Educational Heritage*, p. 283.

5. Because of political ferment, the state of living conditions, and lack of food resulting from repeated crop failures, agrarian disturbances which broke out in Kharkov and Poltava provinces in 1902 spread to labor with the assistance of leftist (primarily Socialist Revolutionary) agitators and irresponsible actions of the right. Dissatisfaction with the unsuccessful involvement in the Russo-Japanese War left few parts of Russia calm, and resulted in a bloodbath which ended, temporarily, only in 1907. The "revolution of 1905" might better be called the "revolutionary period of 1902–1907." Florinsky, *Russia*, 2:1148–1150, 1152–1153, 1159.

6. There was, nevertheless, considerable official concern over political propaganda in the army. See, for example, a letter of November 5, 1903, from Minister of Internal Affairs V. K. von Plehve to Minister of War A. N. Kuropatkin in *Krasnyi arkhiv*, 43 (1930), 171–173.

7. In 1904 both agrarian and industrial (but primarily nationalist) disturbances broke out in Poland. In the Warsaw area, the Russian governor-general restored control by means of the large army units stationed there. Later a declaration of martial law enabled him to take appropriate suppressive measures. Sergei Iu. Witte, *The Memoirs of Count Witte*, p. 261.

8. The system of administrative exile reached its final proportions in the latter years of the reign of Alexander II and that of Alexander III. With approval of a special council in the ministry of internal affairs, governors-general, governors, and municipal police chiefs were allowed to exile suspects without trial. According to the supposed degree of their dangerousness, suspects were confined to labor camps, prison camps, or merely restricted to a certain town or village. If local authorities judged a person's presence to be "prejudicial to the public order" or "incompatible with public tranquillity," he could be arrested without a warrant, held from two weeks to two years in prison, and forcibly relocated to another part of the empire to be kept there under police surveillance for one to ten years. The suspect was not allowed to examine witnesses or to call his own witnesses. He could not demand a trial or even a hearing, or make a public appeal through the press. George Kennan, *Siberia and the Exile System*, 1:242–243; Maxime Kovalevsky, *Russian Political Institutions*, p. 239.

9. A complete account of the false lunacy symptoms and Pilsudski's transfer from the pavilion and subsequent escape may be found in Pilsudski's *Memories*. Madame Marja Paszkowska, an active member of the Polish Socialist Party who claimed to have originated the plot, wrote that she secured Dr. Sabashnikov's complicity. Wladyslaw Mazurkiewicz, a medical student at St. Petersburg University and a member of the P. P. S., arranged to have himself appointed house surgeon at Nikolaevskii hospital and effected Pilsudski's escape on May 14, 1901, while most of the staff were attending a nearby fair. Pilsudski managed to flee the country with his first wife, Maria Juszkiewez, who died in 1921. Pilsudski later married Alexandra Szczerbinska, a long-time fellow revolutionary. Alexandra Pilsudska, *Pilsudski: A Biography by His Wife*, p. 173; Pilsudski, *Memories*, pp. 143–147; W. F. Reddaway, *Marshal Pilsudski*, pp. 149–150.

10. *Bojowka*, the terrorist arm of the P. P. S., was formed in 1905. Pilsudski assumed its leadership later that year and soon built a fully trained and equipped guerrilla force. Pilsudska, *Pilsudski*, pp. 112–115.

CHAPTER 16

1. [A. D.:] Admiral Aleksei Mikhailovich Abaza headed the administrative branch of the Special Committee for the Far East. [A. M. Bezobrazov was appointed *stats-sekretar* in May 1903 and the two men organized concessions for timber exploitation on the Yalu River for which they received over two million rubles in loans and grants from the state treasury. It is uncertain if the small group of shareholders, mostly members of the court circle, were actual subscribers or merely lent their names. Florinsky, *Russia*, 2:1269, n.5.]

2. [A. D.:] Korea was under the protection of China.

3. By the Treaty of Shimonoseki (April 17, 1895), China was forced to cede Formosa, the Pescadores, and the Liaotung peninsula to Japan, recognize Korean independence (implying independence under Japanese protection), pay a large indemnity, open more ports, and negotiate a commercial treaty which gave Japan all the privileges enjoyed in China by Western powers as well as additional ones (which also came to Western powers through most-favored-nation clauses in their treaties with China). Fairbank, Reischauer, and Craig, *East Asia*, 383–384.

4. Russia, alarmed by the Japanese threat to Russian interests in the Far East and encouraged by China, organized joint Russian, German, and French diplomatic intervention in April 1895 which resulted in Japan's relinquishing the Liaotung peninsula in exchange for an additional indemnity. *Ibid.*, p. 384.

5. Li Hung-chang, invited to Russia for the coronation of Nicholas II, agreed on the concessions mentioned by Denikin (Li-Lobanov Treaty) in return for Russian guarantee of China's territorial integrity and arrangements to meet the indemnity to Japan by a Russian loan for which Witte secured funds from France. In 1898 Russia violated the spirit of the treaty by allowing Germany to wrest concessions from China, the lease of Kiaochow following the murder of two German missionaries. Moreover, Russia obtained Port Arthur and Dairen (Dalny, Talien-wan) in lease, the principal ports of the Liaotung peninsula denied to Japan by the 1895 intervention, plus the right to connect Dairen with the main line of the new Chinese Eastern Railway in Central Manchuria. Bernard Pares, *The Fall of the Russian Monarchy; A Study of the Evidence*, p. 68.

6. An anti-Japanese reaction in Korea moved Japan to seek cooperation with Russia. In 1896 the Seoul Protocol provided for maintenance of troops commensurate with their respective interests in Korea. To achieve a balance, Japan decreased while Russia increased its presence there. The same year Japan and Russia signed the Moscow Protocol (Lobanov-Yamagata Agreement) which contained a secret clause stating that neither would send troops to Korea without the other's consent. Fear of Japanese influence, however, caused the Korean king and crown prince to seek refuge in the Russian legation in Seoul for over a year (1896–1897). The two 1896 protocols have been interpreted as establishing a Japanese-Russian condominium in Korea. Later events showed that Russia had no such idea, for Russian military and financial agents began pouring into Korea. Andrew Malozemoff, *Russian Far Eastern Policy, 1881–1904, with Special Emphasis on the Causes of the Russo-Japanese War*, pp. 86–87.

7. In his *Memoirs* (p. 98) Count Witte said that when the Germans landed forces at Kiaochow late in 1897, the "news came to me as a complete surprise." But he added that the foreign minister "was not altogether surprised by Germany's step . . ."

8. The name China erroneously appeared as Korea in the Russian text.

9. Alfred von Waldersee, later chief of the German General Staff, was named by William II as chief commander of the international expedition. He gained the reputation of victor in China although the rebellion was suppressed before he arrived. Martin Kitchen, *The German Officer Corps, 1890–1914*, pp. 92–93.

10. Some of the initial confusion of the Russians in the Russo-Japanese War can be attributed to an unusual division of authority in Manchuria. General A. N. Kuropatkin, while minister of war, had contrived a plan of defense for the Far East based on tactics used against Napoleon in 1812. He planned to employ a gradual fighting retreat for dual advantage: to draw Japanese forces farther from their supply sources while moving Russian troops closer to their own, and to avoid positive confrontation until the army had been built up to full strength. Kuropatkin was named commander in chief of the Manchurian armies while the viceroy in the Far East, Admiral E. I. Alekseev, was commander in chief for the whole Far Eastern theater. And Admiral Alekseev's strategy was quite different. His idea was to hold Port Arthur at all costs, meeting the Japanese on the Yalu River to prevent their further advance. Alekseev's tactical plan seems to have been based on the belief common in St. Petersburg circles that the Japanese would not prove a formidable enemy. The resulting situation was even graver because in addition to their irreconcilable strategic conceptions the two men were personally incompatible. They spent much of their time sending telegrams to St. Petersburg complaining about each other. Roman Romanovich Rosen, *Forty Years of Diplomacy*, 1:247.

11. Aleksei Nikolaevich Kuropatkin was minister of war and Vladimir N. Lamsdorff was minister of foreign affairs. But the man who had the tsar's ear was Viacheslav Konstantinovich von Plehve, minister of the interior. Count Witte recounted a conversation he overheard during this time in which Kuropatkin accused Plehve of wanting war with Japan. Plehve replied, "But Aleksei Nikolaevich, you do not understand the internal situation in Russia. We need a small, victorious war to stem the tide of revolution." Sergei Iulevich Witte, *Vospominaniia; tsarstvovanie Nikolaia II*, 1:262.

12. England was then involved in negotiations with Russia which resulted in the Anglo-Russian Agreement of 1907, eliminating long-standing conflicts on concessions in Persia. Andrew D. Kalmykow, *Memoirs of a Russian Diplomat: Outposts of the Empire, 1893–1917*, pp. 210–212.

13. Japan broke off relations on February 6, 1904. Admiral Togo Heihachiro commanded the night torpedo-boat attack which surprised the Russian Far Eastern fleet in Port Arthur, blockading it there on February 8. According to a popular story, Russian naval officers were ashore celebrating Admiral Alekseev's birthday when the attack occurred. Only on February 10 did the Japanese declare war. With the seas thus secured, Japan was able to land reserves on the mainland in less than twenty-four hours after leaving Japanese ports. Fairbank, Reischauer, and Craig, *East Asia*, p. 480; *New York Times*, February 16, 1904, 2:3.

14. The Rikken Menseito (Constitutional Democratic Society), a relative newcomer, was established in 1927 while the Rikken Seiyukai (Friends of Constitutional Government) dated from 1900. Prince Ito headed the latter party. The ultranationalist Black Dragon (Amur River) Society was formed by Uchida Ryōhei and Toyama Mitsuru in 1901 and favored outright annexation of Korea, contrary to the moderate aims of Prince Ito. Fairbank, Reischauer, and Craig, *East Asia*, pp. 482, 632; Robert A. Scalapino, *Democracy and the Party Movement in Prewar Japan*, pp. 179, 235.

15. [A. D.:] Germany seized Kiaochow, England Weihaiwei, and France the Bay of Hain Chzho-van.

16. The Anglo-Japanese Alliance of 1902, the first equal treaty between a Western and a non-Western nation, provided that each would remain neutral if the other was at war but would expect the other's support if attacked by more than one power. For Japan this forestalled any possible Russo-French or Russo-German combination, which no doubt intensified the boldness of the Japanese attack. The full text of the alliance may be found in G. P. Gooch and H. W. V. Temperley, eds., *British Documents on the Origins of the War, 1898–1914*, 2:115–120.

17. The so-called Tanaka memorial was purported to have been drafted by General Baron Tanaka Giichi, leader of the Seiyukai party and premier in 1927, and presented to the emperor as the conclusions reached by a Tokyo Far Eastern conference held in June–July 1927. The document detailed resources available in Manchuria and Mongolia and suggested methods for strengthening the Japanese position in those areas contrary to restrictions imposed upon Japan by the Nine Power Treaty resulting from the Washington Conference on Limitation of Armaments of 1921–1922. The memorial, of disputed origin, was probably forged by a Japanese and sold to the Chinese. Although no original Japanese text has been uncovered, belief in its authenticity was reinforced by Japanese actions in the 1930s which seemed to follow its outlines. Westel W. Willoughby, *Japan's Case Examined*, pp. 146–153.

18. To those who accepted the authenticity of the Tanaka memorial, hindsight revealed that this passage foreshadowed Pearl Harbor and the Pacific phase of World War II.

19. Fear for the western frontier led to an error in judgment in the Manchurian land campaign. The principal work there was thrown on the reserves, men past their fighting prime who had forgotten their training. Not until the summer of 1905 did the Manchurian armies begin to fill up with drafts from the regular army and young recruits of 1905. These young soldiers arrived at the front in a different frame of mind from that of the reservists who had come out in 1904. Many of them were volunteers and might have performed well had they been given the opportunity. As it was, more than 300,000 of them saw no action due to the "hasty peace." Alexei N. Kuropatkin, *The Russian Army and the Japanese War*, 1:270.

20. Unlike 1863, mobilization was confined to the less explosive areas of Poland. Nevertheless not all Poles were silent. The P. P. S. organized a demonstration on the Plac Grzbowski in Warsaw which attracted widespread attention (and police fire).

Dmowski's Popular Democrats dissociated themselves still more from the P. P. S. after the Warsaw demonstration and followed a program of cooperation with the Russian government. Pilsudski, *Memories*, pp. 153–159.

21. Roman Dmowski was a Polish deputy to the second State Duma in 1907. He led the Popular (or National) Democrats, a Catholic and socially conservative party. They felt that Polish national interests could best be promoted through cooperation with Russia and were thus in opposition to Pilsudski and his P. P. S. for whom Russia was always the primary enemy. During World War I Dmowski and the pianist Ignace Paderewski formed the National Committee, a Polish government-in-exile in Paris. They returned to Poland in 1919 and attempted to upset the socialist government which Pilsudski had established there. The most they were able to accomplish was an uneasy coalition. That was the situation when the Russo-Polish War of 1919–1921 began. Pilsudski's fame in that war as the savior and rebuilder of Poland sustained him in power, openly or behind the scenes, until his death in 1935. Florinsky, *Russia*, 2:762; Pilsudski, *Memories*, pp. 11, 352, 363–365, 372.

22. In early 1905 Pilsudski arrived in Tokyo with Titus Filipowicz (later Polish ambassador to the United States) hoping to form a Polish legion allied with Japan and at Japanese victory to gain an independent Polish republic. Roman Dmowski, his political rival, was already there to discourage the Japanese government from such an arrangement and Pilsudski was able only to secure special treatment of Polish soldiers surrendering without force and his passage home. Pilsudski, *Memories*, p. 159.

23. The famous picture of the Mother of God located in the Częstochowa Paulite monastery on Jasna Góra (Bright Mountain) has a special cult among Polish Catholics, inspiring hundreds of thousands to make pilgrimages there each year. Eric P. Kelly and Dragoš D. Kostich, *The Land and People of Poland*, pp. 78–79; Jerzy Walicki, *Religious Life in Poland*, p. 14.

24. Nor were the Turks involved in revolutionary events of the 1905–1907 period. In comparison with the Russians, Armenians, and Georgians, the Moslems of the Transcaucasus showed little interest in rebellion except for "occasional demonstrations against abuses by the local administration." Serge A. Zenkovsky, *Pan-Turkism and Islam in Russia*, p. 44.

CHAPTER 17

1. The Russian navy was placed under St. Andrew's patronage and sailed under a flag with his symbol, a blue cross.

2. Russia took advantage of the Boxer Rebellion to occupy most of Manchuria. In June 1900, Boxers in Manchuria had attacked the Chinese Eastern Railway then under construction. Russian troops sent there were not withdrawn until 1902, under pressure from Japan, England, Germany, and the United States to open Manchuria to all powers. Even then they were replaced by soldier-woodcutters and soldier-railway guards, the situation which existed when the Russo-Japanese War began. Moderates had considered the occupation an excessive move from the start. Florinsky, *Russia*, 2:1267–1268; *Krasnyi arkhiv*, 14 (1926), 37–38; Boris A. Romanov, *Russia in Manchuria, 1892–1906*, p. 179.

CHAPTER 18

1. Denikin apparently refers here to the Chinese Moslem General Ma Ju-ling. Yuan Shih-kai (1859–1916) of Honan province, Li Hung-chang's protégé, succeeded Li as governor-general of Chihli province and Peiyang commissioner from 1901 to 1907. He was premier, then president (and dictator) of the Chinese Republic from 1911 to 1916, and self-proclaimed emperor for the last six months of his life. Fairbank, Reischauer, and Craig, *East Asia*, pp. 323, 353, 621, 640–646, 649–650.

CHAPTER 19

1. The battle of Tiurenchen was part of a larger action known as the battle of the Yalu. Japan won its first major land victory here when General M. I. Zasulich, contrary to Kuropatkin's orders, engaged a superior Japanese force. The war was disastrous from the start, from the surprise attack on Port Arthur (February 1904), through the untimely loss of Admiral Makarov and the defeat on the Yalu (April 1904), the surrender of Port Arthur (January 1905), and the humiliating defeat at Mukden (March 1905), to the sinking of the Baltic fleet in Tsushima Straits (May 1905).

2. General Hamilton was attached to the Japanese armies. His published observations are available as Sir Ian Standish Monteith Hamilton, *A Staff Officer's Scrap-Book during the Russo-Japanese War*.

3. Colonel Fritz Gertsch published his impressions as *Vom russisch-japanischen Krieg 1904–1905*.

4. *Ho* being a North Chinese word for river, this battle was, therefore, the battle of the Sha River. The battle lines were about 20 kilometers from Mukden. Georges Maurice Paléologue, *Three Critical Years, 1904–05–06*, p. 89.

5. [A. D.:] A *sopka* is a small extinct volcano.

CHAPTER 20

1. Kaoliang is a tall grain sorghum native to China and Manchuria.

2. General Kuropatkin cited, for example, the following comparative figures for 1st Army casualties during the period from November 1904 to September 1905: Losses of officers and men amounted to, respectively, 4.1 and 2.5 percent killed; 23.8 and 14.6 percent wounded; 2.1 and 2.9 percent missing. Total losses were 30 percent of the officers and 20 percent of the soldiers on the 1st Army rolls. Kuropatkin, *Russian Army*, 2:63.

3. General A. M. Stoessel surrendered the fortress after a five-month siege. He said that he had lost three-fourths of the garrison to death and disability, but others claimed that he still had twenty-five thousand able troops and adequate supplies of food and ammunition. Stoessel was court-martialed in 1908 for having surrendered before he had exhausted all possibilities for resistance. He was condemned to death but Nicholas II commuted the sentence to 10 years' imprisonment. Stoessel was pardoned in 1910. Florinsky, *Russia*, 2:1273; Paléologue, p. 154.

4. General Kondratenko was killed two weeks before the surrender.

5. Puns are not readily transferable from one language to another. The noun *nabeg* (raid, incursion) comes from the verb which means "to run." Rennenkampf invented a parallel formation, *napolz*, from the verb meaning "to crawl."

6. General O. K. Gripenberg, commander of the 2nd Manchurian Army, claimed that he was forced to retreat after gaining ground in the Sandepu area when Kuropatkin refused to send reinforcements. He demanded to be relieved of his command because, he said, victory under Kuropatkin was impossible. General Kuropatkin considered, however, that Gripenberg had used poor judgment in allowing independent fire instead of controlled volleys to repulse night attacks and in failing to use the terrain to advantage. By using his own methods, Kuropatkin said, Gripenberg, "got his troops into confusion, gave the enemy time to bring up reinforcements, and retired — to St. Petersburg." Kuropatkin, *Russian Army*, 2:23–24.

CHAPTER 21

1. [A. D.:] General Mishchenko received the title of General of His Majesty's Retinue and later the higher one of Adjutant General.

CHAPTER 22

1. [A. D.:] The conference, under the chairmanship of the sovereign, included Grand Dukes Nikolai Nikolaevich and Aleksei Aleksandrovich, General Dragomirov, and Counts Vorontsov-Dashkov, Frederiks, Roop, and Komarov.
2. General Linevich was sixty-seven years old at this time.
3. Stalingrad, previously called Tsaritsyn, was renamed Volgograd in the late 1950s "de-Stalinization" period.
4. Vice Admiral Zinovii Petrovich Rozhdestvenskii (1848–1908) and the aged Baltic fleet were sent to relieve the paralyzed remnants of the Pacific fleet in October 1904. After a long, tortuous journey around the Cape of Good Hope (England having closed the Suez Canal to them), 42 ships were intercepted by Admiral Togo in the Straits of Tsushima and only 4 survived to limp into Vladivostok harbor. Rozhdestvenskii, severely wounded, was picked up from the wreckage of his flagship *Prince Suvorov* and taken to Japan, from which he was repatriated after the war. The entire venture was foolhardy. The Baltic fleet was little more than a coast guard unit and its sailors were inexperienced because of the ice-locked condition of the Baltic. But nationalist sentiment, endorsed by the tsar, prevailed over the opposition of more practical bureaucrats and naval officers. Florinsky, *Russia*, 2:1276; Richard Hough, *The Fleet That Had to Die*, pp. 120–158; Paléologue, *Three Critical Years*, p. 90.
5. [A. D.:] The staff consisted of five officers at a time.
6. A famous Cossack settlement among the islands of the lower Dnieper (the name means "below the rapids" and "in the clearing"), the setting for Nikolai Gogol's *Taras Bulba*.

CHAPTER 23

1. In mid-August 1905 Nicholas II asked the advice of Count V. N. Kokovtsov, minister of finance, regarding concessions demanded by Japan. Kokovstov replied that peace was an absolute necessity but that the extent of concessions necessary to obtain peace was known only to those familiar with conditions at the front. He realized that General Linevich should be consulted, yet he advised against it because this would mean undue delay and because General Linevich would not be cognizant of all other aspects of the problem. Kokovtsov advised making all concessions consistent with the dignity of Russia short of paying an indemnity, which would have set a precedent. He suggested instead the cession of South Sakhalin island, an area which Japan already possessed, and compensation to Japan for maintenance of the Russian prisoners held by Japan. Count Vladimir N. Kokovtsov, *Out of My Past: The Memoirs of Count Kokovtsov, Russian Minister of Finance 1904–1914, Chairman of the Council of Ministers 1911–1914*, pp. 57–58.
2. [A. D.:] Witte was rewarded with the title of count for his services at Portsmouth. [Witte was not Nicholas II's first choice to send to Portsmouth since he had been out of favor since 1903 for his custom of speaking the truth as he saw it, no matter how unpleasant. Nelidov, ambassador at Paris, refused the mission because of his "incompetence in Far Eastern affairs." Muraviev, ambassador at Rome, begged off for reasons of health. Izvolskii, ambassador at Copenhagen (and formerly at Tokyo) favored Witte as did Count Lamsdorff, minister of foreign affairs. Nicholas yielded. The tsar hoped that Izvolskii would be second plenipotentiary but Witte insisted on Baron R. R. Rosen, Izvolskii's successor at Tokyo. In spite of some animosity between Izvolskii and Witte, Izvolskii considered that Witte obtained the best terms possible and that "public opinion in Russia has shown scant appreciation of the remarkable achievement of M. Witte at Portsmouth." Aleksandr Petrovich Izvolskii, *The Memoirs of Alexander Izwolsky: Formerly Russian Minister of Foreign Affairs and Ambassador to France*, pp. 22–24.]
3. Vladimir Lvovich Burtsev (1862–1942) was arrested as a populist in his youth. Later,

as a Socialist Revolutionary, he became known for exposing double agents such as Evno Azef, head of the Socialist Revolutionary battle organization. Burtsev edited *Byloe* (The Past) from 1900 to 1904 and 1908 to 1912. Moving farther to the right with age, Burtsev accused Lenin and other Bolsheviks in 1917 of being German agents. He worked with the White armies in the civil war and died in French emigration. Florinsky, *McGraw-Hill Encyclopedia*, p. 81.

4. Russian Minister of Finance Count V. N. Kokovtsov was convinced that had the Japanese not relented, the tsar would have continued the war even in the face of disastrous forebodings. Nicholas II informed Kokovtsov that he would never agree to an indemnity "even if I had to continue the war for another two years." Kokovtsov, *Out of My Past*, p. 58.

5. In contrast with the formality of the Japanese mission, Count Witte made himself accessible to the American public and press, treating everyone he met as an equal although such behavior, he said, "was a heavy strain on me as all acting is to the unaccustomed, but it surely was worth the trouble." Of great assistance to Witte was the presence of his friend, the British journalist Emile Joseph Dillon, who wrote reports favorable to the Russians and arranged press interviews for Witte. Another factor affecting American public opinion was undoubtedly an element of racism. Baron Rosen related that a young reporter told him that newspapermen had been 90 percent pro-Japanese and anti-Russian but the proportion was reversed in the course of the negotiations. Rosen asked if the change of attitude could be related to the discovery that the Russians were white. The reporter replied, ". . . that's about the long and short of it." Rosen, *Forty Years of Diplomacy*, 1:267; Witte, *Memoirs*, pp. 141–142.

6. The claim that Russia paid no indemnity has probably been overplayed and is not altogether accurate. Payment for maintenance of prisoners (which was not reciprocal) and transfer without compensation to Japan of Russian technical improvements in the Liaotung (Kwantung) peninsula as well as the property and privileges of the South Manchurian Railway, including coal mines, amounted at least to reparations. Florinsky, *Russia*, 2:1278.

7. The gap around the southern end of Lake Baikal, moreover, had been closed. In July 1905 a "leading Russian commander" (unnamed) at the Manchurian front made the following statement to a *New York Times* correspondent: "I have 150 machine guns and also strong artillery. I have received many men from Russia. All the infantry companies are 250 men strong and all the men are anxious to attack. . . . the army will advance here regardless of the disorder at home. It will fight one, two, or three years, because the end must be victory. The army does not share the peace desires of the Government . . ." *New York Times*, July 21, 1905, 6:6.

8. Letters found on Japanese prisoners and corpses revealed war weariness and privation at home. Actually, Japan's resources were seriously depleted by the end of March 1905, and realistic Japanese observers realized that their country was in no condition to continue fighting. High Japanese military authorities were well aware of the critical nature of their situation and General Kodama, chief of staff of the Manchurian expeditionary forces, returned secretly to Tokyo shortly after the battle of Mukden to tell military and civilian leaders that those who had started the war must know when to stop it. He urged officials to seek an early opportunity to terminate the war. Such an opportunity was the defeat of the Russian Baltic fleet in Tsushima Straits, which gave Japan a good bargaining position. Florinsky, *Russia*, 2:1278; Kuropatkin, "The Treaty at Portsmouth," pp. 239–240; Tatsuji Takeuchi, *War and Diplomacy in the Japanese Empire*, p. 149.

9. A *papakha* is a tall Caucasus hat, usually made of sheepskin.

CHAPTER 24

1. For an English translation of the Manifesto of October 17/30, see Bernard Pares, *The Fall of the Russian Monarchy*, pp. 503–504. Nicholas II, isolated at Peterhof by a

general strike in St. Petersburg, summoned Witte, who had hastened back from the Portsmouth negotiations. Witte outlined for the tsar two alternatives, either to establish a military dictatorship or to grant a constitution. Although Nicholas preferred the former, he trusted no one to act for him. He therefore asked Witte to draft a constitution. Witte too preferred absolutism but was forced by the revolutionary situation and the inadequacies of Nicholas II to favor a constitutional regime. Witte wrote and Nicholas signed the October Manifesto, which granted civil liberties, promised broad franchise for Duma elections, and proclaimed that no law would be valid without the consent of the Duma. But the April 23, 1906, Fundamental Laws and decrees issued in the interim effectively restricted Duma rights and in large measure restored the autocratic principle. Florinsky, *McGraw-Hill Encyclopedia*, p. 476; Florinsky, *Russia*, 2:1184–1188.

2. The Russian Social Democratic Labor Party, founded in 1898, split into the Bolsheviks and Mensheviks in 1903. The two factions cooperated, however, during the revolution of 1905, often working on joint committees to organize and perpetuate the Soviets of Workers' Deputies which were formed in various parts of the empire. Florinsky, *McGraw-Hill Encyclopedia*, pp. 105–106.

3. (Thomas) Mayne Reid (1818–1883) was a British author of adventure fiction.

4. "The History of the Punitive Expeditions to Siberia, 1905–1906" by "V. M." (V. V. Maksakova?), *Krasnyi arkhiv*, 1 (1922), 329–343, contains such documents as instructions from Nicholas II, Premier Witte, Minister of the Interior P. N. Durnovo, and Assistant Minister of the Interior A. A. Polivanov to Generals Rennenkampf and Meller-Zakomelskii, commanders of the two punitive expeditions who were given authority independent of civil and military authorities in Siberia. The author said (p. 329), "Tens of people from Siberia and the Zabaikal region were executed and hanged, hundreds flogged, thousands imprisoned, and so on."

5. [A. D.:] The military governor, General Kholshchevnikov, was later tried and sentenced to imprisonment in a fortress.

6. A three-volume edition of the "Account" was published in Germany as Aleksei N. Kuropatkin, *Zapiski generala Kuropatkina o russkoi-iaponskoi voine: Itogi voiny* (Notes of General Kuropatkin on the Russo-Japanese War: War Totals) (Berlin: I. Ladyschnikoff, 1909). There is also an abbreviated two-volume English version, Aleksei N. Kuropatkin, *The Russian Army and the Japanese War*, trans. A. B. Lindsay (New York: Dutton, 1909; London: John Murray, 1909.) The latter is a complete translation of vol. 4 plus a portion of vol. 3 from a carbon copy of the original typescript.

CHAPTER 25

1. The estrangement of the noble from the peasant is an old theme in Russian history, the result of cultural differentiation, Europeanization, and the adoption of French customs and language by the nobles. In 1909 peasant holdings in the forty-seven provinces of European Russia constituted only about half the land, a situation only slightly improved by 1914. The landlord was usually heir to a former serf owner who lived in a large mansion, the abbot of a monastery, or an official supervising state domains. As Gerold T. Robinson expressed it, "the peasant did not need to be told that he was hungry" and he needed no political agitators to tell him of the economic benefits of keeping the crop harvested from others' lands. Gerold T. Robinson, *Rural Russia under the Old Regime*, pp. 52–55, 144–145, 270.

2. Peter the Great added Estonia and part of Latvia to the empire in the late seventeenth century, leaving the existing system of local authority intact. His successors, who incorporated more of the Baltic region, did not attempt to curb the tyranny of the German barons over Estonian and Lettish peasants until Alexander III (1881–1894) launched an intensive Russification program. Russification, according to Count Witte, introduced liberal ideas among the peasantry as opposed to the medieval German tradition imposed by the aristocracy there. When the revolutionary wave struck the

Baltic area, its immediate impact took the form of agrarian disturbances with Estonian and Lettish peasants pitted against German landowners. Walter Kolarz, *Russia and Her Colonies*, pp. 104–105; Witte, *Memoirs*, pp. 257–258.

3. Russia acquired Finland by the Treaty of Fredrikshamn in 1809 and allowed the Finns to retain the autonomy which they had possessed as a Swedish province. Finland was an autonomous constitutional state, a grand duchy whose grand duke was also emperor of Russia, but which still operated under its own laws and institutions. Nicholas II, like his predecessors, pledged himself to respect Finnish privileges but in 1899 he decreed that all legislation affecting imperial interests had to be approved by the Imperial Council. A 1901 ukase disbanded the Finnish army and made Finns subject to Russian conscription. Meanwhile, Governor-General A. I. Bobrikov introduced an intensive Russification program. Bobrikov's assassination was a expression of nationalist discontent rather than a revolutionary terrorist act. The Empress Mother Maria Fedorovna was instrumental in persuading Nicholas II to restore Finnish autonomy and agitation ceased. Florinsky, *Russia*, 2:665, 703–704, 1158–1159; Witte, *Memoirs*, pp. 258–261.

4. [A. D.:] The "four-tailed formula" consisted of universal, equal, direct, and secret vote.

5. The mutiny aboard the Black Sea battleship *Potemkin* in June 1905 is well known as the subject of a now classic film by the famous Soviet director Serge Eisenstein. The mutineers did not make a clean escape for they surrendered to Romanian authorities at Constanza and Russian officials negotiated successfully for their extradition. Afanasy Matushenko, who led the mutiny, was actually executed but the death sentences of other sailors involved were commuted to fifteen years' imprisonment. Florinsky, *Russia*, 2:1174; *Krasnyi arkhiv*, 8 (1925), 250–254.

6. The first Russian soviet was formed in St. Petersburg in September 1905. Others soon followed in Moscow, Sevastopol, Kiev, Rostov, Samara, Kharkov, and cities of comparable size. After Grand Duke Sergei Aleksandrovich was assassinated, Dubasov, a strong governor-general, was appointed to Moscow in November 1905. Having accidentally learned in advance about the Moscow insurrection, Count Witte persuaded the tsar to send reliable troops there. The army subdued the Moscow rebels quickly and energetically. Louis Fischer, *The Life of Lenin*, p. 50; Witte, *Memoirs*, pp. 280–283.

7. On March 1/14, 1917, a member of the Petrograd Soviet telegraphed Order Number One to all army units (some say that it was meant only for rear garrisons and went to front line units by mistake), instructing them to elect deputies to the soviet and to establish battalion and company committees to control weapons and keep them from officers. Soldiers were not to salute officers off duty and officers were to address soldiers with the polite plural form of "you" instead of the familiar singular. Next day the order was published in *Izvestiia* over the signature of the Petrograd Soviet. L. Fischer, *Lenin*, p. 129; Florinsky, *Russia*, 2:1393–1394.

8. Georgi Stepanovich Khrustalev-Nosar (1879–1932), a lawyer, was elected chairman of the St. Petersburg Soviet of Workers' Deputies in 1905. Premier Witte did not interfere with the soviet because he realized that it exerted little influence beyond St. Petersburg factory workers and he waited for it to outlive its usefulness before arresting its leaders. When Khrustalev-Nosar was exiled to Siberia in 1906 there was little reaction. A joke current in St. Petersburg had it that there were two "governments," that of Witte and that of Khrustalev, and that it was uncertain for a time which would arrest the other. Florinsky, *McGraw-Hill Encyclopedia*, p. 274; Witte, *Memoirs*, pp. 270–278.

9. Mikhail Nikolaevich Pokrovskii (1868–1932) was the official Bolshevik historian whose best-known work *Russkaia istoriia c drevnishikh vremen* (Russian History from the Most Ancient Times) was endorsed by Lenin as a textbook for all Soviet secondary schools. By the mid-1930s Pokrovskii's deterministic description of governments and leaders as pawns of economics clashed with the growing emphasis on the roles of the hero (a reflection of Stalin's self-promotion) and of the state as major factors in history.

In 1936 the Pokrovskii conception of history as "politics applied to the past" was posthumously officially branded anti-Marxist and anti-Leninist. Presently, however, Pokrovskii's reputation has undergone some rehabilitation in the Soviet Union. Jonathan Frankel, "Party Genealogy and the Soviet Historians," p. 571; N. Rubinshtein, "M. N. Pokrovskii: kratkaia biograficheskaia spravka," pp. 79–80.

10. Without a general shift to conservatism the army could not have been popular since troops (particularly Cossack units) were used to subdue internal disturbances, finally calmed by 1907.

11. The Dolgorukii twins, descended from an ancient aristocratic family, were both members of the Union of Liberation and prominent in liberal circles before 1905. Peter, richer and more moderate, was district marshal of the nobility near Moscow while Paul, a militant radical, was board chairman of the Kursk *zemstvo*. Both also belonged to the Moscow *Beseda* (Symposium), a private group of liberal gentry which met from 1899 to 1905 to exchange views on *zemstvo* affairs. George Fischer, *Russian Liberalism*, pp. 124, 149.

12. The Socialist Revolutionaries, agrarian socialists and one of the first modern political parties to use terrorism as a "legitimate" tool to secure political objectives, organized a terrorist section, battle organization, or "flying squad" as it was sometimes called, in 1901. This organization, variously headed by Evno Azef, Boris Savinkov, and others, arranged several political assassinations and other disruptive acts. Their activities were well known to the secret police (*okhranka*). They were effectively immobilized in the "period of Stolypin reaction" and there is evidence to indicate that Premier Stolypin himself directed the counter-terrorist measures carried out by an entire network of double agents. Oliver H. Radkey, *The Agrarian Foes of Bolshevism*, pp. 51, 67–68, 73–74.

13. [A. D.:] The law which abolished serfdom also brought self-administration to the countryside and the cities, judicial reform, and universal military duty instead of recruitment from the lowest, poorest classes of society. [In 1864 Alexander II instituted elective councils (*zemstvos*) as instruments of local self-government. District and provincial assemblies, elected by estates for three-year terms, met annually. Between sessions the executive committee of each conducted business. They were responsible for such local economic and social services as primary education, public health, improvement of agrarian methods, and the training of teachers, doctors, and agronomists. Many liberal political leaders were trained in the *zemstvo* movement, although the membership shifted from a liberal to a conservative position after the 1905 excesses.]

14. The budget rules of 1906 were modeled on the Japanese constitution and excluded approximately a third of national expenditures from legislative authority. For example, the appropriations and expenditures of the Ministry of the Imperial Court could not be discussed by the Duma as long as they did not exceed the sum appropriated in 1906. Nor could appropriation changes under provisions of the Statutes of the Imperial Family be discussed. There was no way that the legislature could reduce expenses for maintenance of the imperial court and imperial family, nor could representatives criticize such expenditures. Florinsky, *Russia*, 2:1187; Paul P. Gronsky and Nicholas J. Astrov, *The War and the Russian Government*, p. 22.

15. On the tsar's orders, Interior Minister Stolypin attempted in the spring of 1906 to negotiate with Kadet leaders to form a coalition government. The Kadets refused to compromise, insisting on a Kadet ministry. Nicholas II had no intention of allowing the formation of an opposition cabinet. He asked the advice of persons whom he trusted and nearly all agreed that such an arrangement was unthinkable. It soon became clear why Stolypin was supervising the negotiations rather than Premier Ivan L. Goremykin. Nicholas II dissolved the recalcitrant first State Duma and replaced Goremykin with Stolypin in July 1906. Maria Petrovna von Bock, *Reminiscences of My Father, Peter A. Stolypin*, p. 141; Florinsky, *Russia*, 2:1192; Kokovtsov, *Out of My Past*, p. 149.

CHAPTER 26

1. The tsar was by definition commander in chief. But when World War I broke out, Nicholas II unexpectedly named his uncle, Grand Duke Nikolai Nikolaevich, as commander in chief. Then, because of his feeling of personal responsibility for Russia (and the empress's jealousy of the grand duke's popularity), the tsar assumed at least nominal command on September 5, 1915, at a time when the military situation was bad and worsening. Sir George Buchanan, *My Mission to Russia*, 1:237–239.

2. [A. D.] *Katorga i ssilka*, no. 2.

3. When the Germans invaded France in 1940, they found Denikin living in the Bordeaux region. The German commander called on him and "offered him favorable living conditions and freedom to work on his memoirs on condition of emigration to Germany." Denikin declined and possibly suffered the more for it. At the end of World War II Denikin settled in the United States. A. I. Denikin, *Put' russkogo ofitsera*, from the N. S. Timashev foreword, p. 8.

4. [A. D.] During the civil war, 1918–1919, in contrast to my Volunteer Army, Don ataman General Krasnov followed a Germanophile policy and during World War II he entered the service of Germany.

5. Article 96 of the 1906 Fundamental Laws originally excluded the Duma and State Council from examination of most new army and navy bills, leaving such legislation virtually the same as under the absolute monarchy. The emperor was authorized to promulgate orders concerning field, technical, and supply regulations as well as the organization and personnel of the army and navy after such questions had been examined (in an advisory capacity) by the councils of the army and navy, bodies retained from the absolutist period. Gronsky and Astrov, *The War and the Russian Government*, pp. 11–12.

6. [A. D.] Guchkov was at one time president of the Duma and Gurko was then chairman of the Commission for Classifying Documents of the Russo-Japanese War and subsequently chief commander of the western front.

CHAPTER 27

1. The State Council was created in 1810 to consider legislative projects assigned by the emperor and to submit recommendations. Members were appointed by the tsar. In 1906 the State Council became the upper chamber, with the State Duma the lower, of the new bicameral legislature. The tsar continued to appoint half of the 180 members, however, as well as the president and the vice-president of the State Council. The remainder were elected by the church, the nobility, the *zemstvos*, and other conservative groups. Florinsky, *McGraw-Hill Encyclopedia*, p. 542; Gronsky and Astrov, *The War and the Russian Government*, pp. 18–19.

2. [A. D.] A reserve brigade consisted of four regiments of two battalions each and the service position in it was the same as in a division.

3. Saratov on the Volga, not Moscow or St. Petersburg, was the original center of the Socialist Revolutionary movement, which may explain why, even before the Russo-Japanese War, Saratov and adjoining provinces were known as the most turbulent in all of Russia. Radkey, *Agrarian Foes of Bolshevism*, pp. 53–54, 67–68.

4. Stolypin, a courageous and conscientious public servant who risked death many times before his assassination in 1911, had little patience with less dedicated individuals. A. P. Izvolskii, his first foreign minister, wrote that Stolypin had "an exalted and chivalrous conception of duty" and was "devoted to the point of martyrdom." Izvolskii, *Memoirs*, p. 100.

5. General Shileiko's name initially appeared in the Russian text (p. 259) as Gileiko. Subsequent entries were spelled correctly.

6. [A. D.] For all military men, certificates were composed by their direct superiors

after "certification conferences" were held, the opinion of the senior superior present being decisive. On this certificate depended all service positions and promotions of officers.

7. [A. D.] The Kazan district was under martial law. For both military and civil political crimes a military court sat, consisting of a chairman, military judges, and two members from troops of the local garrison.

8. "Provisional" rules regarding censorship enacted in 1882 remained in force for more than twenty years. A committee consisting of the Procurator of the Holy Synod and the ministers of education, justice, and internal affairs granted or denied permission to publish. This committee had the authority to suspend publication of any periodical either temporarily or permanently and to prohibit its editors and publishers from publishing or editing other publications. Only in 1905 and 1906 was prior censorship abolished and even then issues of periodicals might be withdrawn from circulation and editors, publishers, and authors penalized for such vague offenses as "spreading false information concerning state agencies and officials" or making "favorable comments on criminal acts." Florinsky, *McGraw-Hill Encyclopedia*, p. 451; Florinsky, *Russia*, 2:1112.

9. [A. D.] The law did not permit collective complaints or ones relayed "from others."

10. [A. D.] This was an authentic phrase from one report.

11. [A. D.] Such certification conferences consisted of the brigade commander, the staff commander, four regimental commanders, and commanders of individual battalions.

12. [A. D.] That is, I.

13. The War Council or Military Council was formed in the War Ministry in 1838. The minister of war was chairman and members were appointed by the emperor. They discussed questions of military legislation, the economic state of the army, and matters of internal administration. The council was enlarged in 1865 and divided into five sections to supervise, respectively, military hospitals, prisons, schools, and codification as well as organization and formation of troops. Gurko, *Features and Figures of the Past*, p. 677, n.16; Kovalevsky, *Russian Political Institutions*, p. 179.

14. [A. D.] During the war there were no field troops in the interior districts, only reserve battalions and rear military institutions.

CHAPTER 28

1. Peter I (the Great, 1682–1725) used hundreds of military and civilian subjects to build his new capital in 1703 on the site of a former Finnish swamp. His incessant wars (mostly with Sweden) gained Russia its shoreline on the Baltic and Gulf of Bothnia as well as the area north of Lake Ladoga. Florinsky, *Russia*, 1:327, 335.

2. [A. D.] See Chapter 14, "In the Brigade Once More." [One of Denikin's obituary notices contained the unsubstantiated comment that "he was reprimanded while a junior officer for the liberalism of his relations with his men." *Times* (London), August 11, 1947, p. 6.]

3. [A. D.] An extreme right organization. [The Union of Russian People, established in October 1905 in St. Petersburg, was largely the creation of Dr. Aleksandr Ivanovich Dubrovin, an ardent monarchist no less addicted to terror than the Socialist Revolutionaries. The tsar, the tsarevich (heir apparent), and several high government officials were said to have been honorary members. The Union of Russian People trained assassination teams to create an atmosphere of revolution in order to establish a right-wing dictatorship. This and other militant rightist groups emerged as a direct result of terrorist acts on the far left. V. P. Viktorov, ed., *Soiuz russkogo naroda, po materialam chrezvychainoi sledstvennoi kommissii vremennogo pravitelstva*, pp. 23–35.]

4. [A. D.] Subsequently Colonel Dukhonin became a general, in 1917 the last commander in chief of the Russian army.

5. [A. D.] Guchkov, a moderate political leader, was at one time chairman of the State Duma. [See Chapter 25, n.14. Expenses for the maintenance of the imperial court and imperial family could be neither reduced nor criticized.]

6. In his published reminiscences Guchkov did not elaborate on the Miasoedov trial and in fact stated that he was unable to judge the accuracy of the charges against Miasoedov. Guchkov was quite explicit, however, about the 1912 incident in which Miasoedov was discharged from leadership of the special political police created by Sukhomlinov to report on the reliability of officers. Guchkov's chief informants at that time were V. S. Botkin, a dragoon officer and brother of the tsar's personal physician, and General N. I. Ivanov, then troop commander of the Kiev military district. Miasoedov had been dismissed from active service in 1907 for smuggling contraband from Germany in a consular automobile. Evidence offered by Guchkov indicated, moreover, that as late as 1915 Sukhomlinov was, even if unwittingly, furnishing information to a certain Altschiller, head of Austrian espionage in Russia, and was still friends with Miasoedov. A. I. Guchkov, "Iz vospominaniia A. I. Guchkova," *Poslednaia novosti*, no. 5630 (August 23, 1936), p. 2; no. 5633 (August 26, 1936), p. 2.

7. [A. D.] Statistics on the officer corps were never published by nationality or native origins. Instead there was noted just the religious creed, which gave only an approximate indication of nationality. In the general lists of 1912, 86 percent were Orthodox.

8. According to the witty assessment of the elder Baron Wrangel, to be a Pole in tsarist Russia was only a misdemeanor but to be a Jew was a crime. Before 1827 Jews normally paid a special tax in lieu of military service but Nicholas I decreed in 1827 that Jews must serve in person. The object was both punitive and missionary, to promote conversion to Christianity. Jewish communities were made responsible for assigned quotas of recruits, higher than the ratio of the total Jewish population. A specified number of Jews were drafted at the age of eighteen for 25-year terms but they could be taken at the age of twelve for several years of preparatory training which were not subtracted from the regular term. Many Jewish males of draft age fled to the forests or mutilated themselves to become physically ineligible. There were so many evaders that communal authorities often hired kidnappers to pick up boys from the streets or private homes. Russian administrators treated the prospective soldiers almost as criminals, often keeping them in chains until the respective draft boards could administer physical examinations. Baron, *The Russian Jew*, pp. 35–36; Baron N. E. Wrangel, *From Serfdom to Bolshevism*, p. 132.

9. [A. D.] The line of Jewish settlement, the Jewish Pale, went through the Polish southwest and northwest provinces, a territory twice that of France. Merchants of certain guilds, well-educated individuals, students at institutions of higher learning, qualified artists, and such people were permitted to live in districts of inner Russia.

10. Many believed that the Ural Executive Committee, isolated from Moscow by approaching White forces, acted independently in executing the tsarist family in an Ekaterinburg cellar in July 1918. P. M. Bykov, chairman of the Ekaterinburg Soviet, confirmed this theory but there is considerable evidence that the Politburo in Moscow was involved. P. M. Bykov, *The Last Days of Tsardom*, pp. 75–82; Leon Trotsky, *Trotsky's Diary in Exile*, pp. 80–81.

11. The imperial party was in Kiev to attend the unveiling of a monument to Alexander III. At one of the many festive events celebrating the occasion, Stolypin was leaning against the orchestra balustrade during the second intermission of a theater performance, talking with the minister of the nobility, Baron Frederiks. Although guests were admitted by invitation only, Dmitri Grigorevich Bogrov entered unchallenged and shot Stolypin twice. Bock, *Reminiscences of Stolypin*, p. 277; Kokovtsov, *Out of My Past*, pp. 268, 271, 575, n.1.

12. [A. D.] The first time was at my academic graduation. The second was the presentation after receiving a regiment at a reception in the Winter Palace.

13. Kadet leader Pavel N. Miliukov called the new electoral law the coup d'etat which

ended the first Russian revolution. Stolypin violated the Fundamental Laws by dissolving the second State Duma, then passing the electoral reform by Article 87, which provided for emergency legislation by the tsar between Duma sessions. Stolypin's aim was to give the landed proprietors and those with a material interest in the state a preponderant voice in the Duma. The resulting legislation, drafted by the assistant minister of the interior, Sergei Efimovich Kryzhanovskii, and promulgated extralegally, gave advantage to conservatives and moderate liberals and reduced non-Russian representation. Buchanan, *My Mission to Russia*, 1:158–160; Florinsky, *Russia*, 2:1199; Gronsky and Astrov, *The War and the Russian Government*, pp. 12–13; Paul Miliukov, *Political Memoirs, 1905-1917*, p. 158.

14. Stolypin also passed his agrarian reform of November 9, 1906, under Article 87 of the Fundamental Laws following dissolution of the first State Duma. The longstanding Russian agrarian problem, complicated by climate and insufficient arable land, resulted from fragmented strip farming, uneconomical use of serf labor, absentee landlordship, traditional Slavophile glorification of the commune, and overpopulation of European Russia. Alexander II's serf reforms had assigned lands to communes to be reapportioned periodically among members. Stolypin's agrarian law aimed toward gradual conversion of communal landownership into individual holdings, his "wager on the strong" to provide the peasant with incentive to develop the land. He also established peasant banks to facilitate peasant purchase of state and imperial appanage lands and subsidized emigration to Asiatic Russia. When Stolypin was killed in 1911 nearly nineteen million acres of land had already been assigned to peasant proprietors. Stolypin's basic agrarian program, his plan of building an independent Russian peasantry based on private ownership of plots, succeeded to such an extent that Stalin in the 1930s was forced to wage all-out war against the *kulaks* to undo all that Stolypin had created. Buchanan, *My Mission to Russia*, 1:161; Isaac Deutscher, *Stalin: A Political Biography*, pp. 317–325; George Pavlovsky, *Agricultural Russia on the Eve of Revolution*, p. 117.

15. [A. D.] All peasant self-government was separate from the general system of administration and subject to rural marshals of the nobility. In civil cases peasants were tried by an elected peasant court on the basis of customary law. But in regard to the private peasant ownership of land, only 20 percent of the peasants had actually succeeded in establishing their own farms before the revolution.

16. Most of the radical remedies were offered by the leftist parties. All were based on increasing peasant property by expropriating the land of large proprietors, either with or without compensation. Stolypin stood firm for the need to create a stable peasant propertied class, for private property purchased on easy terms, and for improved agrarian techniques. He replied to the left in a famous speech on May 10/23, 1907, before the State Duma: "To adversaries of the government who have chosen the path of radicalism, the path of deviation from Russia's historic course, deviation from cultural tradition, I say 'To you a great cataclysm is necessary, to us a Great Russia!' " Nor did Stolypin harbor any sentimental attachment for the *mir*. Although he was himself a large landowner, he had observed the efficiency of smallhold tenure in Western Europe. He recognized the stultifying effect of the repartitional commune on Russian agriculture. Therefore he said in a speech before the State Duma on December 5/18, 1908: ". . . we must give the peasant freedom in fixing his labor to the land . . . freedom to work for himself, to gain wealth, to manage his own property. We must give him authority over land and rescue him from the slavery of working off the debts of the commune." Bock, *Reminiscences of Stolypin*, pp. 304–305; Pavlovsky, *Agricultural Russia*, pp. 115–116; Sergei G. Pushkarev, *The Emergence of Modern Russia, 1801-1917*, pp. 265–266.

17. Bogrov was executed but the circumstances of Stolypin's death caused indignant protests. An official inquest revealed that Assistant Minister of the Interior Kurlov, who was responsible for police security, was grossly negligent. Minister of Justice Shche-

glovitov favored bringing Kurlov and three others to trial. Count V. M. Kokovtsov, who replaced Stolypin as chairman of the Council of Ministers, recommended such legal action to the tsar but Nicholas II had just undergone another near-fatal crisis with his hemophiliac son and declared that he could not punish anyone at such a time. Although most people believed that Bogrov was a double agent, a Socialist Revolutionary employed by the *okhranka*, the matter was closed except for speculation. Buchanan, *My Mission to Russia*, 1:156; Kokovtsov, *Out of My Past*, pp. 274, 341; Pares, *Fall*, p. 125.

18. In 1920 Metropolitan Antonii established the "Orthodox Synod Abroad" at Sermski Karlovtsy, Yugoslavia. Since renamed the "Orthodox Church Abroad," the organization has never recognized the authority of either the Russian or the Greek patriarch. In 1960 it claimed some 300 parishes in various countries, still awaiting the restoral of a "legitimate" patriarch in Moscow. Florinsky, *McGraw-Hill Encyclopedia*, p. 492.

19. In October 1912 the first Balkan War broke out, with Bulgaria, Serbia, and Greece pitted against Turkey. The war was complicated by the interests of the great powers, but the Balkan allies were largely successful in expelling Turkey from Europe. In June–July 1913 Serbia and Greece, joined by Romania and Turkey, fought Bulgaria over division of the spoils. Although fighting soon ended, conferences and realignments continued until World War I among both the Balkan allies and the great powers. Russia was, of course, vitally interested. The minister of war wanted partial mobilization in 1912, but Kokovtsov and Sazonov were able to discourage Nicholas II even though Austria had massed troops on the Serbian frontier and reinforced Galician garrisons. To alleviate tension Franz Joseph sent Prince Gotfried Hohenlohe (a former military attaché at St. Petersburg who was welcome at the Russian court) to Nicholas II. Friendly exchanges between the two emperors resulted in dismissal of Russian reservists retained past discharge time. Austria in turn reduced troops on the Russo-Galician frontier. Austria refused to reduce its troop buildup on the Serbian border, but the Austrian ambassador authorized a statement in Russian newspapers that Austria had no territorial designs on Serbia.

20. [A. D.] "Army Notes," *Razvedchik*, no. 72.

CHAPTER 29

1. In December 1912 Wilhelm II ordered the press to prepare the German people for war and informed his foreign ministry that the inevitability of struggle to the death of Teutons against Slavs and Gauls must be made the "basis of our policy." Fritz Fischer, *Germany's Aims in the First World War*, p. 35.

2. [A. D.] Long before the war, in 1906 if I am not mistaken. [General Friedrich von Bernhardi's more specific expression of German aims was published in 1912, *Deutschland und der nächste Krieg* (Germany and the Next War), which ran to five editions by the end of that year. Bernhardi promoted the right and duty of Germany to make war for reasons of Social Darwinism, militant Christian morality, the need for *Lebensraum*, and Germany's historical mission to keep her superior culture intact and spread it throughout the world. "Without war," he said, "inferior or dying races could easily choke the growth of healthy budding elements and a universal decadence would follow." Friedrich A. J. von Bernhardi, *Germany and the Next War*, pp. 20, 22, 29, 73; F. Fischer, *Germany's Aims*, p. 34. *Kriegsbrauch* (The Customs of War) to which Denikin refers was published in 1902 in Berlin by the German General Staff. It is included in English translation in Friedrich A. J. von Bernhardi's *Britain as Germany's Vassal*.]

3. An argument raged in the Reichstag over increases in the German army requested by the General Staff in the spring of 1913. Because of dissension the necessary appropriations were not voted until several months later. F. Fischer, *Germany's Aims*, pp. 35–36.

4. In reply to those who interpreted Russia's initial participation in World War I as part of the traditional Russian drive for the Straits, Serge Sazonov put forward Russia's offer,

before Turkey joined Germany, to guarantee Turkey's territorial integrity if Turkey would remain neutral. M. F. Schilling, *How the War Began in 1914, Being the Diary of the Russian Foreign Office from the 3rd to 20th (Old Style) of July, 1914*, from the S. D. Sazonov foreword, p. 10.

5. Gavrilo Princip, a young Bosnian revolutionary, was an agent of the Serbian society Union or Death (the Black Hand), a terrorist organization founded in 1911 for Slavic agitation against Austria.

6. On July 24, however, the German ambassador to St. Petersburg, Count Pourtales, handed Sazonov a note which stated that the "German Government had no knowledge of the Austrian note prior to its dispatch, and exercised no influence whatever upon its contents." But as Austria's ally, Count Pourtales added, Germany "naturally supports the demands presented by the Vienna Cabinet to Serbia, which are, in her opinion, justified." Schilling, *How the War Began*, p. 34.

7. Austria carefully timed delivery of the ultimatum so that President Raymond Poincaré and Premier René Viviani, who were both visiting Russia, had departed and were committed to at least four days of travel before they reached France. Buchanan, *My Mission to Russia*, 1:190.

8. Baron Moritz Fabianovich Schilling, chief of the Foreign Ministry chancellery, kept a diary to supplement official ministry documents from June 1914 to July 1916. The diary remained in the ministry and fell into Bolshevik hands. It was published in part in *Krasnyi arkhiv*, no. 4 (1923), and from this the English translation previously cited (see note 4 above) was made of July 1914 entries. Schilling made extensive notes on Russia's attempts to find an honorable, peaceful solution to the Austro-Serbian problem.

9. Even so, on July 25, 1914, General Nicholas Golovine estimated the shortage of Russian officers at approximately 8,000. Minister of Finance Kokovtsov saw little improvement in the army during the period mentioned and ascribed Russian failure to meet the German challenge to War Minister Sukhomlinov's negligence. Only in 1914, Kokovtsov said, did Sukhomlinov present a comprehensive plan to the Duma and "even then, there were still omissions and errors." Golovine, *Russian Army*, p. 29; Kokovtsov, *Out of My Past*, pp. 362–364.

10. Only the retreat from Galicia, which began in April 1915, and the subsequent rapid advance of Germans onto Russian territory made Russians realize that military success depended on necessary war materials and that some overall economic-political coordination was needed. Since the idea of compulsory mobilization of industry was distasteful to industrial circles and political groups, the little mobilization which actually occurred was voluntary and directed primarily by local committees set up by *zemstvos*. By late 1915, 28 such provincial war industry boards had been formed in districts of Russia as scattered as Arkhangelsk, Odessa, and Vladivostok. S. O. Zagorsky, *State Control of Industry in Russia during the War*, pp. 82–89.

11. [A. D.] Incidentally, there was only one case in my journalistic career when an article of mine was suppressed. This was an article opposing abolition of the fortresses. And it was forbidden not by the censor but by Sukhomlinov himself, to whom the editor of *Razvedchik*, Berezovskii, showed it beforehand. [General Brusilov called abolition of fortifications on the western frontier thoughtless and contributory to 1915 reverses. The plan was to abandon the western frontier to the enemy, but when the crisis came Russia was unable to do so and was forced to improvise. The guiding concept was apparently to create a buffer zone in which an invading army could capture nothing of value and would find movement and supply difficult. The neglect of transport and supply routes was, of course, detrimental to Russian forces as well. Aleksei A. Brussilov, *A Soldier's Notebook, 1914–1918*, p. 12.]

12. The current definitive work proving this point is Fritz Fischer, *Germany's Aims in the First World War* (1967).

13. General Helmuth von Moltke was chief of the German General Staff from 1906 to 1914. The basic plan was, however, the work of General Alfred von Schlieffen, his predecessor (1892–1906). F. Fischer, *Germany's Aims*, p. xxvii.

CHAPTER 30

1. Emphasizing that it was against Austria only, the Russian War Ministry improvised mobilization of four southern districts, a symbolic act since no arrangements were made to call up reservists from other districts. But the delay in ordering general mobilization stemmed more from the tsar's fervent peace hopes than from Sukhomlinov's known incompetence. By July 30 Sukhomlinov and the chief of the General Staff, Yanush-kevich, begged Foreign Minister Sazonov to intercede with the tsar and urge general mobilization. They convinced Sazonov of the necessity for positive action and he in turn persuaded the tsar. Serge D. Sazonov, *Fateful Years, 1909–1916: Reminiscences of Serge Sazonov*, pp. 199–205.

2. In the historiography of the origins of World War I, Bernadotte Schmidt and Pierre Renouvin were the first to challenge the prevailing opinion that Russia, Austria-Hungary, and Germany in that order were primarily responsible for the war. Luigi Albertini's two-volume work, translated into English in 1952, converted many non-German historians to the view of Germany's basic guilt. Fritz Fischer in 1961 was the first eminent German historian to reexamine German history during the World War I period in the light of new official sources and to reach the Albertini conclusion (in *Griff nach der Weltmacht*). F. Fischer, *Germany's Aims*, from the Hajo Holborn introduction to the American edition, pp. x–xi.

3. See note 1 above.

4. Late on the evening of August 4 German Chancellor Bethmann-Hollweg received the English ambassador in Berlin. During the meeting Bethmann-Hollweg called the 1879 Belgian neutrality pledge signed by England, Prussia, and France "a scrap of paper." The treaty pledge had serious significance for England, for German violation of Belgian neutrality galvanized British public opinion. Previously one-third to one-half of the British cabinet had opposed entering the war but the German ultimatum to Belgium made the cabinet favor war almost unanimously. David Lloyd George, *War Memoirs of David Lloyd George*, 2:40; Sazonov, *Fateful Years*, p. 219.

5. [A. D.] The Constitutional Democrats, a liberal political party. [*Rech* was the Kadet daily newspaper published in St. Petersburg from 1906 to 1917. It was suppressed by the Soviets but reappeared under various names (*Nasha rech, Svobodnaia rech, Vek, Novaia rech, Nash vek*) until finally closed in 1918. Iosif Vladimirovich Hessen was chief editor for the entire period, but Kadet leader Pavel N. Miliukov was also active when his political work permitted. Miliukov utilized the period of negotiations following Sarajevo to campaign in *Rech* against Russia's participation in the war because it seemed to him "more than probable that Russia would be defeated." But on August 1 the staff prepared the August 4 issue containing "sharp issues against Germany." That night they learned that their paper had been banned because of its outspoken opposition to the war. Conferences proved fruitful and the issue was printed. Miliukov did not blame the Russian government for the war. "Given William's disposition," he said, "the war would have occurred all the same, whether Russia mobilized or not." Florinsky, *McGraw-Hill Encyclopedia*, p. 214; Gurko, *Features and Figures of the Past*, pp. 671–672, n.49; Miliukov, *Political Memoirs*, pp. 293, 298–299.]

6. "In the present situation, it is impossible to determine, from the standpoint of the international proletariat, the defeat of which of the two groups of belligerent nations would be the lesser evil for socialism. But to us Russian Social-Democrats there cannot be the slightest doubt that, from the standpoint of the working class and of the toiling masses of all the nations of Russia, the defeat of the tsarist monarchy, the most reactionary and barbarous of governments, which is oppressing the largest number of nations and the greatest mass of the population of Europe and Asia, would be the lesser evil." V. I. Lenin, "The War and Russian Social-Democracy," *Collected Works*, 21:32–33.

7. The resolution adopted by the State Duma appeared in *Pravitelstvenny vestnik*, no. 165 (August 9, 1914). It read: "Having heard the explanations of the Government, and having satisfied itself that all means were exhausted for the preservation of peace in

keeping with Russia's dignity as a great power, the State Duma expresses its unshakable conviction that in this grave hour of trial, in the face of the approaching war storm, all nationalities of Russia, united in the common sentiment of their cause, are prepared, at the summons of the Sovereign, to stand up in defense of their country, its honor, and its possessions." The same day the resolution was published, *Rech* editors observed that the resolution was unanimous only because the extreme left withdrew from the Duma hall to avoid voting "nyet." Frank A. Golder, ed., *Documents of Russian History, 1914–1917*, p. 37.

CHAPTER 31

1. [A. D.] Field Marshal von Moltke had led the rout of Austria in 1866 and of France in 1871. [Count Helmuth Carl Bernhard von Moltke's relationship to the younger Moltke was actually that of uncle.]

2. Bitter accusations were hurled at both Zhilinskii and Rennenkampf but according to Golovine the Russian reverses were "entirely due to the overwhelming preponderance of the German batteries." Golovine, *The Russian Army*, p. 133.

3. [A. D.] Born a princess of Hesse-Darmstadt, Elizaveta Fedorovna was the widow of Grand Duke Sergei Aleksandrovich, who was murdered by a revolutionary. [The grand duke, both uncle and brother-in-law of the tsar, was governor-general of Moscow when he was assassinated by a Socialist Revolutionary in 1905. By 1915 his widow was estranged from her sister the empress, having tried to influence Alexandra to repudiate Rasputin's influence. Bolsheviks shot the grand duchess and five other members of the Romanov family and threw them into a mine shaft near Alapaevsk in the Northern Urals on July 17, 1918, the day after Nicholas II and his family were killed at Ekaterinburg. Elizaveta's body and that of a nun-companion killed with her were recovered by White forces and ultimately reinterred in Jerusalem. William Henry Chamberlain, *The Russian Revolution, 1917–1921*, 2:93–94.]

4. Alexandra herself suffered from Germanophobe sentiment. Hated and misunderstood by her subjects, she was called "that German woman" and accused of treason by complicity with Germany. The accusation was an invention, according to those who knew her, but it satisfied the urge to find a scapegoat for Russian reverses. Izvolskii, *Memoirs*, pp. 279–280.

5. [A. D.] Before the war 9.2 percent Protestants appeared in lists of Russian generals, undoubtedly persons of German descent. But since many had adopted Orthodoxy the actual percentage was higher.

6. [A. D.] If memory does not betray me, it was General Pantaleev.

7. [A. D.] Units of the rifle brigades were excluded from infantry divisions, having their own divisional organization although fewer personnel: four regiments of two battalions each instead of four and a division of artillery, three batteries instead of six.

8. [A. D.] In 1915 it was expanded into a division during military action.

CHAPTER 32

1. [A. D.] Kaledin subsequently commanded the 8th Army and at the beginning of the revolution was a Don ataman.

2. [A. D.] Future supreme commander and leader of the White movement.

3. Golovine held General Ruzskii and his staff responsible for failure to contain the Germans, encircled near Lodz in November 1914. This blunder, said Golovine, was known neither to the troops nor to the public and General Ruzskii retained his position because of his popularity with the State Duma and with the Russian people. Golovine, *The Russian Army*, p. 215.

4. [A. D.] General Brusilov remained in Soviet Russia and collaborated with Soviet authorities.

5. [A. D.] Regular battle personnel of the brigade was 4,000 bayonets.

CHAPTER 33

1. [A. D.] At the most critical moment in February, we had only twelve to fourteen ordnance depots in all. Toward spring 1916 we had thirty to forty and by fall, ninety to a hundred.

2. Denikin quoted excerpts (here retranslated from the Russian) from David Lloyd George's 6-volume *War Memoirs* (London, 1933–36), 1:470–471, 478. Lloyd George, then British minister of munitions, stated that allowing a road to Russia to be opened through the Balkans was an error offset only by American entry into the war. Had France and Britain equipped Russia and Romania, he believed, Russian armies would not have been beaten and the Russian revolution would not have occurred before the war's end. The Russian military justifiably felt abandoned and betrayed by their allies, who wasted ammunition on the western front while the Russians were left without shells to defend themselves. "Militarily it was foolish," he said, "psychologically it was insane." Lloyd George, *War Memoirs*, 2:2033–2034.

3. Nicholas II designated Grand Duke Mikhail Aleksandrovich as his heir when he abdicated in March 1917 but Mikhail refused. Following the Bolshevik revolution the grand duke was banished to Perm, near which he was shot on June 12, 1918. Chamberlin, *Russian Revolution*, 2:94; Gurko, *Features and Figures of the Past*, p. 615, n. 18.

4. [A. D.] Radko-Dmitriev was a Bulgarian, hero of the Balkan Wars of 1911–1913, who had come over to Russian service because of the Germanophile tendencies of Bulgaria.

5. [A. D.] Only later did I learn that Brusilov supported our left flank at the request of [General D. G.] Shcherbachev, commander of the army, whose troops were able to withdraw in time.

CHAPTER 34

1. Although the leadership of Turkey during World War I was technically a triumvirate, Enver Pasha (Enver Bey) actually ruled. When Turkey collapsed Enver Pasha was sentenced to die (1919) but he escaped to Soviet Russia. He claimed to despise Germany, to favor revolution, and to admire the new Soviet state. The Bolsheviks did not believe him and supported his political rival, Mustapha Kemal. Enver Pasha formed a rebel band and fought the Bolsheviks, hoping to found a Pan-Turanian empire. In August 1922 a Red Army patrol killed Enver and his band. Louis Fischer, *The Soviets in World Affairs: A History of Relations between the Soviet Union and the Rest of the World, 1917–1929*, pp. 280–286.

2. By mid-November 1915 the Serbs, virtually encircled by Austrian, German, and Bulgarian forces, had no escape route except to the southwest. Leaving their women and children at Prishtina, they fled in the depths of winter through the mountains of Albania. Only the Bulgarians pursued them. Survivors reached the Adriatic port of San Giovanni di Medua but could not be rescued because the Austrian fleet was near. Through December they made their way down the Albanian coast and were finally transported by British and French vessels to safety on Corfu. Winston S. Churchill, *The World Crisis*, 6:345–347.

3. General Count Franz Conrad von Hötzendorff (1852–1925) recorded his experiences in *Aus meiner Dienstzeit, 1906–1918* (From My Military Career, 1906–1918), 5 v. in 7.

4. During the winter of 1915–1916 General Klembovskii replaced General Savich as chief of staff of the southwest front and in March 1916 General Brusilov replaced Ivanov as commander there. Brussilov, *Soldier's Notebook*, p. 204, n.1.

5. At a meeting on August 20, 1915, over which the tsar presided, the Russian ministers to a man attempted to dissuade the tsar from taking personal command. Chairman of the Council of Ministers Goremykin, elderly and never courageous, apparently cited only

the potential danger to the tsar's person but others were more outspoken, both then and in individual appeals to the tsar. Seven ministers who feared being left with Goremykin in charge and who were unable to unseat him submitted a collective resignation to the tsar. Through Goremykin, the tsar expressed his displeasure at their action and, comparing it to a strike, ordered them to remain in their posts. By the following year, six of them had been replaced. Sazonov, *Fateful Years*, pp. 291–295.

6. [A. D.] Goremykin was on the friendliest of terms with Rasputin and in all matters followed the advice of the empress. [The "report" of the "opposition ministers" was drafted at Sazonov's house and was signed by seven ministers and the Procurator of the Holy Synod, A. D. Samarin, on August 21, 1915. The signers opposed not Nicholas but his decision to assume supreme command of the army and leave the government in Goremykin's hands. Besides Goremykin, only the ministers of war and the navy were absent from the meeting but they expressed sympathy with the action. *Ibid.*, p. 294.]

7. [A. D.] I will write about Rasputin's personality and role in Chapter 36. [Denikin died after completing only part of Chapter 35.]

8. By the pejorative nickname *galki* (crows) Alexandra referred to Grand Duchesses Anastasia Nikolaevna and Militsa Nikolaevna, wives of Grand Dukes Nikolai Nikolaevich and Peter Nikolaevich respectively. Both were daughters of Montenegrin King Nicholas. "Anna" was Anna Vyrubova (née Taneeva), Alexandra's confidante. Inconsistencies between these excerpts and printed versions of the correspondence come from the fact that Denikin apparently quoted from a Russian translation of Alexandra's letters. The imperial couple customarily corresponded in English, dating and numbering their letters. The empress's letters were found in the last Ekaterinburg residence of the imperial couple and have been reproduced in several sources. The wartime letters of Nicholas and Alexandra are now available in a convenient single-volume edition, *The Nicky-Sunny Letters: Correspondence of the Tsar and Tsaritsa, 1914–1917* (Hattiesburg, Miss.: Academic International, 1970).

9. The noun *starets* comes from the adjective *starii* (old) and is a title of respect meaning "elder," not necessarily in age but in wisdom.

10. Grand Duke Nikolai Nikolaevich was known to despise Rasputin. The story of his threat to hang Rasputin may be apocryphal but it nevertheless appears in many memoirs of the period.

11. "Khodynka" refers to the tragedy which occurred during the official coronation of Nicholas II in Moscow in 1896. The tsar was to appear and distribute small favors to common people assembled at Khodynka field. In the eager press of the crowd, hundreds of people fell and were trampled to death. Many bitter words were written about the fact that Nicholas unfeelingly danced that evening at the French ambassador's ball. Evidence indicates, however, that officials whisked him away from Khodynka and he was not informed about the disaster until the next day. Nicholas's son, Aleksei Nikolaevich, was, of course, a hemophiliac.

CHAPTER 35

1. Denikin did not live to complete his book, and the account breaks off at this point. The Brusilov offensive, originally scheduled for June 15 to coincide with the Joffre offensive on the Somme, was moved forward to assist the Italians, attacked by Austrians in the Trentino. When the Russian offensive began on June 4, the surprised Austrians fell back, leaving many prisoners. Although Russia retook Lutsk and Chernovits, advancing deep into Austrian territory, their lack of adequate north-south railroad lines prevented suitable troop movement. The offensive stopped when fifteen German divisions arrived from the western front. The Russians failed to take Kovel, the major target to the south, or Lvov; they had lost a million men and the army was demoralized and discontented.

BIOGRAPHICAL SKETCHES

BIOGRAPHICAL SKETCHES

Alekseev, General Mikhail Vasilievich (1857–1918), actually directed Russian forces during most of World War I and with General Kornilov founded the White movement after the Bolshevik revolution. He had served in the Russo-Turkish War and attended the General Staff Academy, becoming a lecturer there in 1896. In the Russo-Japanese War he was quartermaster general of the 3rd Manchurian Army, after which he returned to the General Staff Academy to teach the history of military science. When the tsar assumed personal command in 1915, he chose Alekseev as his chief of staff. Although Alekseev's knowledge was primarily theoretical and his experience limited to the management of small forces, he was fearless, energetic, and intelligent, directing *Stavka* (supreme headquarters) to the best of his ability. In March 1917 Alekseev became chief commander until he was replaced by Brusilov in early June. When the Bolshevik revolution came, he made his way from his Smolensk residence to the Don and organized the White forces. He was one of the first prominent fatalities in the civil war. Kenez, *Civil War in South Russia, 1918*, pp. 25–26; Kokovtsov, *Out of My Past*, p. 590, n.7; *Krasnyi arkhiv*, 1 (1922), 265.

Brusilov, Adjutant General Aleksei Alekseevich (1853–1926), was a cavalryman who served in the Russo-Turkish War and afterward became head of the cavalry officers' school. In 1906 he commanded a division and in 1909 a corps. He was assistant troop commander of the Warsaw military district in 1912–1913. At the outbreak of World War I, Brusilov was named commander of the 8th Army, then replaced General Ivanov as commander of the southwest front. In June–July 1917 he replaced General Alekseev as supreme commander but was himself replaced by Kornilov. In the Bolshevik revolution Brusilov fought for the insurgent government and was seriously wounded. During the Russo-Polish War he served the Bolsheviks and later was rewarded with the sinecure post of chief inspector of the State Stud Farm. Brusilov's account of his activities in World War I and the 1917 revolutions is available in English as *A Soldier's Notebook*. *Krasnyi arkhiv*, 1 (1922), 268.

Dragomirov, General Mikhail Ivanovich (1830–1905), graduated from the Imperial Military Academy in 1856 and taught in the Nicholas Academy of the General Staff. From 1864 to 1866 he was tutor to the future Alexander III and in 1866 he was attached to the Prussian army as military observer in the Austro-Prussian War. Later he was named chief of staff of the Kiev military district and served in the Russo-Turkish War of 1877–1878. He moved through several posts from chief of the Nicholas Academy of the General Staff in 1878 to troop commander of the Kiev military district in 1889. In 1903 he was named to the State Council. He wrote several treatises on tactics, officer education, and troop training. Florinsky, *McGraw-Hill Encyclopedia*, p. 138; Gurko, *Features and Figures of the Past*, p. 671, n.43.

Dragomirov, General Vladimir Mikhailovich, born in 1867, completed the Corps of Pages school and the General Staff Academy and entered the elite Semenovskii

Guards Regiment in 1881. By 1904 he was chief of staff of a corps and in the Russo-Japanese War commanded a regiment. In 1914 Dragomirov was chief of staff of the 3rd Army and in 1915 chief of staff of the southwest front. Because of illness he went into reserve ranks and in 1917 he retired. *Krasnyi arkhiv*, 1 (1922), 271.

Dukhonin, Nikolai Nikolaevich (1876–1917), one of the youngest generals in the tsarist army, was commander of all Russian forces at the time of the Bolshevik revolution. Dukhonin helped a number of imprisoned generals, including Denikin, to escape south to the Don. When he refused to begin truce negotiations with the Germans, he was shot by mutineering soldiers. Florinsky, *McGraw-Hill Encyclopedia*, p. 139.

Guchkov, Aleksandr Ivanovich (1862–1936), became chairman of the third State Duma in March 1910 and resigned a year later. Guchkov had always been a man of action. He fought with the Boers against England and with the Macedonians against Turkey. In 1904–1905 he represented the Russian Red Cross in the Manchurian theater. Subsequently he was head of the Moscow City Duma, a founder of the Octobrist Party, and a member of the first, third, and fourth State Dumas. In 1914 he was head of the St. Petersburg City Duma. During World War I Guchkov was chairman of the Central War Industries Committee and a member of the State Council. In March 1917 he and Bruce Shulgin accepted the act of abdication from Nicholas II at Pskov. Guchkov was minister of war and navy in the Provisional Government and went into French emigration following the Bolshevik revolution. Gurko, *Features and Figures of the Past*, p. 667, n.8; *Krasnyi arkhiv*, 1 (1922), 267–268.

Gurko, General (later Field Marshal) Iosif Vladimirovich (1828–1901), gained fame in the battles of Shipka, Turnov, and Gorny Dubniak during the Russo-Turkish War of 1877–1878. As governor-general of Poland in the 1890s, he supported the policy of Russification and suppressed revolutionary movements. Florinsky, *McGraw-Hill Encyclopedia*, p. 213.

Gurko, General Vasilii Iosifovich (1864–1937) was chief of the General Staff from November 1916 to March 1917 and commander in chief of the western front under the Provisional Government from March to June 1917. Kerensky turned against Gurko and ordered his arrest, then released him in care of the British who accepted him for British emigration. General and Mrs. Gurko went, however, to France, where his wife continued her work as a nurse. In March 1918 she was killed by a German shell. General Gurko left an account of his experiences in World War I and the first 1917 revolution in Basil Gourko, *War and Revolution in Russia, 1914–1917*.

Ivanov, Adjutant General Nikolai Iudovich (1851–1919), had participated in the Russo-Turkish and Russo-Japanese wars. He served as governor-general of Kronstadt (1906–1907) and troop commander of the Kiev military district (1908–1914). At the outbreak of World War I, Ivanov was named commander of the southwest front but as the British military observer General Alfred Knox expressed it, "As a leader, he belonged to a past generation, and had to make way for younger men." Nicholas II named Ivanov to the State Council in 1916. Since this obviously amounted to forced retirement, the tsar, who was fond of Ivanov, then called him to *Stavka* (supreme headquarters) where Ivanov remained, idle and unhappy, until the February/March revolution. Nicholas ordered Ivanov to lead a selected force to Petrograd but he was unable to get there because of railway strikes. Arrested by Kerensky, he was later released and joined the White movement after the Bolshevik revolution. He died of wounds in 1919. Alfred W. F. Knox, *With the Russian Army, 1914–1917*, 2:403; Kokovtsov, *Out of My Past*, pp. 575–576, n.5; *Krasnyi arkhiv*, 1 (1922), 264.

Kaledin, Aleksei Maksimovich (1861–1918), replaced Brusilov as commander of the 8th Army in 1916 when Brusilov was named commander of the southwest front. He resigned in May 1917 but soon after was elected ataman of the Don Cossacks. According to a British military observer, General Alfred Knox, "Kaledin was shy and silent, more of a student than a man of the world like his chief," Brusilov; he gave the impression of being a "hard thinker" but perhaps lacked the vitality "to carry a difficult operation through." Unhappy, unable to adjust to changed conditions, Kaledin committed suicide in February 1918. Knox, *With the Russian Army, 1914–1917*, 2:437–438; Kokovtsov, *Out of My Past*, p. 590, n.6.

Kaulbars, General Baron Aleksandr Vasilievich (1844–1929), became a General Staff officer in 1869. In 1901 he was appointed a general of cavalry and participated in the Russo-Japanese War as assistant commander of the 3rd Manchurian Army. After the war he became troop commander of the Odessa military district and in 1909 was named to the War Council. *Krasnyi arkhiv*, 1 (1922), 266.

Kerensky, Alexander Fedorovich (1881–1970), first achieved prominence as a defense attorney in political trials. As leader of the Trudovik (Labor) group of Socialist Revolutionaries, he was a deputy to the third and fourth State Dumas. In March 1917 Kerensky was vice-chairman of the Petrograd Soviet, then minister of justice, minister of war and of the navy, and finally prime minister in the Provisional Government. He barely escaped from Petrograd during the Bolshevik revolution and emigrated to the United States where he died in New York in 1970. He devoted his long life in emigration to writing and speaking against the Bolshevik regime. Kokovtsov, *Out of My Past*, p. 280, n.2.

Kornilov, Lavr Georgievich (1870–1918), son of a Siberian Cossack, graduated from the Nicholas Academy of the General Staff and served in Central Asia and in the Russo-Japanese War. From 1907 to 1911 he was Russian military attaché to China. During World War I he was captured by the Austrians in May 1915 but escaped and made his way back to Russia in 1916. Kornilov commanded the southwest front for a week in July 1917 and was chief commander from July to September 1917. Kerensky turned against him and had him imprisoned in September 1917 following the dubious "Kornilov rebellion," an alleged officers' plot to unseat Kerensky and form a military dictatorship. Released in December 1917, Kornilov went to the Don where with General Alekseev he formed the Volunteer army. Kornilov was killed by enemy fire in April 1918. Gurko, *Features and Figures of the Past*, p. 641, n.2; Kokovtsov, *Out of My Past*, p. 590, n.7; Leonid I. Strakhovsky, "Was There a Kornilov Rebellion? A Re-appraisal of the Evidence," *Slavonic and East European Review* (London), 32, no. 81 (June 1, 1955), 372–395.

Krasnov, General Petr Nikolaevich (1869–1947), a graduate of the General Staff Academy, advanced from colonel to general in World War I. He was appointed by Alexander Kerensky in October 1917 to command Cossack forces against the Bolshevik Red Guards. Krasnov's 3rd Corps fought the only battles in defense of the Provisional Government in the October (November) revolution. In May 1918 he was elected Don Cossack ataman and participated in the battle of Tsaritsyn (later Stalingrad, now Volgograd) in the winter of 1918. Following the civil war Krasnov lived in Germany and in World War II fought in the German army. After the war the Soviets captured him and he was executed in 1947. Florinsky, *McGraw-Hill Encyclopedia*, pp. 289–290; Kenez, *Civil War in South Russia, 1918*, p. 140.

Kropotkin, Prince Peter Alekseevich (1842–1921), fulfilled his military obligation as an officer in an Amur Cossack division, then joined a scientific expedition to investigate glaciers in Finland and Sweden. In 1872 on a visit to Switzerland he joined the First International but later adopted his anarchist philosophy. He was arrested in 1874 in Russia for participation in revolutionary circles but escaped to England in

1876. Kropotkin was expelled from Switzerland in 1881 after three years' residence, then arrested and imprisoned for five years in France for membership in the International. In 1886 he settled near London where he wrote political pamphlets and his *Memoirs of a Revolutionist* (which first appeared serially in the *Atlantic Monthly*, September 1898–September 1899, as "Autobiography of a Revolutionist"). Kropotkin returned to Russia in June 1917 but took no further political role. Gurko, *Features and Figures of the Past*, p. 632, n.16.

Kuropatkin, General Aleksei Nikolaevich (1848–1925), a product of the Pavlovsk Military School and the General Staff Academy, served with distinction as General Skobelev's chief of staff in the Russo-Turkish War, 1877–1878. In 1897 he became commander in chief in the Caucasus and in 1898 minister of war. At the outbreak of the Russo-Japanese War in 1904 he was sent to Manchuria to share supreme command with Admiral E. I. Alekseev, viceroy of the Far East. After the disastrous Mukden defeat General Kuropatkin relinquished his post to General N. P. Linevich and accepted command of one of the Manchurian armies. He urgently requested participation in World War I and was named commander of a grenadier corps, then commander of the western front. In 1916, however, he was troop commander of the Turkestan military district. Arrested in 1917 by the Provisional Government, he was transferred to Petrograd but was soon freed. He settled on his former estate in Pskov province where he served as a village teacher until his death in 1925. Kokovtsov, *Out of My Past*, p. 542, n.16; *Krasnyi arkhiv*, 1 (1922), 266; Sydney V. Utechin, *Everyman's Concise Encyclopedia of Russia* (New York: Dutton, 1961), p. 298.

Linevich, General Nikolai Petrovich (1838–1908), had served in the Russo-Turkish War and in 1900 had commanded the Russian contingent of an international force for suppression of the Boxer Rebellion. In 1904 he was governor-general of Amur province. In November 1904 Linevich assumed command of the 1st Manchurian Army under General Kuropatkin, a position of subordination which was to be reversed the following year. Following the Russian defeat at Mukden, Linevich replaced Kuropatkin as commander in chief of Russian land forces in the Far East and Kuropatkin, by his own request, was given command of the 1st Army. Florinsky, *Russia*, 2:1267, 1275; Kokovtsov, *Out of My Past*, p. 552, n.10.

Makarov, Vice Admiral Stepan Osipovich (1848–1904), was a scientist and explorer as well as an outstanding naval commander. He was the founder of the Russian torpedo-boat fleet and used these vessels against Turkish ironclads in the Russo-Turkish War of 1877–1878. Makarov designed and supervised the building of the first powerful icebreaker *Ermak* and invented the armor-piercing point for projectiles. As commander of the Russian Pacific fleet, he went down with his flagship *Petropavlovsk* when it struck a Japanese mine in April 1904. Florinsky, *McGraw-Hill Encyclopedia*, p. 328.

Maklakov, Vasilii Alekseevich (1869–1957), a graduate of Moscow University, was a well-known attorney in both Moscow and St. Petersburg. He was elected as a Kadet deputy to the second, third, and fourth State Dumas. In 1917 he was appointed Provisional Government ambassador to Paris and in 1919 represented White forces at a political conference there. After the civil war Maklakov headed the Russian Emigrants Committee in France and published several works on the Duma period. He died in Switzerland in 1957. Kokovtsov, *Out of My Past*, p. 590, n.1.

Markov, General S. L., had been a lecturer at the General Staff Academy and his background was primarily academic when he became Denikin's chief of staff in 1914. But he proved to be an excellent field commander. Markov was arrested with Denikin in September 1917 as part of the Kornilov affair, and they escaped together to the Don in December 1917. Markov was killed by hostile fire on June

25, 1918, in the second Kuban campaign near the Cossack village of Torgovaia. Richard Luckett, *The White Generals*, pp. 84, 115, 179.

Meller-Zakomelskii, General Baron Aleksandr Nikolaevich (1844–1928), participated in the Polish campaign of 1863 after which he attended the General Staff Academy and served in the Russo-Turkish War. From 1906 to 1909 he was governor of the Baltic region and in 1909 was appointed to the State Council. Gurko, *Features and Figures of the Past*, pp. 670–671, n.41.

Miasoedov, Sergei Nikolaevich (1867–1915), was called "A. D." Miasoedov in the Russian text, a pardonable error since Denikin was writing from memory much of the time. Miasoedov served in the gendarme corps from 1892 to 1907 when he was suspected of being a German agent and put on the reserve lists. In 1909, because of his friendship with Minister of War Sukhomlinov, he returned to active duty in intelligence and counterespionage. He was again dismissed in 1912 after Guchkov accused him from the Duma tribune of secret dealings with Germany. In 1914 Sukhomlinov assigned Miasoedov to the 10th Army as interpreter. When Russia's military reverses began in Galicia and Poland in 1915, Miasoedov was among those suspected of treason. His court-martial produced no conclusive evidence of guilt but he was hanged nevertheless. Certainly the incident reinforced rumors of treason in high office, both military and civilian. Gurko, *Features and Figures of the Past*, pp. 682–683, n.5; Edward G. Thaden, *Russia Since 1801: The Making of a New Society*, p. 417.

Mikhail Nikolaevich, Grand Duke (1832–1909), the fourth son of Nicholas I, had served as viceroy of the Caucasus, then commander of Caucasus forces in the Russo-Turkish War, 1877–1878. He was an uncle of Alexander III and represented the imperial family in government as chairman of the State Council for a time. Kuropatkin, *Russian Army*, 1:26; Kokovtsov, *Out of My Past*, p. 541, n.7.

Mishchenko, General Pavel Ivanovich, born in 1853, participated in the Russo-Turkish War, 1877–1878, the Chinese campaign of 1900, and the Russo-Japanese War, after which he became governor-general and troop commander of the Turkestan military district. He was also elected ataman of the Don Cossacks. Unlike his role in the Russo-Japanese War, he failed to distinguish himself in World War I. *Krasnyi arkhiv*, 1 (1922), 264.

Pantaleev, General A. I., born in 1838, had served in the Russo-Turkish War, been assistant chief and then chief of gendarmes (1897–1900), and military governor-general of Irkutsk (1900–1903). In 1903 he was named to the State Council. He was often called upon to investigate matters of a delicate nature. *Krasnyi arkhiv*, 1 (1922), 269.

Pilsudski (Ginet-Pilsudski), Joseph Kiemens (1867–1935), a Russian Pole, was born on the family estate of Zulow, Lithuania, and educated in Vilna. He was arrested and exiled to Siberia for five years for involvement with his brother Bronislas in an attempt on the life of Alexander III in 1887 (Lenin's brother Aleksandr Ilyich was executed for his part in the plot). Back in Vilna in 1892 Pilsudski became an active member of the Polish Socialist Party, dedicated to changing it from an internationalist to a nationalist organization. In 1904 he traveled to Japan where he failed to get Japanese agreement to make Polish independence a condition for peace with Russia. At the outbreak of World War I Pilsudski formed a Polish legion with Austrian approval and by the war's end had attained an independent Polish republic. The war which he led against Bolshevik Russia in 1919–1920 was ended by the Treaty of Riga, 1921. Except for a brief period of retirement (1922–1926) Pilsudski, as president, premier, or chief of army staff, was virtual dictator of Poland until his death in 1935. Pilsudska, *Pilsudski*; Pilsudski, *Memories*; Reddaway, *Marshal Pilsudski*.

Polivanov, General Aleksei Andreevich (1855–1922), a graduate of the Nicholas Academy of the General Staff, participated in the Russo-Turkish War, was chief of the General Staff in 1905, and assistant minister of war from 1906 to 1912. In 1912 he became a member of the State Council and was briefly minister of war in 1915 following Sukhomlinov's dismissal. Polivanov remained with the Bolsheviks, serving as Soviet military expert in Soviet-Polish negotiations for the 1921 Treaty of Riga. Gurko, *Features and Figures of the Past*, p. 683, n.5a.

Radko-Dmitriev, General, had been trained at the General Staff Academy. After the Balkan Wars he was named Bulgarian envoy to St. Petersburg. In World War I he remained with Russia and commanded the 8th Army Corps, then the 3rd Army, the 7th Cavalry Corps, and the 7th Army. Transferred to reserve ranks in 1917, he resided in Kislovodsk until he was arrested and killed after the Bolshevik revolution. *Krasnyi arkhiv*, 1 (1922), 270.

Rennenkampf, General Pavel Karlovich (1854–1918), was chief of staff of the Zabaikal district troops and served, as indicated, in the Russo-Japanese War. In January 1906 he commanded one of two punitive expeditions into Siberia. In 1911 as an adjutant general, he was named troop commander of the Vilna military district. As commander of the 1st Army in 1914 he was blamed by many of his contemporaries for the Russian defeat in East Prussia during the early stages of World War I. Florinsky, *McGraw-Hill Encyclopedia*, p. 475; *Krasnyi arkhiv*, 1 (1922), 265.

Ruzskii, General Nikolai Vladimirovich (1854–1918), was wounded in the Russo-Turkish War. Subsequently he completed the General Staff Academy and served as quartermaster general of the Kiev military district under General Ivanov and as chief of staff of the 2nd Manchurian Army. Before World War I he was a member of the Military Council. In 1914 he commanded the 3rd Army on the southwest front, then replaced Zhilinskii as northwest front commander. After the first 1917 revolution he resided in Kislovodsk and was killed there after the Bolshevik revolution. Knox, *With the Russian Army, 1914–1917*, I, 47; *Krasnyi arkhiv*, 1 (1922), 265.

Sakharov, Lieutenant General Viktor Viktorovich (1848–1905), a graduate of the Nicholas Academy of the General Staff, served in the Russo-Turkish War, then in the Warsaw military district first as assistant chief of staff, then as quartermaster general. Before being named chief of the General Staff, 1898–1904, he served as chief of staff of the Odessa military district. He replaced General Kuropatkin as minister of war, 1904–1905, and in 1905 was assassinated in the residence of then Governor Peter A. Stolypin in Saratov, where he had been sent to investigate agrarian disorders. Gurko, *Features and Figures of the Past*, p. 651, n.33; Bock, *Reminiscences of Stolypin*, pp. 120–121.

Samsonov, General Aleksandr Vasilievich (1859–1914), served in the Russo-Turkish War and was appointed to the General Staff in 1884. He was commandant of the cavalry school at Elizavetgrod from 1896 to 1904 and commanded a brigade in the Russo-Japanese War. In 1909 Samsonov became military governor-general in Turkestan. In August 1914 his 2nd Army was destroyed in the battle near Tannenberg (at Soldau), in the Masurian Lakes region, and he committed suicide. Kokovtsov, *Out of My Past*, p. 574, n.8.; *Krasnyi arkhiv*, 1 (1922), 264.

Savinkov, Boris Viktorovich (1879–1925), was a leading member of the Socialist Revolutionary battle organization who planned such terrorist acts as the assassination of Minister of the Interior von Plehve in 1905 and Moscow Governor-General Grand Duke Sergei Aleksandrovich in 1905. He was briefly assistant minister of the interior in the Kerensky government and later a counterrevolutionary opposing the Bolsheviks. In 1924 Savinkov was apprehended in Soviet Russia and sentenced to execution. The sentence was commuted to ten years at hard labor and Savinkov died in 1925, the Soviets alleged by suicide. Savinkov wrote several novels about his revolutionary experiences as well as poetry. Florinsky, *McGraw-Hill Encyclopedia*, pp. 496–497.

Skobelev, General Mikhail Dmitrievich (1843–1882), a product of the Nicholas Academy of the General Staff, was promoted to general at the age of 34 for distinguished service in the Khiva campaign of 1873 and the Kokand expedition of 1875–1876. In the Russo-Turkish War of 1877–1878 he was the hero of the battles of Plevna and Shipka. Florinsky, *McGraw-Hill Encyclopedia*, p. 517; Gurko, *Features and Figures of the Past*, p. 671, n.42.

Sokolov, Nikolai Dmitrievich (1870–1928), like Kerensky, gained recognition defending those accused of political crimes. In 1906, for example, he defended the Kronstadt sailors involved in the mutiny aboard the cruiser *Pamiat Azova* (Memory of Azov). With Kerensky and 22 other members of the St. Petersburg bar, Sokolov was arrested in 1913 for passing a resolution protesting the Mendel Beylis trial, a case in which a Jew was accused of the ritual murder of a Christian boy. Although Beylis was judged innocent a few days later, Kerensky and Sokolov, as leaders, were sentenced to eight months' imprisonment and barred from political office. Credited by some with drafting Order Number One (See above, Chapter 25, n.7), Sokolov remained in Soviet Russia and worked in Soviet judicial institutions. Alexander F. Kerensky, *Russia and History's Turning Point*, pp. 74, 85–87; Kokovtsov, *Out of My Past*, pp. 488, 589, n.13.

Sukhomlinov, General Vladimir Aleksandrovich (1848–1926), graduated from the Nicholas Academy of the General Staff in 1867 and served on General Skobelev's staff in the Russo-Turkish War. He was troop commander and governor-general of the Kiev military district (1904–1908) and chief of the General Staff (1908–1909). From 1909 to 1915 Sukhomlinov was minister of war. He was dismissed by request of the State Duma and tried for treasonable negligence but was merely placed under house arrest. Tried again by the Provisional Government, he was sentenced to life at hard labor. The Bolsheviks released him in 1918 and he fled to Finland, then to Germany where he died in 1926. Probably he was innocent of the deliberate "malfeasance, corruption, and treason" with which he was charged, but he was unquestionably incompetent and mismanaged the war. Gurko, *Features and Figures of the Past*, p. 677, n.2; Florinsky, *Russia*, 2:1331–1332, n.5; *Krasnyi arkhiv*, 1 (1922), 263.

Suvorov, Field Marshal Aleksandr Vasilievich (1730–1800), originated the Russian school of military strategy based on bold attack, rapid troop movement, and attrition of enemy forces. He won worldwide fame in the 1799 Italian and Swiss campaigns against the French for his legendary crossing of the St. Gothard pass of the Alps. Florinsky, *McGraw-Hill Encyclopedia*, p. 550.

Ulianov, Aleksandr Ilyich (1866–1887), Lenin's older brother, became a member of the People's Will revolutionary movement while a student at St. Petersburg University. He was involved with Joseph and Bronislas Pilsudski and others in a plot to assassinate Alexander III in 1887. Ulianov was arrested, sentenced, and executed in Schlüsselburg Fortress that same year. Florinsky, *McGraw-Hill Encyclopedia*, p. 588.

Zhilinskii, General Yakov Grigorevich (1853–1919), was appointed to the General Staff in 1885. After serving as Admiral Alekseev's chief of staff, he commanded a cavalry division in Poland. Zhilinskii was chief of the General Staff from 1911 to 1914 and in early 1914 replaced General Skalon as military governor-general of the Warsaw district. In 1914 Zhilinskii was appointed commander of the northwest front but was replaced after Tannenberg and sent as *Stavka* representative to the Anglo-French armies. He lacked both talent and warmth and was generally unpopular. Knox, *With the Russian Army, 1914–1917*, 1:45; Kokovtsov, *Out of My Past*, p. 583, n.7; *Krasnyi arkhiv*, 1 (1922), 264.

BIBLIOGRAPHY

BIBLIOGRAPHY

Baron, Salo W. *The Russian Jew under Tsars and Soviets*. New York: Macmillan, 1964.
Basseches, Nikolaus. *The Unknown Army: The Nature and History of the Russian Military Forces*. New York: Viking, 1943.
Bernhardi, General Friedrich A. J. von. *Germany and the Next War*. Trans. Allen Powles. New York: Longmans, Green, 1914.
Bock, Maria Petrovna von. *Reminiscences of My Father, Peter A. Stolypin*. Ed. and trans. Margaret Patoski. Metuchen, N.J.: Scarecrow Press, 1970.
Bolshaia sovetskaia entsiklopediia. 51 vols. 2d ed. Moscow: Gosudarstvennoe nauchnoe izdatel'stvo "Bolshaia sovetskaia entsiklopediia," 1949–1958.
Brussilov, A. A. *A Soldier's Notebook, 1914–1918*. London: Macmillan, 1930.
Buchanan, Sir George. *My Mission to Russia*. 2 vols. Boston: Little, Brown, 1923.
Bykov, P. M. *The Last Days of Tsardom*. Trans. Andrew Rothstein. London: Martin Lawrence, 1934.
Chamberlin, William Henry. *The Russian Revolution, 1917–1921*. 2 vols. New York: Grosset and Dunlap, 1965.
Churchill, Winston S. *The World Crisis*. 6 vols. New York: Scribner's, 1931.
Conrad von Hötzendorff, Count Franz. *Aus meiner Dienstzeit, 1906–1918*. 5 vols. in 7. Vienna: Rikola Verlag, 1921–1925.
Denikin, Anton Ivanovich. *Ocherki russkoi smuty*. 5 vols. Berlin: Russkoe natsional'noe knigoizdatel'stvo, 1921–1925.
————. *Put' russkogo ofitsera*. New York: Izdatel'stvo imeni Chekhova, 1953.
————. *The Russian Turmoil; Memoirs: Military, Social, and Political*. London: Hutchinson, 1922.
————. *The White Army*. Trans. Catherine Zvegintsov. London: Jonathan Cape, 1930.
Deutscher, Isaac. *Stalin: A Political Biography*. 2d ed. New York: Oxford University Press, 1967.
Fairbank, John K., Edwin O. Reischauer, and Albert M. Craig. *East Asia: The Modern Transformation*. Boston: Houghton Mifflin, 1965.
Fischer, Fritz. *Germany's Aims in the First World War*. New York: Norton, 1967.
Fischer, George. *Russian Liberalism*. Cambridge, Mass.: Harvard University Press, 1958.
Fischer, Louis. *The Life of Lenin*. New York: Harper and Row, 1964.
————. *The Soviets in World Affairs: A History of Relations between the Soviet Union and the Rest of the World, 1917–1929*. New York: Knopf, Vintage Books, 1951.
Florinsky, Michael T., ed. *McGraw-Hill Encyclopedia of Russia and the Soviet Union*. New York: McGraw-Hill, 1961.
————. *Russia: A History and An Interpretation*. 2 vols. New York: Macmillan, 1968.
Frankel, Jonathan. "Party Genealogy and the Soviet Historians." *Slavic Review*, 25, no. 3 (September 1966), 563–603.
Gertsch, Oberst Fritz. *Vom russisch-japanischen Krieg 1904–1905*. 2 vols. Bern: Verlag Christian Künzi-Locher, 1907–1910.
Golder, Frank A., ed. *Documents of Russian History, 1914–1917*. Trans. Emanuel Aronsberg. Gloucester, Mass.: Peter Smith, 1964.

Golovine, Nicholas N. *The Russian Army in the World War*. New Haven: Yale University Press, 1931.

Gooch, G. P., and H. W. V. Temperley, eds. *British Documents on the Origins of the War, 1898–1914*. 11 vols. London: H. M. Stationery Office, 1926–1938.

Gourko, Basil. *War and Revolution in Russia, 1914–1917*. New York: Macmillan, 1919.

Greene, Francis V. *Sketches of Army Life in Russia*. New York: Scribner's, 1881.

Gronsky, Paul P., and Nicholas J. Astrov. *The War and the Russian Government*. New Haven: Yale University Press, 1929.

Guchkov, A. I. "Iz vospominaniia A. I. Guchkova." *Poslednaia novosti*, no. 5630 (August 23, 1936) and no. 5633 (August 26, 1936).

Gurko, Vladimir Iosifovich. *Features and Figures of the Past: Government and Opinion in the Reign of Nicholas II*. Trans. Laura Matveev. Stanford: Stanford University Press, 1939.

Hamiliton, Sir Ian Standish Monteith. *A Staff Officer's Scrap-Book during the Russo-Japanese War*. 2 vols. London: Edward Arnold, 1905–1907.

Hough, Richard. *The Fleet That Had to Die*. New York: Ballantine Books, 1958.

Izvolskii, Aleksandr Petrovich. *The Memoirs of Alexander Izwolsky: Formerly Russian Minister of Foreign Affairs and Ambassador to France*. Ed. and trans. Charles Louis Seeger. London: Hutchinson, 1920.

Johnson, William H. E. *Russia's Educational Heritage*. Pittsburgh: Carnegie Press, 1950.

Kalmykow, Andrew D. *Memoirs of a Russian Diplomat: Outposts of the Empire, 1893–1917*. Ed. Alexandra Kalmykow. New Haven: Yale University Press, 1971.

Kelly, Eric P., and Dragoš D. Kostich. *The Land and People of Poland*. Rev. ed. Philadelphia and New York: J. P. Lippincott, 1964.

Kenez, Peter. *Civil War in South Russia, 1918: The First Year of the Volunteer Army*. Berkeley: University of California Press, 1971.

Kennan, George. *Siberia and the Exile System*. 2 vols. New York: Century, 1891.

Kerensky, Alexander F. *Russia and History's Turning Point*. New York: Duell, Sloan and Pearce, 1965.

Kitchen, Martin. *The German Officer Corps, 1890–1914*. Oxford: Clarendon Press, 1968.

Kizevetter, Aleksandr Aleksandrovich. *Na rubezh dvukh stoletii (vospominaniia 1881–1914)*. Prague: Izdatel'stvo Orbis, 1929.

Knox, Sir Alfred W. F. *With the Russian Army, 1914–1917*. 2 vols. London: Hutchinson and Co., 1921.

Kokovtsov, Count Vladimir N. *Out of My Past: The Memoirs of Count Kokovtsov, Russian Minister of Finance 1904–1914, Chairman of the Council of Ministers 1911–1914*. Ed. H. H. Fisher. Trans. Laura Matveev. Stanford: Stanford University Press, 1935.

Kolarz, Walter. *Russia and Her Colonies*. n. p.: Archon Books, 1967.

Kovalevsky, Maxime. *Russian Political Institutions*. Chicago: University of Chicago Press, 1902.

Krasnyi arkhiv. Leningrad, 1922–1941.

Kropotkin, Prince Peter. *Memoirs of a Revolutionist*. Boston and New York: Houghton Mifflin, 1899.

Kuropatkin, Aleksei N. *The Russian Army and the Japanese War*. 2 vols. Trans. A. B. Lindsay. New York: Dutton, 1909.

———. "The Treaty at Portsmouth." *McClure's Magazine*, 32 (January 1909), 237–246.

———. *Zapiski Generala Kuropatkina o russko-iaponskoi voine: Itogi voiny*. 3 vols. Berlin: I. Ladyschnikoff, 1909.

Lenin, V. I. "The War and Social-Democracy." *Collected Works*, 21:27–34. Moscow: Progress Publishers, 1964.

Lloyd George, David. *War Memoirs of David Lloyd George*. 2 vols. London: Odhams Press, 1938.

Luckett, Richard. *The White Generals: An Account of the White Movement and the Russian Civil War*. New York: Viking Press, 1971.

Malozemoff, Andrew. *Russian Far Eastern Policy, 1881–1904, with Special Emphasis on the Causes of the Russo-Japanese War.* Berkeley: University of California Press, 1958.

Miliukov, Paul. *Political Memoirs, 1905–1917.* Trans. Carl Goldberg. Ed. Arthur P. Mendel. Ann Arbor: University of Michigan Press, 1967.

Monas, Sidney. *The Third Section: Police and Society in Russia under Nicholas I.* Cambridge, Mass.: Harvard University Press, 1961.

Mosse, W. E. *Alexander II and the Modernization of Russia.* Rev. ed. New York: Collier Books, 1962.

Odinetz, Dimitrii M., and P. J. Novgorotsov. *Russian Schools and Universities in the World War.* New Haven: Yale University Press, 1929.

Paléologue, Georges Maurice. *Three Critical Years, 1904–05–06.* New York: Robert Speller, 1957.

Pares, Bernard. *The Fall of the Russian Monarchy: A Study of the Evidence.* New York: Knopf, 1939.

———. *A History of Russia.* New York: Knopf, 1956.

Pavlovsky, George. *Agricultural Russia on the Eve of Revolution.* New York: Howard Fertig, 1968.

Pilsudska, Alexandra. *Pilsudski: A Biography by His Wife.* New York: Dodd, Mead, 1941.

Pilsudski, Joseph. *The Memories of a Polish Revolutionary and Soldier.* Ed. and trans. D. R. Gillie. London: Faber and Faber, 1931.

Pushkarev, Sergei G. *Dictionary of Russian Historical Terms from the Eleventh Century to 1917.* Eds. George Vernadsky and Ralph T. Fisher, Jr. New Haven: Yale University Press, 1970.

———. *The Emergence of Modern Russia, 1801–1917.* Trans. Robert H. McNeal and Tova Yedlin. New York: Holt, Rinehart and Winston, 1963.

Radkey, Oliver H. *The Agrarian Foes of Bolshevism.* New York: Columbia University Press, 1958.

Reddaway, William F. *Marshal Pilsudski.* London: George Routledge, 1939.

Robinson, Geroid T. *Rural Russia under the Old Regime.* New York: Macmillan, 1949.

Romanov, Boris A. *Russia in Manchuria, 1892–1906.* Trans. Susan Wilbur Jones. Ann Arbor: J. W. Edwards, 1952.

Rosen, Baron Roman Romanovich. *Forty Years of Diplomacy.* 2 vols. New York: Knopf, 1922.

Rubinshtein, N. "M. N. Pokrovskii: kratkaia biograficheskie spravka." *Istorik-Marksist,* 9 (1928), 80–83.

Sazonov, Serge D. *Fateful Years, 1909–1916: Reminscences of Serge Sazonov.* London: Jonathan Cape, 1928.

Scalapino, Robert A. *Democracy and the Party Movement in Prewar Japan: The Failure of the First Attempt.* Berkeley: University of California Press, 1953.

Schilling, Baron M. F. *How the War Began in 1914: Being the Diary of the Russian Foreign Office from the 3rd to the 20th (Old Style) of July, 1914.* Trans. W. Cyprian Bridges. London: George Allen and Unwin, 1925.

Strakhovsky, Leonid I. "Was There a Kornilov Rebellion? A Re-appraisal of the Evidence." *Slavonic and East European Review,* 32, no. 81 (June 1, 1955), 372–395.

Takeuchi, Tatsuji. *War and Diplomacy in the Japanese Empire.* Chicago: University of Chicago Press, 1935.

Thaden, Edward G. *Russia Since 1801: The Making of a New Society.* New York: Wiley, 1971.

Trotsky, Leon. *Trotsky's Diary in Exile, 1935.* Trans. Elena Zarudnaya. Cambridge, Mass.: Harvard University Press, 1958.

Troyat, Henri. *Daily Life in Russia under the Last Tsar.* Trans. Malcolm Barnes. London: George Allen and Unwin, 1961.

———. *Tolstoy.* Trans. Nancy Amphoux. Garden City: Doubleday, 1967.

Turgenev, Ivan. *Virgin Soil.* Trans. Isabel F. Hapgood. New York: Scribner's, 1917.

Utechin, Sydney V., ed. *Everyman's Concise Encyclopedia of Russia*. New York: Dutton, 1961.

Viktorov, V. P., ed. *Soiuz russkogo naroda, po materialam chrezvychainoi sledstvennoi kommissii vremennogo pravitel'stva 1917 g.* Moscow: Gosudarstvennoe izdatel'stvo, 1929.

Walicki, Jerzy. *Religious Life in Poland*. Warsaw: Interpress Publishers, 1970.

Willoughby, Westel W. *Japan's Case Examined*. Baltimore: Johns Hopkins Press, 1940.

Witte, Count Sergei Iu. *The Memoirs of Count Witte*. Ed. and trans. Abraham Yarmolinsky. Garden City: Doubleday, Page, 1921.

———. *Vospominaniia; tsarstvovanie Nikolaia II*. 2 vols. Berlin: Knigoizdatel'stvo slovo, 1922–1923.

Wrangel, Baron Nikolai Egorovich. *From Serfdom to Bolshevism: The Memoirs of Baron N. Wrangel, 1847–1920*. Trans. Brian and Beatrice Lunn. Philadelphia: Lippincott, 1927.

Zagorsky, S. O. *State Control of Industry in Russia during the War*. New Haven: Yale University Press, 1928.

Zenkovsky, Serge A. *Pan-Turkism and Islam in Russia*. Cambridge, Mass.: Harvard University Press, 1960.

INDEX

INDEX

Material from the notes has been included extensively in the following index. Where the same note number appears more than once on a page, references to such notes appear as 280n1(1), 280n1(2), and so on.